THE ENCYCLOPEDIA OF ARCADE VIDEO GAMES

BILL KURTZ

4880 Lower Valley Road, Atglen, PA 19310 USA

DEDICATION

This book is dedicated to my mother, Lillian Kurtz, who always had faith in me and what I could accomplish.

Some of the items pictured in this book may be covered by various copyrights, trademarks, and logos. Their use herein is for identification purposes only. All rights are reserved by their respective owners. This book is not sponsored, endorsed, or otherwise affiliated with any of the companies whose products are represented herein. This book is derived from the author's independent research.

Copyright © 2004 by Bill Kurtz
Library of Congress Control Number: 2003108563

All rights reserved. No part of this work may be reproduced or used in any form or by any means—graphic, electronic, or mechanical, including photocopying or information storage and retrieval systems—without written permission from the publisher.
The scanning, uploading and distribution of this book or any part thereof via the Internet or via any other means without the permission of the publisher is illegal and punishable by law. Please purchase only authorized editions and do not participate in or encourage the electronic piracy of copyrighted materials.
"Schiffer," "Schiffer Publishing Ltd. & Design," and the "Design of pen and ink well" are registered trademarks of Schiffer Publishing Ltd.

Designed by Joseph M. Riggio Jr.
Type set in Lithograph/Souvenir Lt BT

ISBN: 0-7643-1925-6
Printed in China
1 2 3 4

Published by Schiffer Publishing Ltd.
4880 Lower Valley Road
Atglen, PA 19310
Phone: (610) 593-1777; Fax: (610) 593-2002
E-mail: Info@schifferbooks.com
Please visit our web site catalog at
www.schifferbooks.com
We are always looking for people to write books on new and related subjects. If you have an idea for a book, please contact us at the above address.

This book may be purchased from the publisher.
Include $3.95 for shipping.
Please try your bookstore first.
You may write for a free catalog.

In Europe, Schiffer books are distributed by
Bushwood Books
6 Marksbury Avenue
Kew Gardens
Surrey TW9 4JF England
Phone: 44 (0) 20 8392 8585
Fax: 44 (0) 20 8392 9876
E-mail: Bushwd@aol.com
Free postage in the UK. Europe: air mail at cost.

CONTENTS

Introduction 4
Part 1: The Birth of Video Games 1972-1976 5
Part 2: Invaders From Space 1977-1979 45
Part 3: The Pac Man Years 1980-1982 79
Part 4: The Experimental Years 1983-1985 149
Part 5: The Modern Era 1986-Present 196
Part 6: Video Games of the World 219
Part 7: Video Game Collectibles 224
Part 8: Owning Your Own Machine 232
Notes 239

ACKNOWLEDGMENTS

The author would like to thank the following:

James Brown (Kirtland, Ohio)
Karen Feldman (Shaker Heights, Ohio)
Balint Kocsis (Phoenix, Arizona)
Kopy-Kwik Printing (Eastlake, Ohio)
Martin Krongold (Brooklyn, New York)
Fran Kurtz (Eastlake, Ohio)
Warren Kurtz (Lake Tahoe, Nevada)
Walter Lazuka (Mentor, Ohio)

David Marshall (Oxford, Ohio)
Dennis Matejka (Cleveland, Ohio)
Theresa Myllykoski (Kirtland, Ohio)
Dave Ondrey (Pittsburgh, Pennsylvania)
Laurie Ruck (Brunswick, Ohio)
Jeff Siegel (Cincinnati, Ohio)
Jack Smith (Florence, Kentucky)

INTRODUCTION

Welcome to a magical world, a world where anything is possible. Welcome to the world of arcade video games. Is there anyone under the age of twenty who hasn't heard of PAC MAN? Or dropped a quarter into the coin slot of one of these machines to experience the feeling of blasting alien invaders out of the sky?

Until a few years ago, words like "classic" and "vintage" were never associated with video games. Today, some collectors are paying several times more for old, used video games than these same machines sold for when they were new. People now collect the same machines that were once hauled out to the landfills and disposed of by game operators two decades ago. The generation that grew up with SPACE INVADERS, ASTEROIDS, DONKEY KONG, and PAC MAN has fond memories of the time spent on these and other popular electronic wonders, and today, there's a new appreciation for these classic video games. From their shaky start (the first coin-operated video game was considered a flop when it was released) to their explosive popularity in the late 1970s and early '80s, video games are not a passing fad – they're here to stay.

Today, collecting video arcade games is a growing hobby, with conventions and Internet newsgroups available to keep enthusiasts informed and knowledgeable. While some people own more than three hundred machines, these people can probably be considered hoarders rather than collectors; true collectors appreciate the thrill of restoring and playing their games, instead of merely accumulating warehouses full of neglected machines. For many collectors, locating and painstakingly restoring a classic game to its former beauty is the most enjoyable part of the hobby.

In this book, we'll be looking at the evolution of video games – where they began and how they became a part of American society. Nearly every video game produced before 1986 is included here – you'll find lots of old favorites, a few games you've probably forgotten, and some that you've never heard of before. Although a few machines from the late 1980s and 1990s are also included, most video game collectors agree that these modern video games are too recent to be considered collectible – yet.

You'll also find a value range listed along with the machines. This price range will give you a general idea of how much you might expect to pay for the game in complete working condition. The lower price reflects a machine in average condition with some fading, nicks, or wear on the cabinet, while the higher price would be the value of the game in excellent or near mint condition. Non-working games will generally sell for less than half of the lower price, although that will depend on what is wrong with the machine. Remember that video game prices are fluid; what's hot today may be a giant paperweight tomorrow. And of course the reverse is also true. In the late 1980s, you could pick up an Atari ASTEROIDS for $50 from just about any video game operator; some operators even staged tournaments on ASTEROIDS with the machine itself as the grand prize, just to get rid of these machines. Today, an ASTEROIDS video game will cost you between $400 and $600.

Whether you've been collecting video games for years or are just getting started in the hobby, you're sure to find valuable insights into the fascinating world of arcade video games, along with nostalgic photos sure to delight you. Enjoy the journey!

Part 1
THE BIRTH OF VIDEO GAMES
1972-1976

Walk into any arcade at the beginning of the 1970s and you would find an assortment of electromechanical games eager to swallow your dimes. You could shoot at the flying ducks on a gun game, race a grand prix car around the track on a driving game, or aim for the high-scoring drop targets and spinners on a pinball machine. Arcade games had been around since the turn of the century, and nearly all of them were designed with the same electromechanical solenoids and relays for decades. New features were always introduced to keep players coming back, but the arcade games of the 1960s were remarkably similar to their predecessors.

But everything changed in 1971 when a strange-looking game began to appear in arcades. This machine didn't look like any other coin-op game. With its bright yellow fiberglass cabinet and rounded top, COMPUTER SPACE looked like it had come right out of a science fiction movie. And in a way, it had. Because COMPUTER SPACE heralded the beginning of a new era in arcade games – the video game era. Instead of relays and solenoids, COMPUTER SPACE had a circuit board inside. Instead of manipulating a silver ball around a playfield, you piloted a tiny space ship through an asteroid belt. COMPUTER SPACE was perfectly suited to the baby boomer generation which had grown up in front of a television screen.

Actually, the idea for COMPUTER SPACE had been floating around since 1965 when Nolan Bushnell, an engineering student at the University of Utah, programmed the school's computer to play several games that he had designed. Computer technology was still in its infancy, though, and there was no economical way to apply Bushnell's concepts to arcade games. By 1970, the technology needed to create a coin-operated TV computer game had become both practical and affordable, and

This 1971 trade ad for Nutting's COMPUTER SPACE describes the game as "innovative" without ever mentioning the fact that it was the first arcade video game ever made.

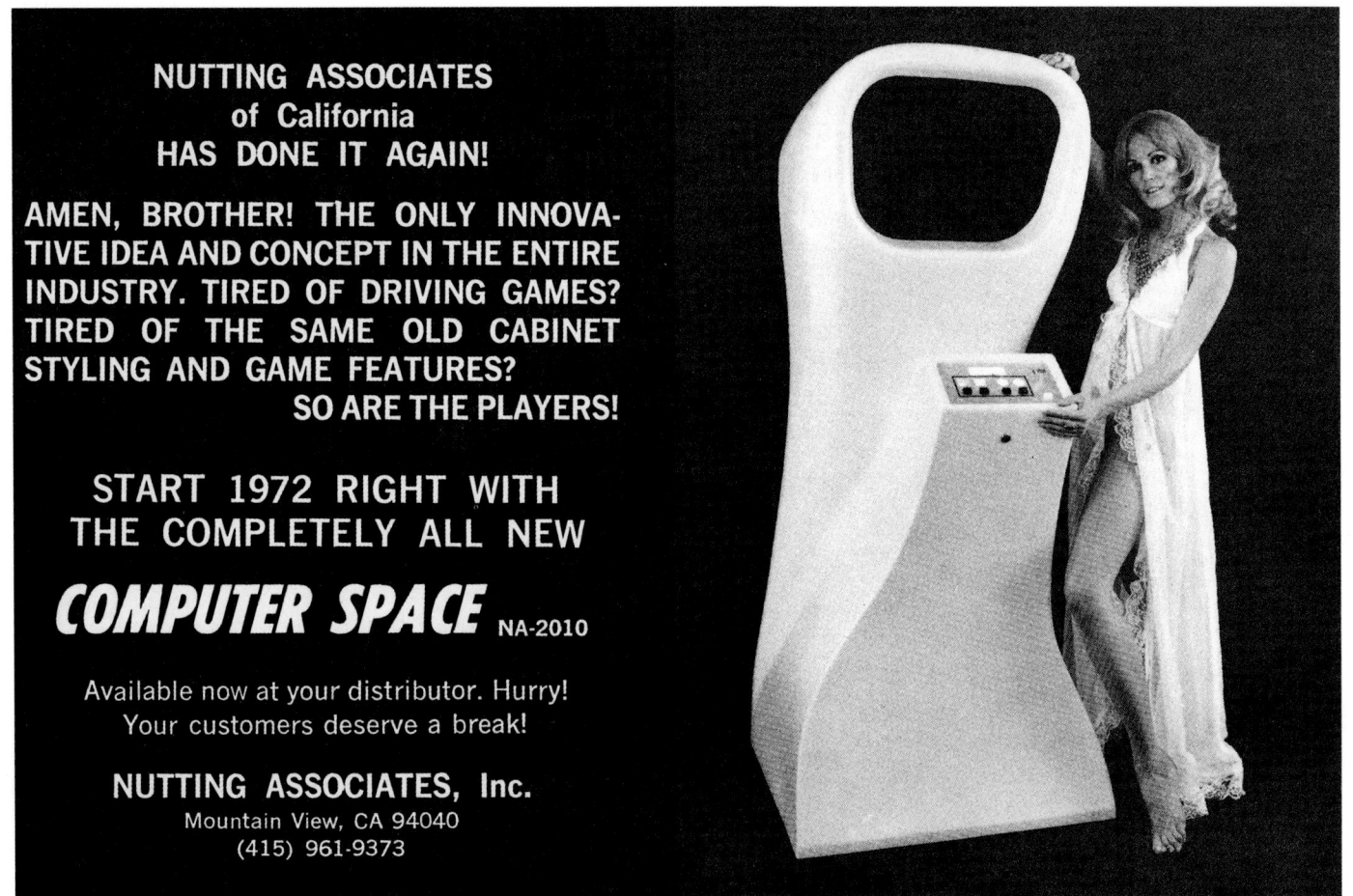

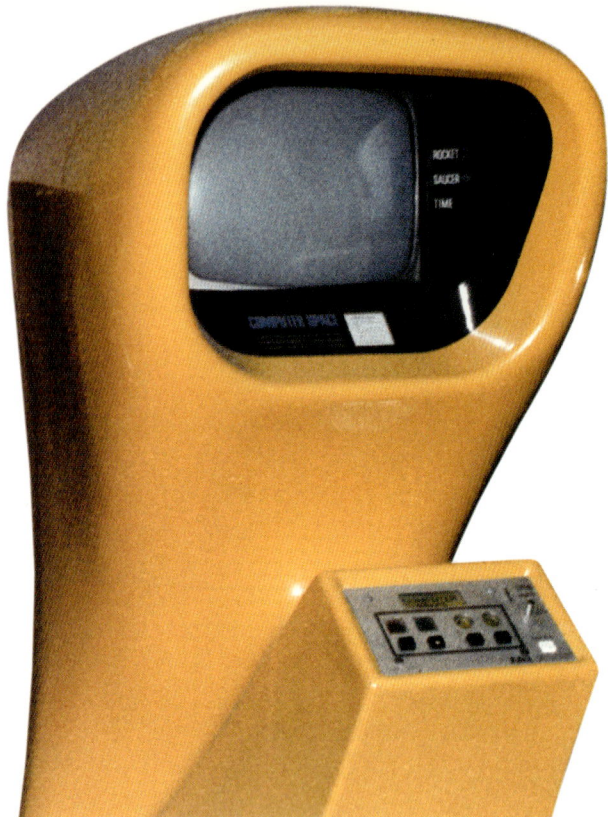

COMPUTER SPACE was produced in a variety of colors including yellow, blue, and red; because of the lightweight design of the fiberglass cabinet, the entire machine weighed less than 100 pounds! $1,500-$2,500.

Bushnell decided to market his idea. Although he initially planned to create his own company to produce the game, all of Bushnell's prospective investors withdrew their backing before the prototype was built. Bushnell then approached Dave Nutting of Nutting Associates Inc., a newly formed company which had produced a handful of novelty arcade games, most notably an electromechanical quiz game which was popular with players. And in the fall of 1971, COMPUTER SPACE was unveiled.

The game play of COMPUTER SPACE was simple: Maneuver your spaceship though an asteroid field while blasting the asteroids into rubble. Players used to the simplicity of electromechanical arcade games didn't know what to make of COMPUTER SPACE, though. Many players were intimidated by the high-tech appearance and strategy of the game, which was the tenth arcade machine produced by Nutting. After building about 1,500 COMPUTER SPACE machines, Dave Nutting concluded that video games were a passing fad at best and decided to focus the company's attention on the more successful mechanical quiz games.

Undeterred, Bushnell decided to try again. He approached Bally, one of the largest arcade game manufacturers, with his idea for a different video game, one that would be simple enough for every player to understand. This time, Bushnell's game would simulate the game of ping pong, with an electronic "ball" that was bounced between two video paddles. Bally rejected the game because it couldn't be played by just one player, and thought that the game should feature video men instead of paddles.

Bushnell had confidence in his game (which he had named PONG), and started building the machines in his garage. The internal components were simple, and included a black and white television set (video game monitors didn't exist yet) and a homemade cabinet. Bushnell placed the first PONG in Andy Capp's Tavern in California on November 29, 1972, and the earnings were phenomenal. Word of mouth about the game's success spread quickly, and a few weeks later, Bushnell opened a factory for his new company which he had named Atari, taken from the Japanese board game Go. (The term Atari in Go is approximately the same as the term check in chess.)

One reason for PONG's success was its versatility. PONG could be operated in locations such as upscale night clubs which couldn't accommodate large, noisy mechanical arcade games like pinball machines and gun games, as well as arcades and taverns. PONG was also available in a cocktail table format, as well as in a high-tech futuristic cabinet. Atari even produced a few PONG games with a wooden barrel as a cabinet!

Less than a month after PONG's introduction, video game mania started spreading as clones of the game began appearing. New video game manufacturers sprang up out of nowhere to produce "TV paddle games," as they were called, and even established arcade game companies jumped into the ring. Williams Electronics (PADDLE BALL), Midway Manufacturing (WINNER), and Chicago Coin (TV PING PONG) were just a few of the coin-op firms scrambling to cash in on the popularity of PONG.

By the beginning of 1973, the popularity of paddle games had still not subsided, so new twists on the old

COMPUTER SPACE used a standard black and white TV set rather than a custom-built video monitor, and even had an attract mode with moving saucers to catch your attention when the game wasn't being played.

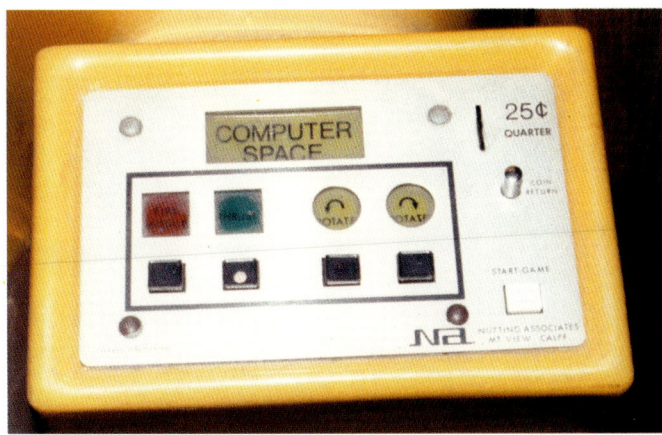

Operators could adjust the length of the game on COMPUTER SPACE for anywhere from one to two minutes, and the machine could be set for either one or two plays for a quarter.

concept were introduced. Atari's PONG DOUBLES was one of the first video games that let four players compete simultaneously, and before long, four-player paddle games were the norm. These paddle games were often named after sports like tennis, hockey, and soccer, but most offered essentially the same game play. Over thirty different companies produced at least one coin-operated paddle-style video game in 1973.

Some interesting paddle game variations did appear, though, most notably Chicago Coin's 1973 TV PINBALL. This game had virtually nothing in common with pinball, as the object was simply to bounce the ball off the paddle which moved horizontally across the bottom of the screen to hit all of the sixteen targets. Midway's TV FLIPPER was virtually identical to TV PINBALL, although Midway's version used a joystick to control the paddle rather than a knob.

By 1974, interest in paddle games had started to wane, and many of the tiny manufacturers who had set up shop the previous year to cash in on the PONG craze disappeared as quickly as they had sprung into being. Atari and Midway emerged as the industry leaders and began producing video gun and driving games to simulate the action of these longtime arcade favorites; space-themed games were also popular. As the technology developed, players found that they could do much more than simply bounce an electronic ball off a paddle.

Video game operators found themselves with a glut of PONG-style games after the initial paddle-game craze had worn off by the end of 1974. By most estimates, over 70,000 of these PONG clones were produced, and most of these games were scrapped by operators who didn't have the space to store all of these outdated machines. Most of these games have little or no value today, although original PONG machines are still in demand.

As interest in the early paddle games dropped, manufacturers produced enhancement kits to squeeze a few extra dollars out of the old machines. Atari's SUPER PONG, released in 1974, was little more than a speed-up chip which could be added to the printed circuit board to liven up the game. GYRO-PONG, which put an unpre-dictable spin on the ball, was another enhancement kit made by a small independent firm. Other enhancement kits were designed to simply add additional paddles to the screen or to serve the ball each time from a random spot on the screen. These enhancement kits usually cost about $50 to $200 at a time when new machines sold for about $1,250.

The popularity of these early video games made 25 cent pricing standard for all coin-operated machines. Since the mid 1950s, most arcade games had cost a dime per play, but virtually every video game starting with COMPUTER SPACE and PONG was set at 25 cents per game. Players didn't seem to mind paying a quarter for a shot at these high-tech machines – and video game operators were both amazed and delighted at the public's acceptance of this pricing. Before too long, 25 cents per play became standard on pinball machines and other arcade games.

By late 1974 and early 1975, a new generation of imaginative video games was introduced, many of which are regarded as classics today. Kee Games' TANK, for example, let you drive a tiny tank through a maze while firing at attacking vehicles and dodging enemy fire. TANK had a unique joystick control system which required you to move two joysticks simultaneously during the game.

Atari sold thousands of PONG video games in 1972 but most of these machines were destroyed years ago when thousands of PONG clones flooded the market and players lost interest in paddle-style games. Game shown in this period ad is $800-$1,200.

Most collectors prefer the upright version of PONG to the cocktail-table design shown in this 1972 factory promo photo. Notice that the table model has the same yellow color motif as the upright game. $600-$800.

Midway's TV BASKETBALL was the first video basketball game, and featured stick-figure basketball players on the screen. Another popular game from this era was Midway's WHEELS, originally released under the name RACER. Midway also released a two-player version called WHEELS II, which was available with an optional molded plastic seat attached to the cabinet.

Although no one realized it at the time, Midway's GUNFIGHT (1975) represented a turning point for video games. GUNFIGHT was an old west shoot-'em-up video game which used a gunhandle-style trigger joystick to control the action. The idea was to move your cowboy up and down the screen between the chuck wagons and the cactus plants, dodging the bullets fired by the bad guys while hitting as many of the desperados as you could. But it was what was inside the machine that would change the shape of things to come. GUNFIGHT was the first video game to use a microprocessor rather than the first-generation circuit boards that had been used in every machine since COMPUTER SPACE. Players might not have noticed the difference, but video game manufacturers certainly took note.

GUNFIGHT represented another radical departure for video games as well. Midway Manufacturing had purchased the rights to produce GUNFIGHT from Taito, a Japanese arcade game manufacturer. Several Japanese firms had come out of nowhere a couple of years earlier to build PONG-style games for the Japanese market, and the technological development of video games in Japan quickly outpaced the U.S. industry. Taito, a Tokyo-based firm which had been in business since the early '70s, was one of the leaders in video game development in Japan, and GUNFIGHT represented the first time that a U.S.

game manufacturer had licensed a game from overseas. Such licensing arrangements would become commonplace later in the decade and throughout the 1980s, but GUNFIGHT marked the first time that a U.S.-produced video game was not built in-house.

Video games also took a cue from Hollywood for the first time. The blockbuster film *Jaws*, released in 1975, triggered a shark frenzy across the country and a fledgling manufacturer called Project Support Engineering

PADDLE BALL (1973) was Williams Electronics' first venture into video games and is of little historical significance except to fans of Williams' later video games. $150-$250.

(PSE) was quick to capitalize on the interest. MANEATER got attention not for the game play but for the unique fiberglass cabinet designed to look like the open mouth of a giant shark! The controls were placed in the shark's lower jaw, and you had to reach inside the shark's mouth to play the game! MANEATER was the first of only a handful of machines produced by PSE, which closed its doors less than three years later.

Another *Jaws*-inspired game was Atari's SHARK JAWS, also produced in 1975. Atari's game was housed in a conventional video game cabinet, and featured "realistic sound effects" such as screaming divers, according to the

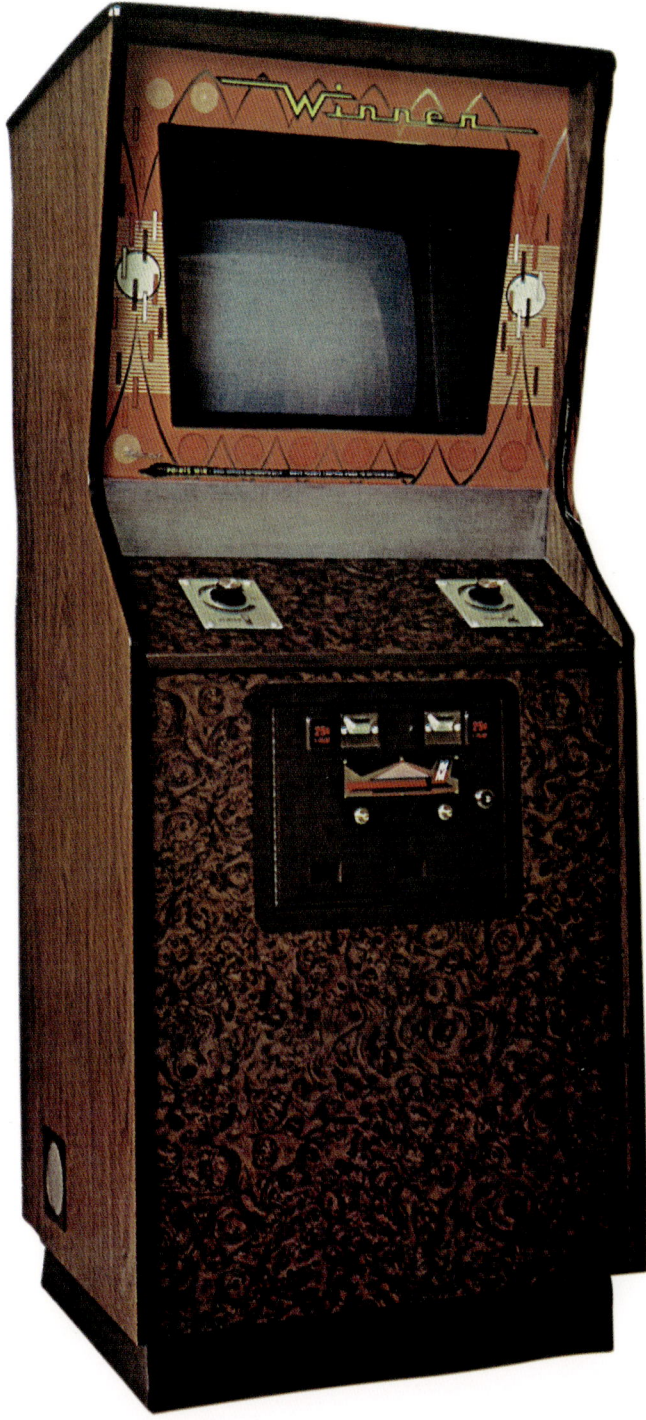

Midway jumped into the video game market with a winner – its two-player WINNER video game, released in 1973. $100-$150.

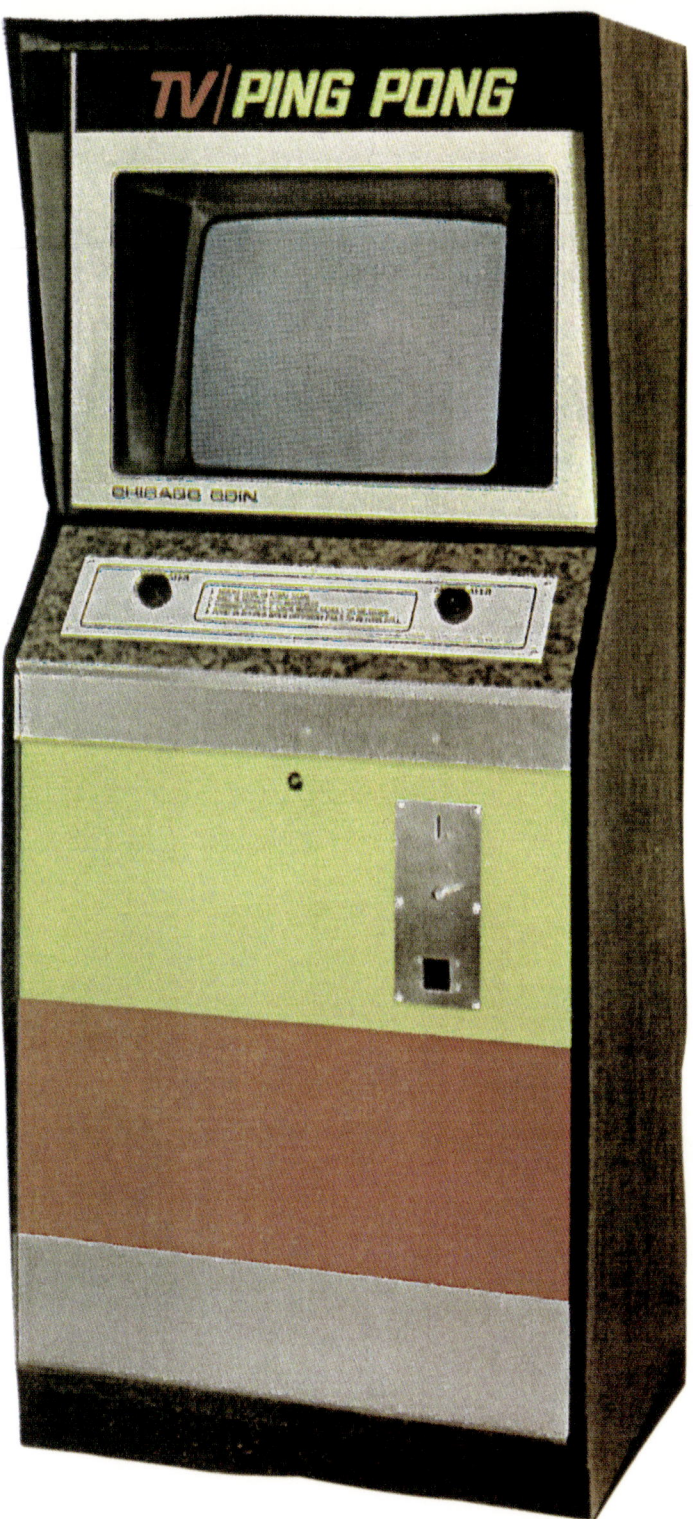

Longtime pinball manufacturer Chicago Coin jumped on the video game bandwagon with TV PING PONG in 1973. Notice the lack of artwork and plain cabinet design. $50-$75.

company's literature. SHARK JAWS was not officially licensed from the movie, so Atari designed the game's logo with the word "Shark" in small lettering beside the word "Jaws" in much larger lettering to attract fans of the movie while not infringing on the film's copyright.

The video game industry was taking full advantage of the adaptability of the machines by 1975. Cocktail table video games had been around since the introduction of PONG, and these machines offered two advantages over their upright cabinet counterparts. First, as noted earlier, cocktail-style games could be operated in locations where a full-size machine wouldn't be practical, either because of space or because of the décor. And cocktail table video games were generally less expensive than upright games, usually selling for about 25 percent less than full-size arcade video games. Some games were sold only in a cocktail table format, most notably Atari's 1975 GOAL FOUR video game.

On the other hand, other games featured huge cabinets that commanded attention from players. One of the largest was Allied Leisure's F-114, a monstrous widescreen video game that was 63 inches high and 46 inches wide. Released during the summer of 1975, F-114 had a huge wooden swivel chair with a joystick control attached to it. The game weighed 470 pounds, considerably more

Yet another game called TV PING PONG, this one from Amutronics (1973). Early video games were often referred to as "TV games" by players and operators. $25-$50.

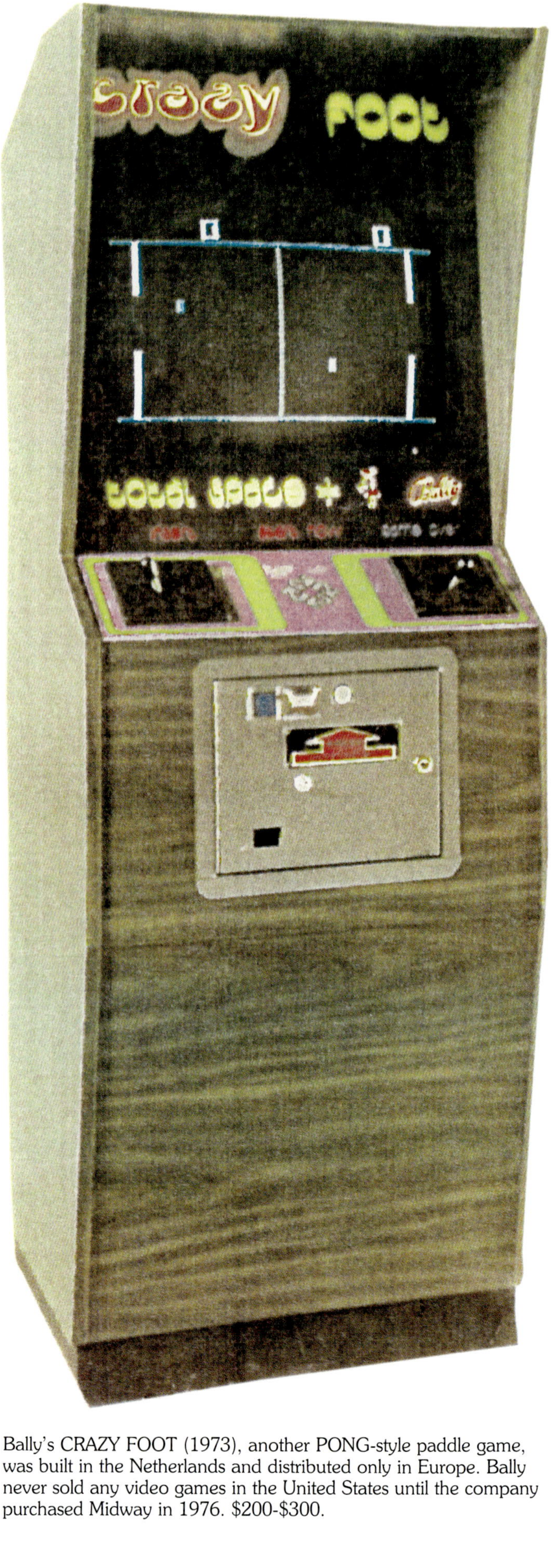

Bally's CRAZY FOOT (1973), another PONG-style paddle game, was built in the Netherlands and distributed only in Europe. Bally never sold any video games in the United States until the company purchased Midway in 1976. $200-$300.

than the 250-pound weight of most upright video games. And F-114 was the first video game ever shipped with a factory-set pricing of 50 cents per play, although operators could drop it down to a quarter a game. Atari's HI-WAY, also released that same year, was the first sit-down driving game. Produced in a red fiberglass cabinet, HI-WAY was described by the company as "The ultimate driving experience."

Late in 1975, the first national controversy involving an arcade video game dealt a blow to the reputation of the industry. Exidy's DEATH RACE was a driving game with a new twist – the object was to drive over as many

Released in 1973, Allied Leisure's PADDLE BATTLE was the firm's first video game. $50-$100.

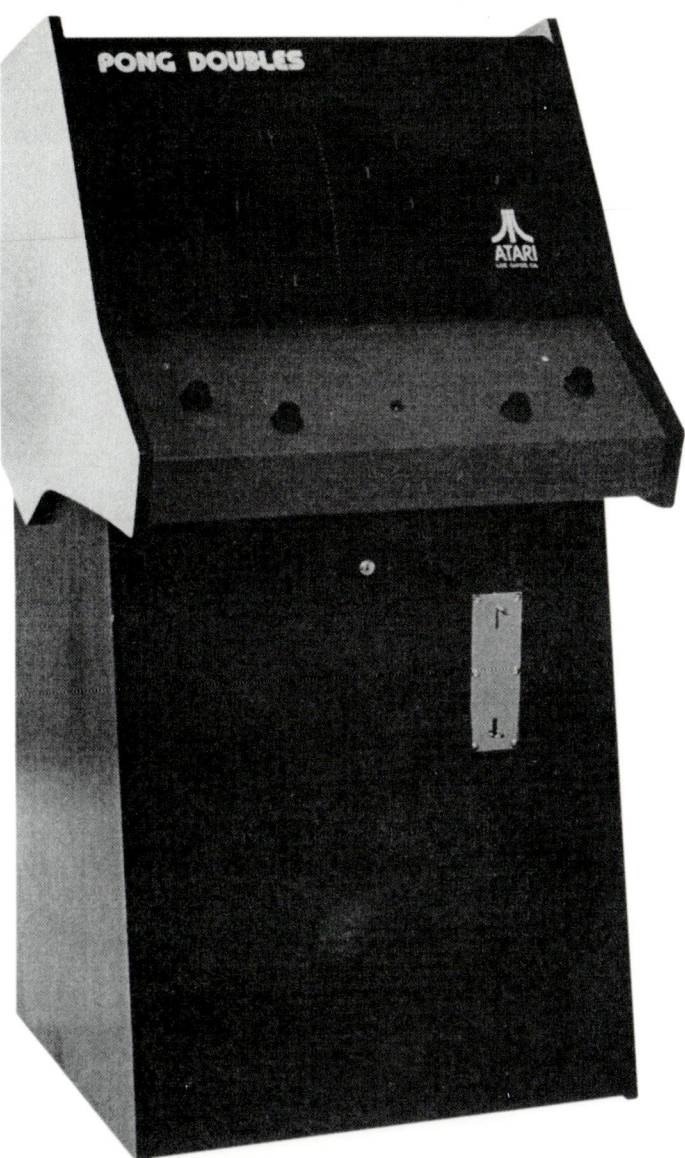

Atari's PONG DOUBLES (1973) was one of the first video games that could be played by either two or four players; notice the width of the cabinet, which was designed to accommodate four people standing side by side. $100-$150.

pedestrians as possible to score points. Parents were outraged at what they perceived to be the inherent violence in the game, although Exidy claimed that the video victims were monsters rather than people so the carnage was acceptable. The artwork for the game featured a pair of hooded skeletons reminiscent of the Grim Reaper racing each other down a deserted road past a cemetery. Adding to the effect was the fact that the T in the game's logo was designed to resemble a grave marker. Many PTAs around the country called on video game operators to pull the plug on the games, but the protests did little except to generate publicity for DEATH RACE, making it one of the top-earning games of 1976. Exidy shelved plans for a sequel called SUPER DEATH CHASE, which had been scheduled for production early in 1976; only a few prototypes were built.

Throughout the rest of 1976, Atari and Midway were the undisputed leaders in the video game industry, although a number of smaller manufacturers were also trying to carve a niche for themselves. Exidy, Ramtek, Meadows, and Gremlin were just a few of the firms hoping to produce a game that would capture players' interest the way that PONG had done only a few years earlier, but there didn't seem to be any game that had the same universal appeal. Video game earnings had started to drop and it looked like players were beginning to tire of the games now that the novelty of these "TV games" had worn off. The consensus among industry veterans was that video games were destined to become filler pieces in arcades, a passing fad whose time had come and gone.

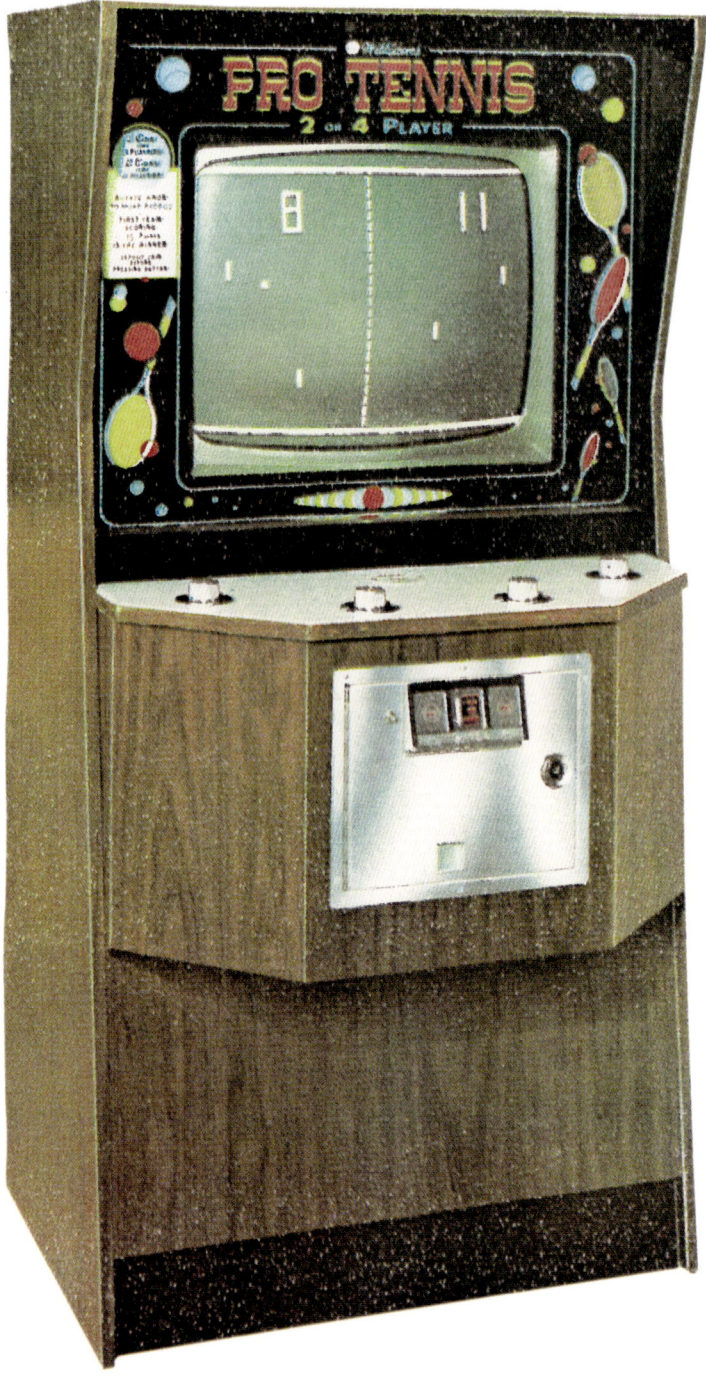

ATARI

After Nolan Bushnell tried unsuccessfully to sell the concept for PONG to established arcade game manufacturers like Bally, Chicago Coin, and Midway, Bushnell decided to form his own company. Atari was the first major coin-op game manufacturer located outside of Chicago, which had always been the center of the coin-op game industry. The high-tech environment of the Silicon Valley in California was ideally suited as the birthplace of the video game industry, and nearly every major video game company followed Bushnell's lead and set up shop in California.

Atari quickly established itself as the leading producer of arcade video games, and within two years, had bought out one of its competitors, Kee Games, which had been founded by several ex-Atari employees. Atari's growth was phenomenal throughout the rest of the 1970s and early 1980s, although Bushnell left the company by the end of the '70s. By the early 1980s, Atari was the leading manufacturer of home video game systems, and also manufactured home computers for a short time. Atari continued building coin-op video games well into the 1990s; near the end of the decade, the company's assets were purchased by Williams Electronics, and Atari faded into memory as Williams closed its amusement game division in 1999. Interestingly enough, a new generation of teens is wearing T-shirts emblazoned with the old familiar Atari logo, which is now considered cool among young video game players who weren't even born when Atari was building its hits like ASTEROIDS and CENTIPEDE.

Two players could compete on Williams' 1973 PRO TENNIS for a quarter, but it would cost 50 cents for four players to test their skill. $75-$100.

For players who weren't yet tired of batting an electronic ball back and forth, Chicago Coin introduced TV TENNIS in 1973. $25-$50.

This four-player TV HOCKEY (1973) was the final game produced by Amutronics, a short-lived video game manufacturer based in Cherry Hill, New Jersey. $25-$50.

Midway's WINNER IV, unveiled in the fall of 1973, was simply a four-player version of the firm's two-player WINNER video game released earlier that year. $100-$150.

Bailey's FUN FOUR (1974) offered a choice of four player-selectable paddle-style games. Notice the control knobs positioned at the corners of the cabinet. $25-$50.

Mirco's CHALLENGE (1973) was the first video game which offered players a chance to win a free game. Mirco produced only a few video games, although the company was better known for its table soccer games – notice the row of table soccer players in the company's logo in the lower right corner of the top panel. $25-$50.

Few players chose to play PLAYERS CHOICE, a run-of-the-mill four-player paddle game from PMC in 1973. $25-$50.

Some players found Digital Games' KNOCK-OUT (1974) difficult to operate because the control knobs were positioned below the table top and out of the players' line of sight. $25-$50.

14

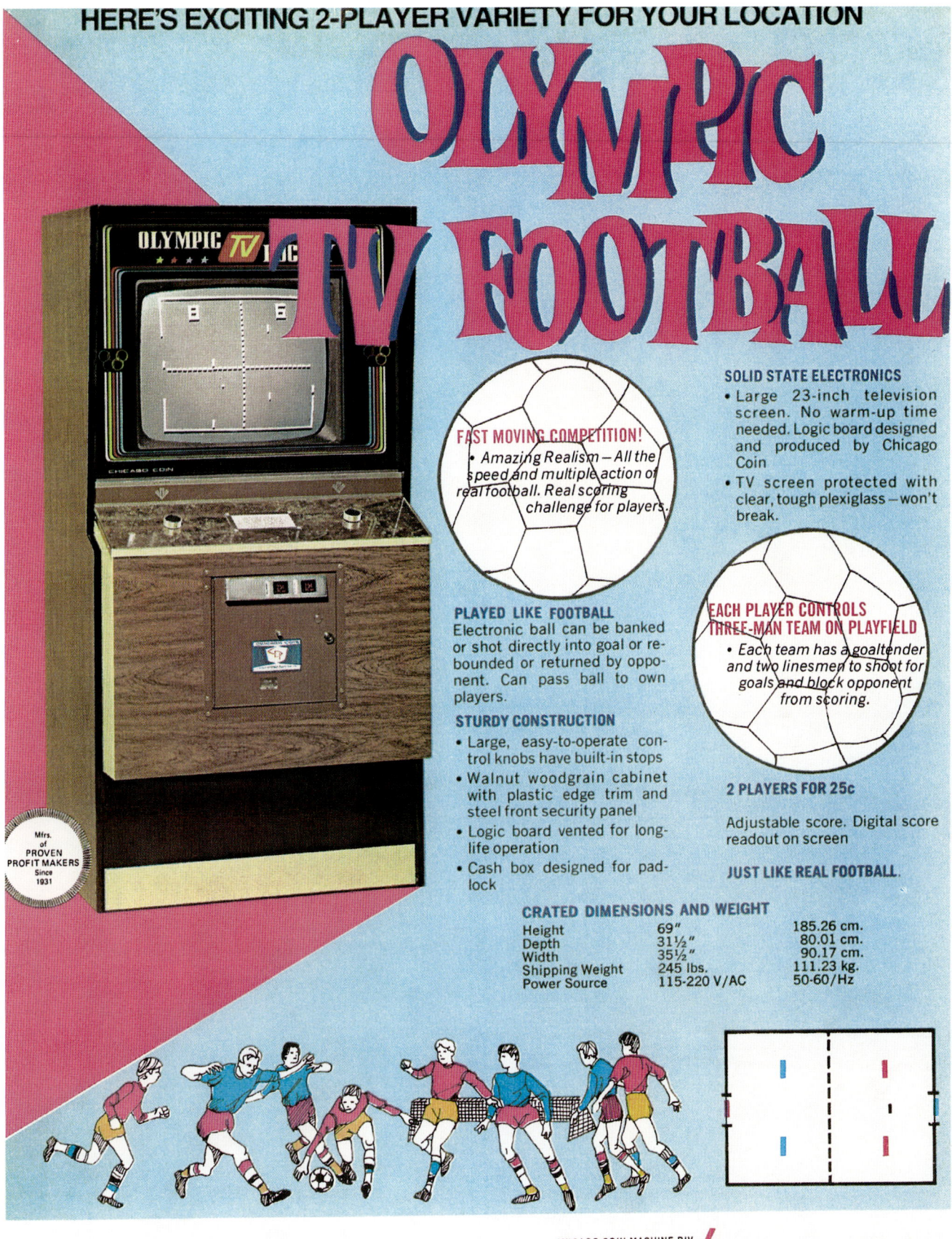

Look closely at the name of the game in the photograph and you'll see that it reads OLYMPIC TV HOCKEY, even though the flyer is advertising OLYMPIC TV FOOTBALL. This 1973 flyer was designed for the European market where the American game of soccer is called football; whether named hockey, tennis, soccer, or football, all of these early paddle games offered essentially the same game play. Game shown in this period ad is $25-$50.

Atari's 1973 QUADRAPONG came in a stand-up table cabinet so four people could play at once without having to line up side by side; according to the brochure, "its low profile allows room for 4 players and a congenial group of spectators." Game shown in this period ad is $100-$150.

Midway's LEADER, produced in 1974, was advertised as "a TV knock-out!" in the company's literature, although the game attracted few players. $50-$75.

Cocktail table version of Midway's LEADER. $50-$75.

Instead of knobs, Midway's 1974 PLAYTIME featured mini joysticks which could move the paddles up, down, sideways, diagonally, and in circles. $50-$75.

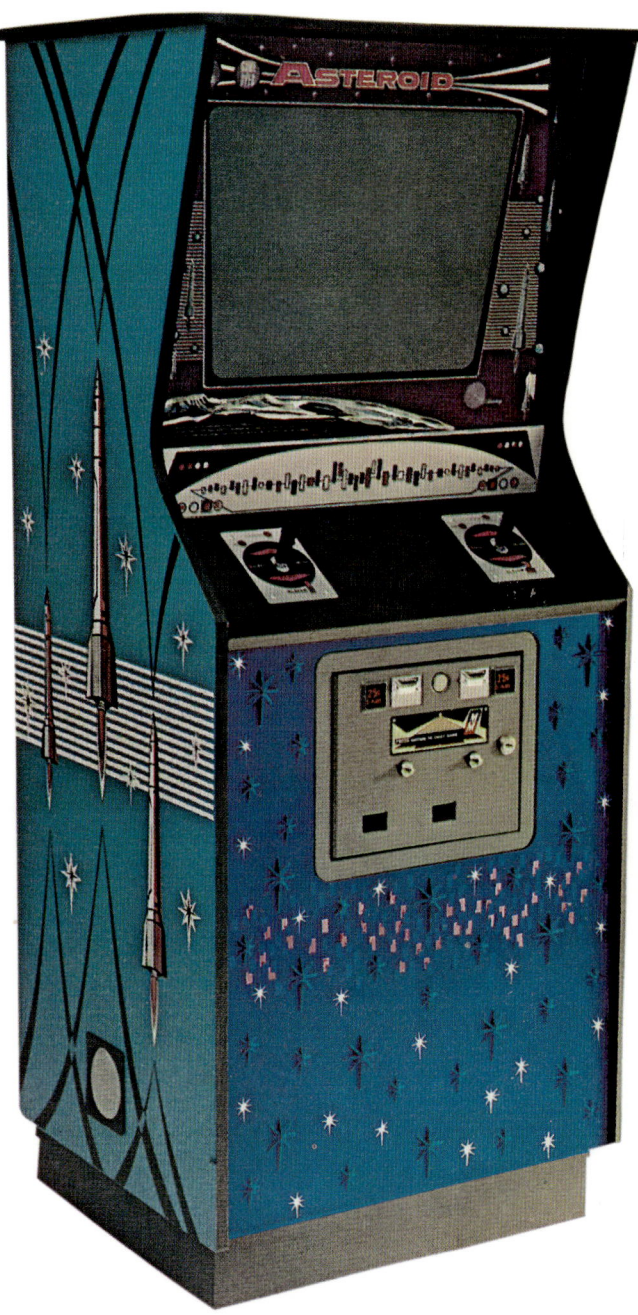

Don't confuse Midway's ASTEROID (1974) with Atari's classic ASTEROIDS video game from 1979. $75-$100.

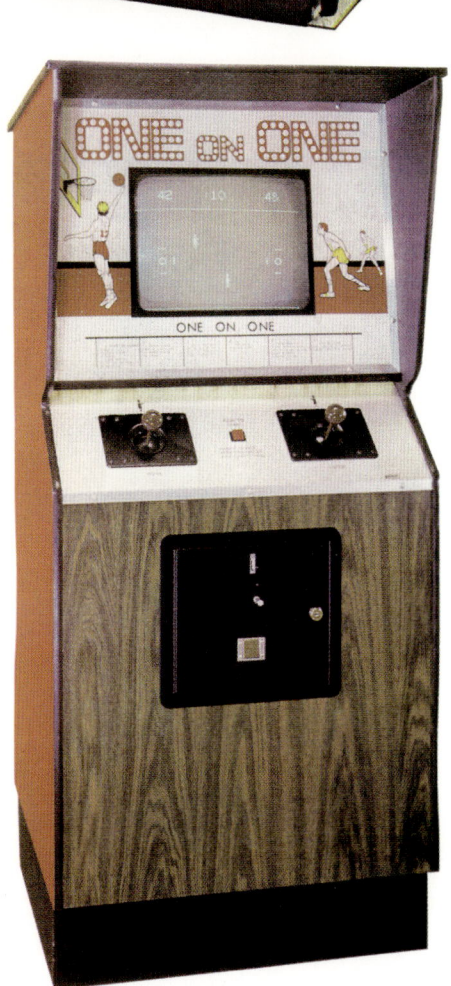

The name and graphics may lead you to believe that PMC's ONE ON ONE (1974) simulates a game of basketball, but the game offered little more than the usual paddle-game action. $25-$50.

17

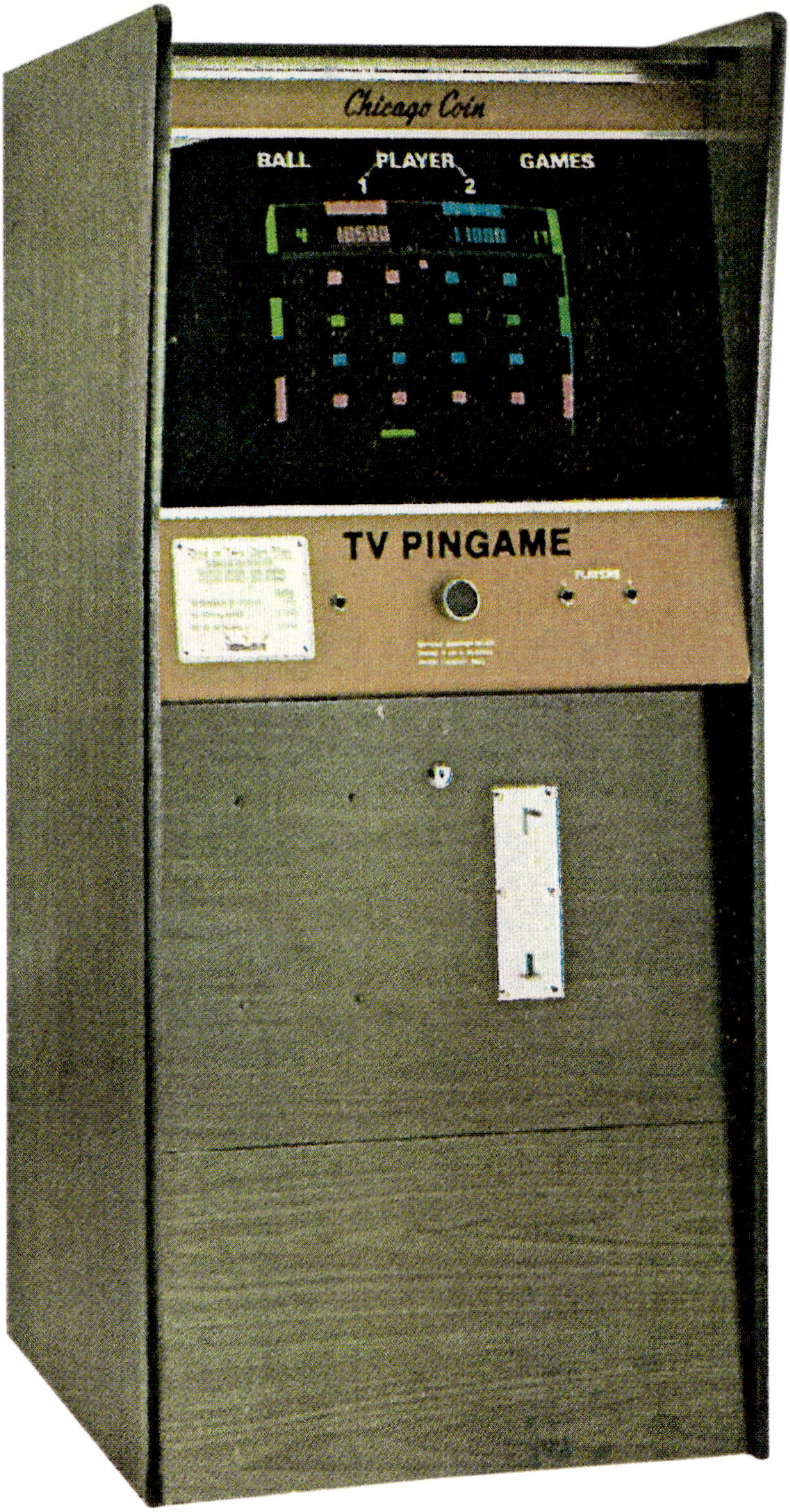

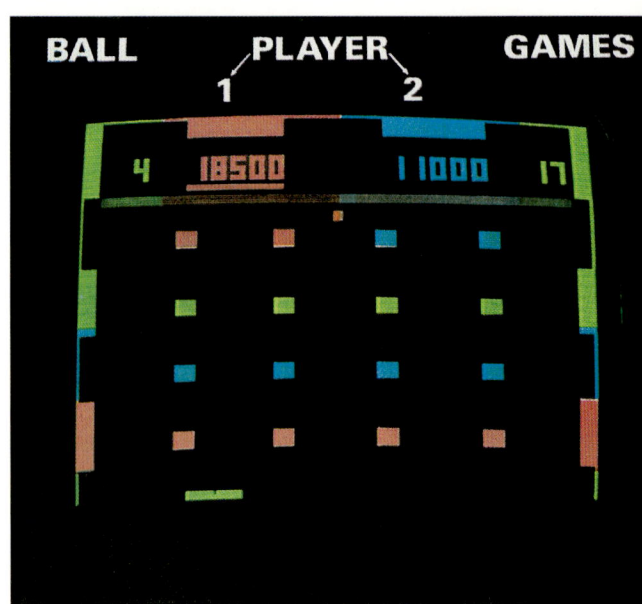

The colors on the screen of Chicago Coin's TV PINGAME were created using a plastic overlay positioned over the black and white monitor.

How do you get pinball players to try a video game? Call it TV PINGAME! This 1974 video game from Chicago Coin had nothing in common with pinball except the name. $100-$150.

Midway's TV FLIPPER (1974) was nearly identical to Chicago Coin's TV PINGAME except that Midway's game used a joystick to control the paddle at the bottom of the screen rather than a knob. $100-$150.

Atari's PINPONG was the first video pinball game to use a pair of "flippers" rather than a paddle at the bottom of the screen to control the game play. $150-$200.

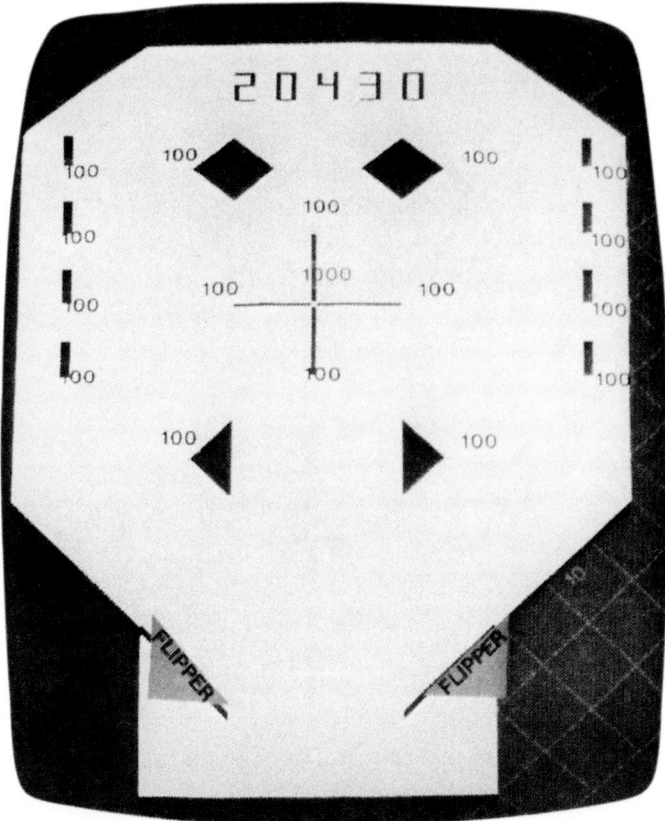

PINPONG had targets along each side of the "playfield," along with bumpers in the middle of the screen.

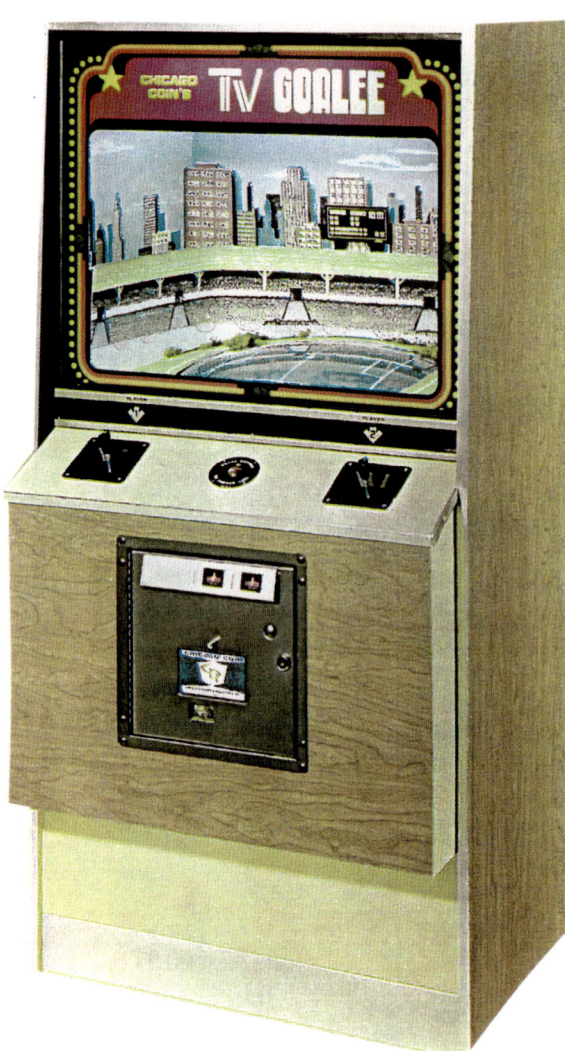

Released in 1974, TV GOALEE had a colorful city skyline as the backdrop around the screen.

TV GOALEE by Chicago Coin was the first video game to have the monitor mounted horizontally in the cabinet, rather than vertically at eye level. $75-$100.

Atari's SPACE RACE offered "just enough frustration to encourage replay after replay," according to the company's literature. Produced in 1973, this game was the first to use a joystick control. Game shown in this period ad is $150-$250.

20

For-Play's STAR TREK (1972) was an outer space shoot-'em-up similar to COMPUTER SPACE; the game was never properly licensed from Paramount Pictures (which owns the rights to *Star Trek*), and only a few prototypes were produced before Paramount halted production of the game. $1,500-$2,000.

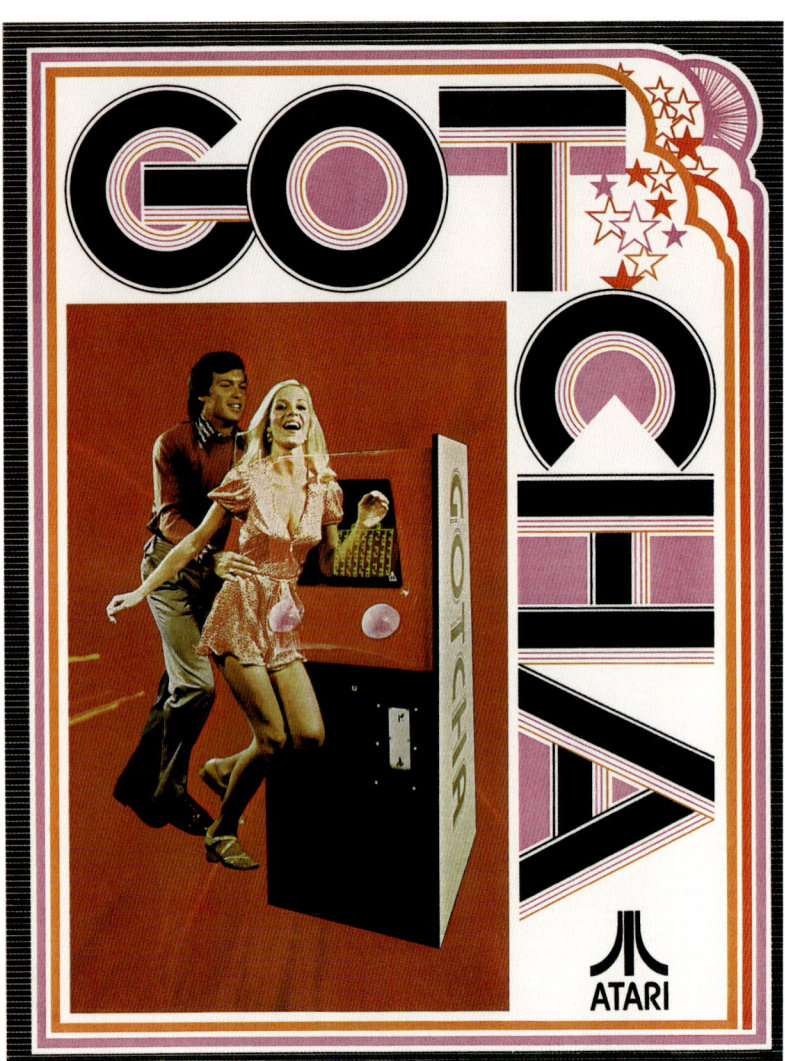

One of the first maze games, Atari's GOTCHA (1973) let players alternate between being the pursuer and being the pursued. Check out those huge player-control bubbles on the control panel! Game shown in this period ad is $150-$250.

Think that Atari made only video games? The company produced TOUCH ME in 1974, an electronic novelty arcade game which asked you to reproduce a random sequence of musical tones selected by the machine. $250-$350.

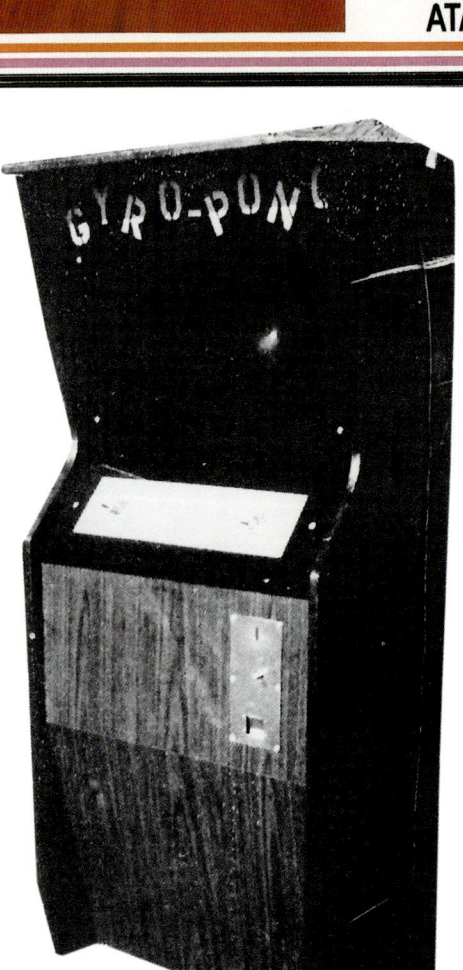

For about $200, you could convert a low-earning PONG game into GYRO-PONG with an enhancement kit that put an unpredictable spin on the electronic ball. $100-$150.

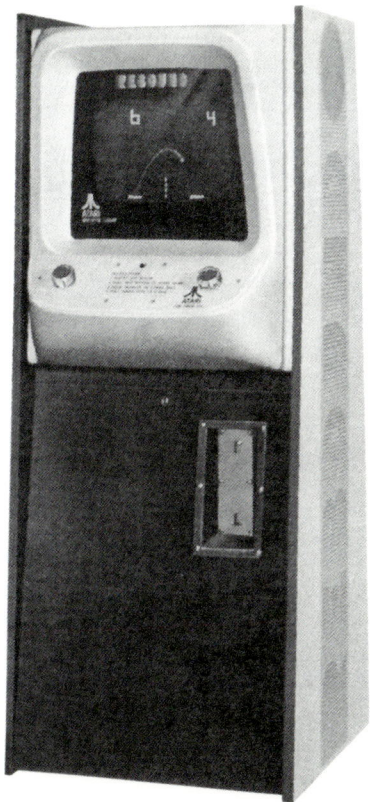

Atari's 1974 REBOUND was based on the game of volleyball rather than tennis or hockey. $100-$150.

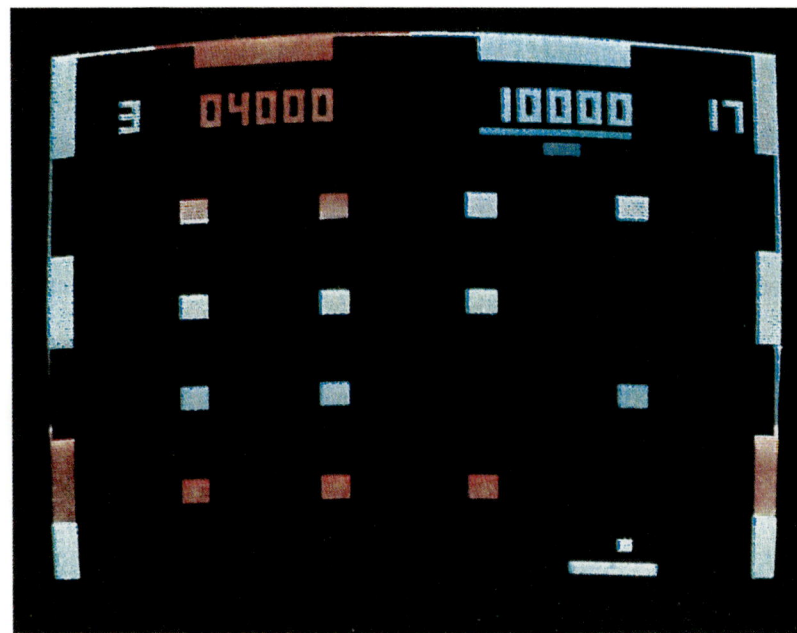

Screen shot of Exidy's TV PINBALL.

TV PINBALL (1974) was one of the first video games produced by Exidy, and was strikingly similar to Chicago Coin's TV PINGAME and Midway's TV FLIPPER. $100-$150.

Atari's GRAN TRAK 10 (1974) featured revving engines and squealing tires – quite a departure from the electronic blip sounds that players had been listening to. Game shown in this period ad is $100-$150.

Either two or four players could shoot for the hoops on Midway's TV BASKETBALL (1974). $100-$150.

Either one or two players could compete on Atari's GRAN TRAK 20, which had the same race track as GRAN TRAK 10. If you scored 40 points, you received a free game – and if either player scored 40 points in a two-player game, both players would receive free games! Released in 1974, this game weighed 400 pounds. $150-$200.

Released in 1974, Atari's QWAK! had a replica rifle attached to the game by a steel cable. The game was featured in the cult horror film *Dawn of the Dead*. $150-$200.

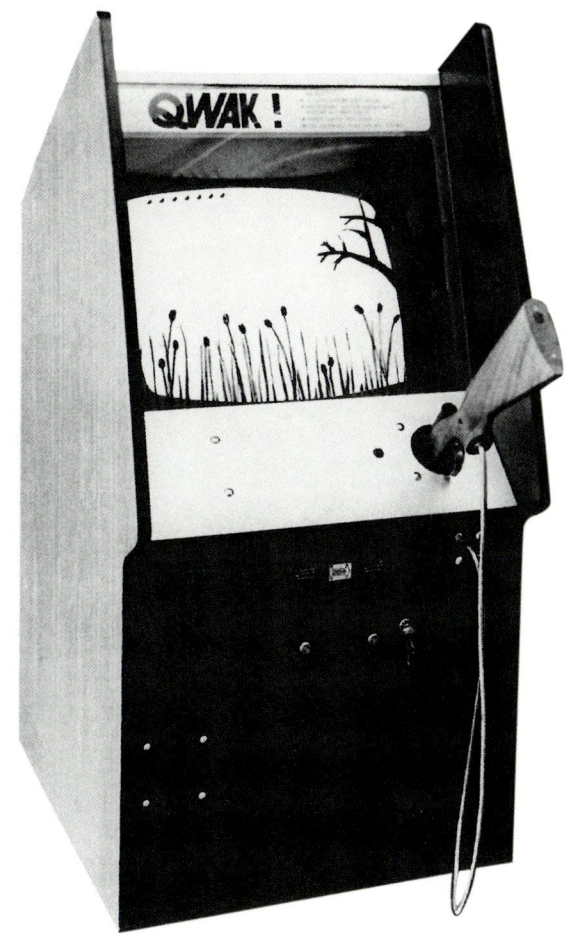

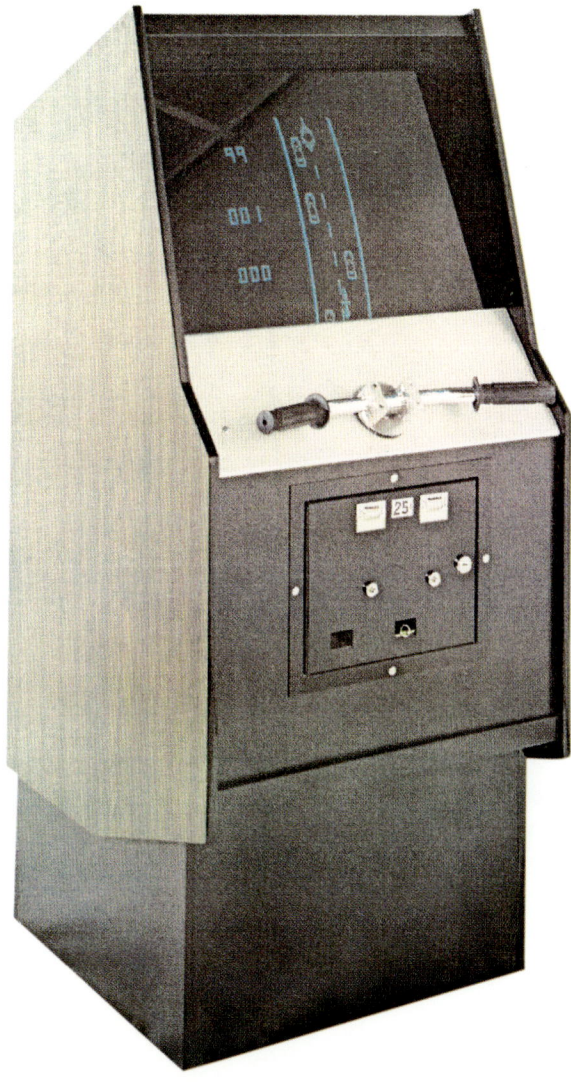

Digital Games' HEAVY TRAFFIC (1975) was one of the first video games to use motorcycle handlebar controls. $50-$75.

Kee Games produced the upright version of TANK, but Atari built the cocktail version of the game after Atari bought out Kee Games in 1975. Game shown in this period ad is $200-$250.

Midway's RACER (1975) was sold with an optional molded plastic seat. The game was renamed WHEELS. Game shown in this period ad is $100-$125.

Released in the summer of 1975, Midway's WHEELS II was simply a two-player version of WHEELS, not a sequel. Game shown in this period ad is $100-$125.

Notice the unusual cabinet configuration on the cocktail-table version of Midway's GUNFIGHT; players sat side by side, rather than opposite each other. $200-$250.

Midway's GUNFIGHT (1975) marked the first time a U.S. manufacturer ever licensed a game from overseas – in this case, from Taito of Tokyo, Japan. The game was a hit for Midway. $250-$300.

Up to six players could compete simultaneously on Atari's STEEPLECHASE horse racing game, released in 1975. $100-$125.

27

Meadows' BOMBS AWAY (1975) had wartime graphics to go along with the game's aerial bombing theme. $50-$75.

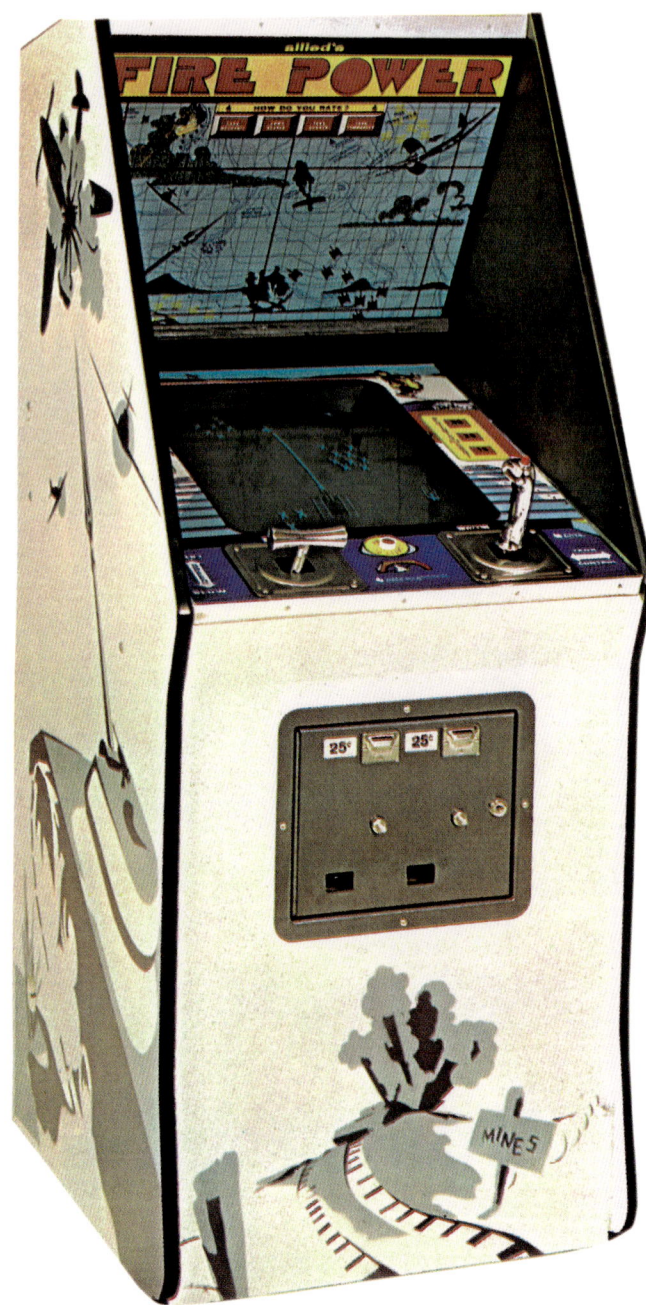

In Allied Leisure's FIRE POWER (1975), you controlled a ground-based tank and shot at enemy aircraft while trying to avoid the minefields in your path. $50-$100.

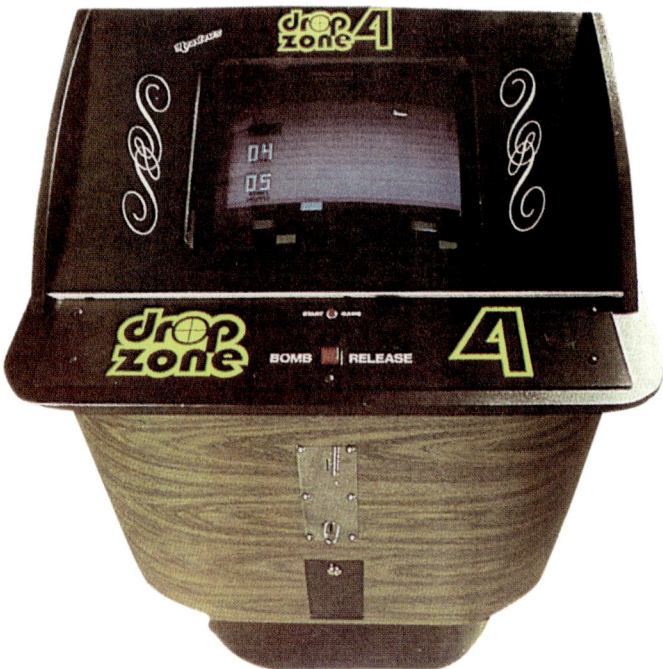

Meadows' DROP ZONE 4 (1975) was a cocktail-table version of the company's BOMBS AWAY game. $25-$50.

Elektra's PACE CAR PRO (1975) was a four-player driving game that used joysticks rather than steering wheels to control the action. Elektra produced only ten video games in 1975 and 1976 before the company folded. $50-$75.

The colorful (but purely decorative) artwork panel at the top of Atari's 1975 JET FIGHTER could be removed to make the game appear less gaudy. $50-$100.

You have to look closely to see that the name of this 1975 Atari game is actually SHARK JAWS rather than simply Jaws. Another attempt to capitalize on the shark frenzy sweeping the country in 1975. $100-$150.

MANEATER!
VIDEO TERROR
GIANT ATTRACTION AT THE M.O.A.

DERIVE MAXIMUM PROFITS THRU-

- Creative fiberglass cabinet
- 25¢ per player (1 or 2 players)
- Operator adjustable timer
- Solid State digital component reliability
- Extensive realistic animation

Also available in wooden upright cabinet and cocktail tables.

> "I have a hunch that this game will still be taking in quarters in arcades 5 years from now."
>
> C. Marshall Caras, General Manager
> Rowe Int'l, Dedham, Massachusetts

Units Are Now Being Shipped — Contact Your Local Distributor

FROM:
PROJECT SUPPORT ENGINEERING
750 N. MARY AVENUE, SUNNYVALE, CA 94086 / (408) 739-8550

Trade ad for P.S.E.'s MANEATER. Cashing in on the shark craze following the release of the movie *Jaws* in 1975, this game featured an *eye-catching* fiberglass cabinet but not much else. The first of a half dozen games produced by this company in the mid '70s, its collectibility is based primarily on its unusual cabinet rather than the game play. Game shown in this period ad is $1,500-$2,000.

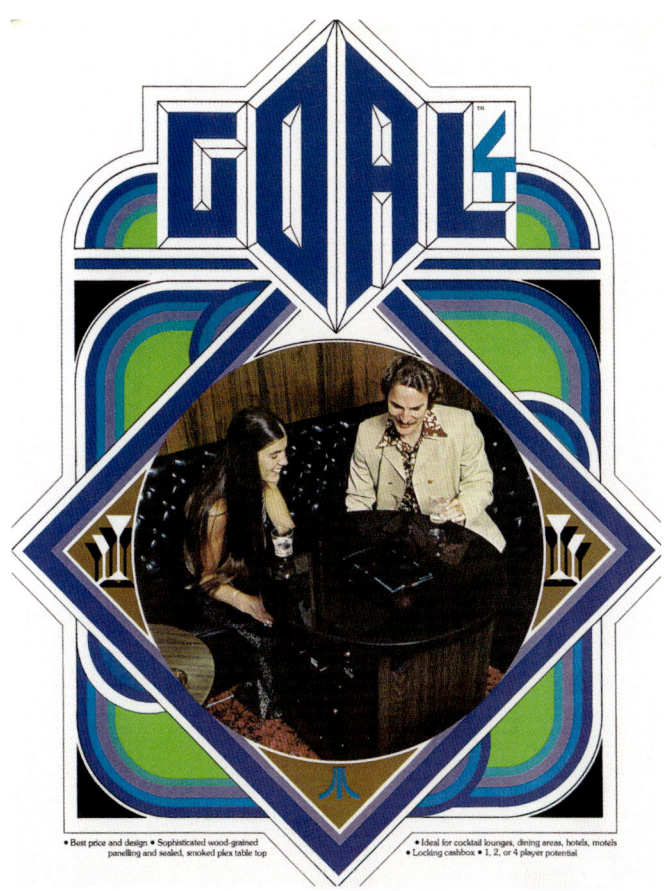

Atari's GOAL 4 (1975) was the only video game ever produced by Atari that was sold only in a cocktail table format; no upright version was ever produced. It was also one of the last paddle-style video games ever made. Game shown in this period ad is $50-$75.

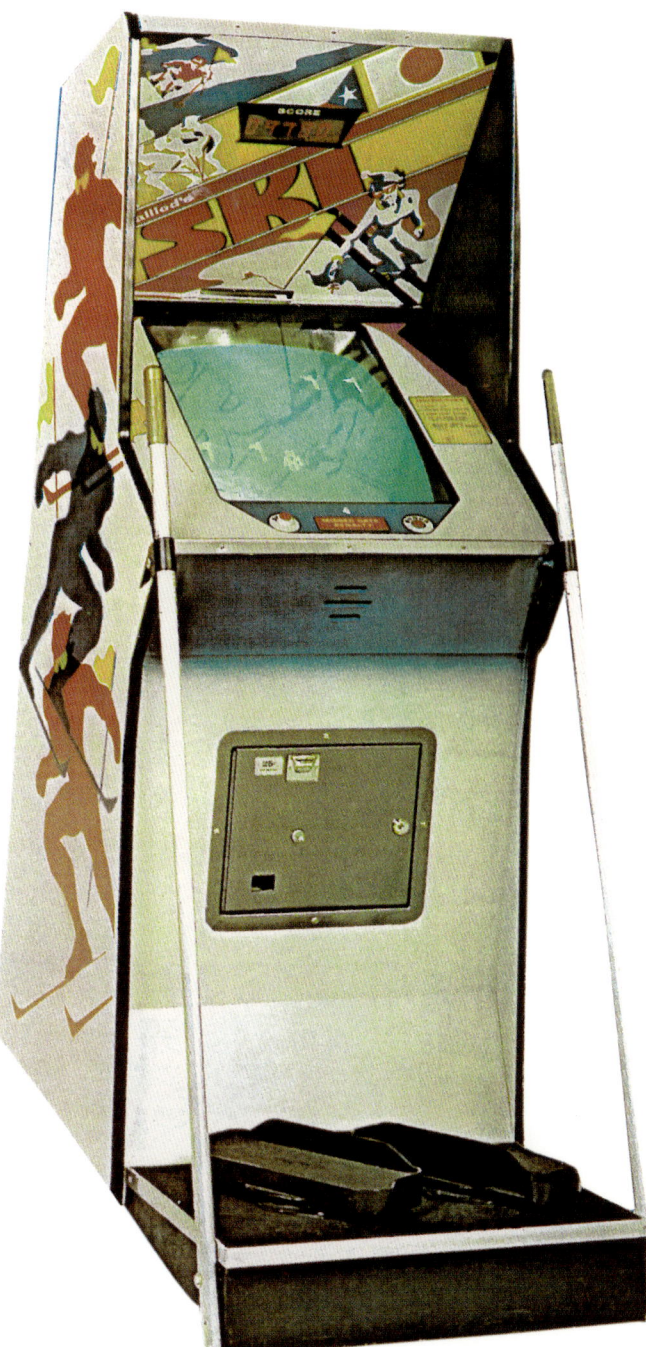

Allied's 1975 SKI had one of the most creative and imaginative cabinets used on any video game to that time; you held on to the poles and moved your feet from side to side to guide the skier down the hill. It was also one of the first games to use a digital score readout. $200-$350.

ROBOT, from Allied Leisure, was one of the few paddle games which let one player compete against the machine; two or four players could also compete on this 1975 game. $50-$75.

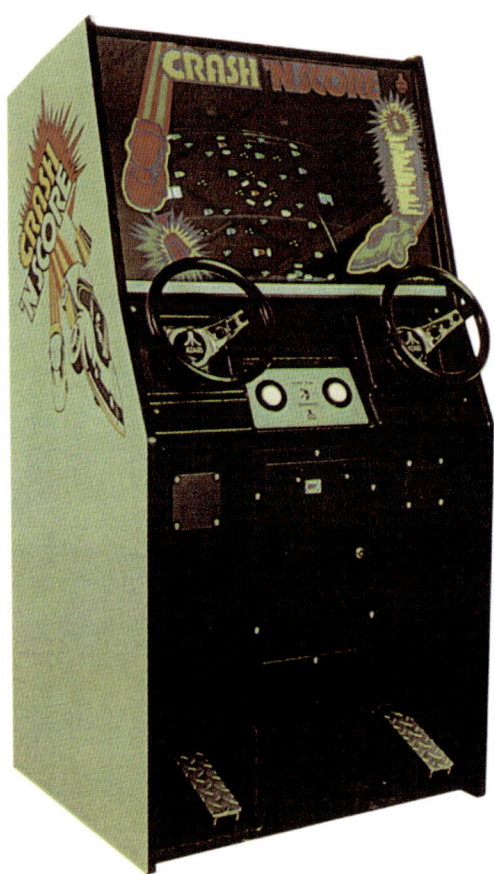

You could choose to play Atari's CRASH 'N SCORE (1975) either with or without the barriers on the screen of this demolition derby game. $75-$100.

Released in 1975, Exidy's DESTRUCTION DERBY was the first two-player driving game. The object was to smash into your opponents' cars at a demolition derby. $100-$150.

Atari's HI-WAY was available only in this molded fiberglass cabinet designed for arcades and bowling alleys rather than street locations like bars and taverns. $200-$300.

You sat in the control chair and used the triggered joystick to play Allied's F-114 (1975). The game came set from the factory at 50 cents per play and featured the largest monitor ever used on a video game to that time. $200-$300.

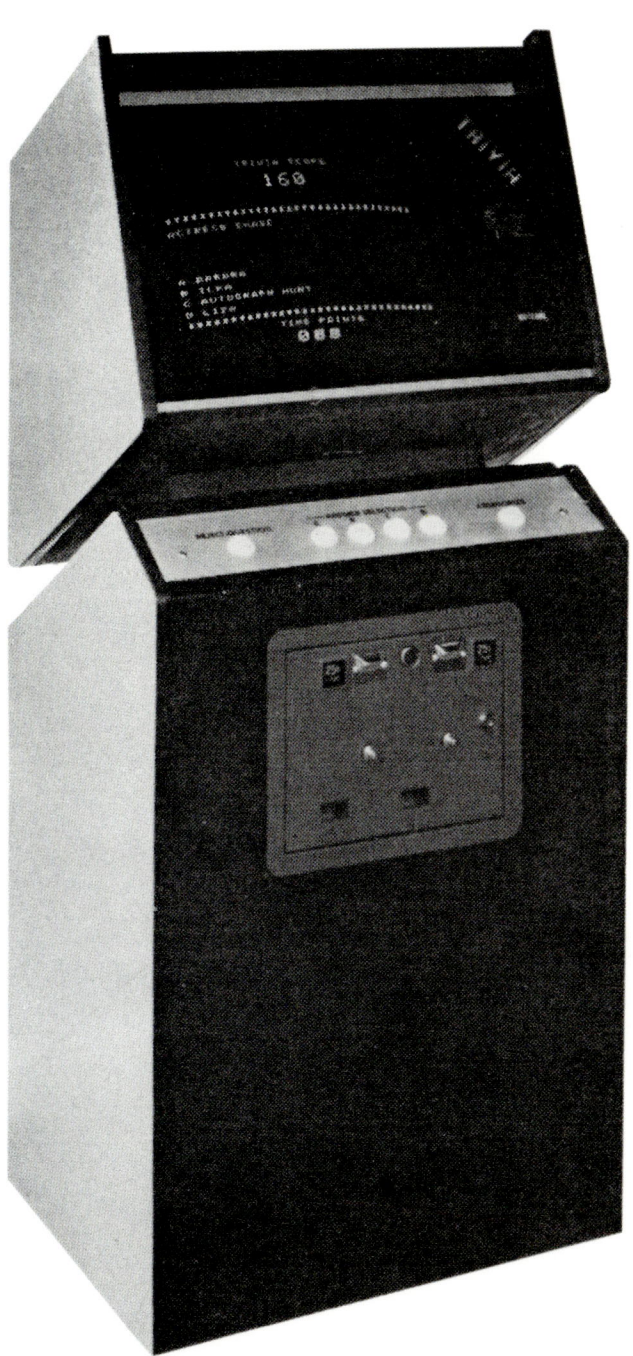

Ramtek's TRIVIA (1976) was the first video quiz game. Although popular in bars, most quiz games have little collectible value today. $25-$50.

Atari's 1975 ANTI AIRCRAFT was a land-to-air shooting game. $100-$150.

You shot the bad guys on Atari's OUTLAW (1976) using the replica Colt 45 which was attached to the cabinet by a steel cable. You could even select your desired skill level by gunning against either Half-Fast Pete (beginner) or Billy the Kid (advanced). $150-$250.

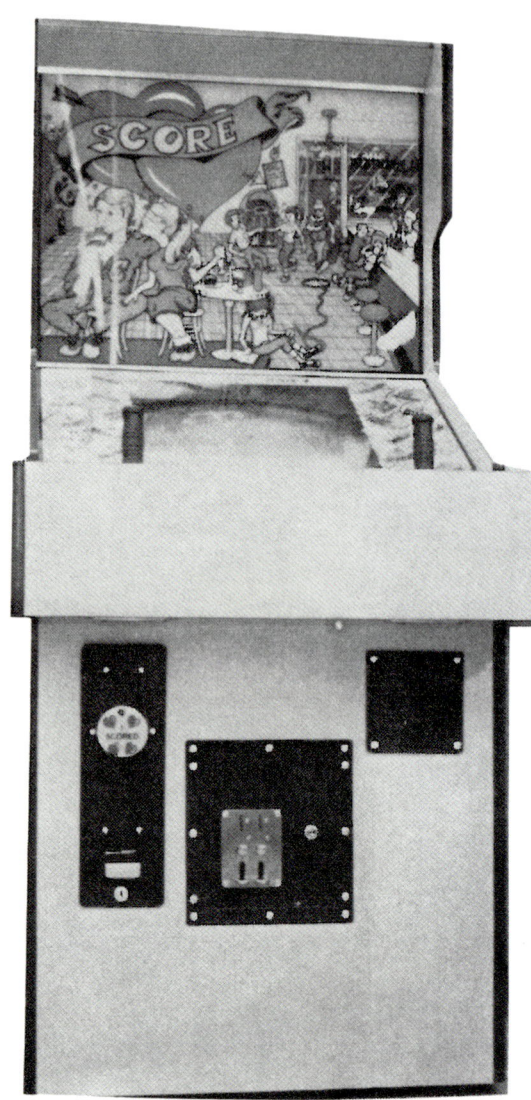

Exidy's SCORE (1976) awarded a free play token for skillful play; the token dispenser is located just to the left of the coin door. $100-$150.

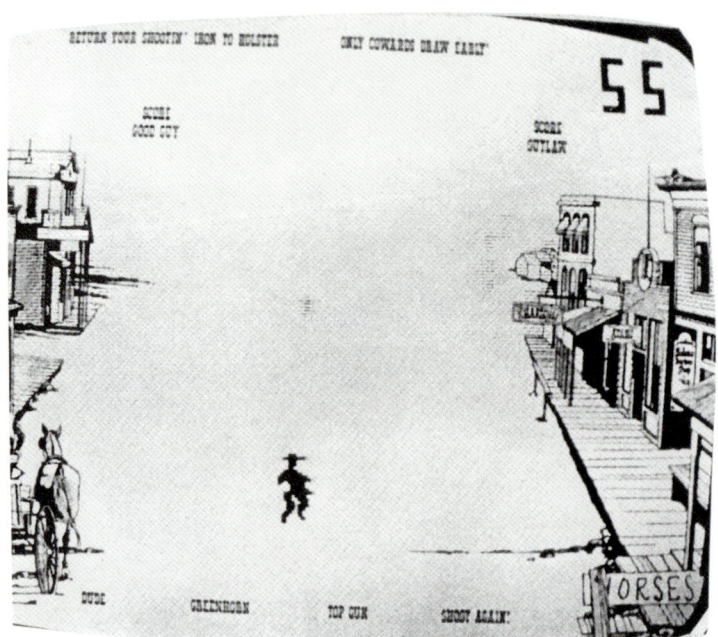

OUTLAW screen shot.

34

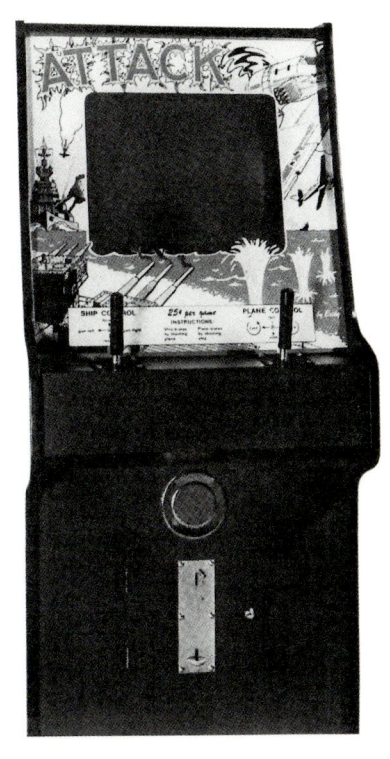

ATTACK, an air-sea combat game, was produced by Exidy in 1976. $75-$100.

Allied Leisure's FOTSBALL (1976) was a video adaptation of foosball; notice the table soccer player stenciled on the front of the cabinet. $75-$100.

Although two could play Chicago Coin's DEMOLITION DERBY simultaneously, a single player had to use the controls on the left of the cabinet when playing alone; the right pedal and steering wheel were only used when two players were competing. Arcade owners received many complaints from players who tried using the controls on the right and thought that the game wasn't working properly. $75-$125.

Instead of a rifle, P.S.E.'s BAZOOKA (1976) featured a replica of a bazooka in this war-themed game, one of the last games made by this company. $75-$125.

Produced in 1976, Gremlin's BLOCKADE was a one- or two-player maze game. $100-$125.

Midway's 1976 TORNADO BASEBALL gave you one inning with three outs for a quarter, but you could deposit up to nine quarters and play a full nine-inning game! $100-$150.

CO-MOTION (1976) was one of the first games produced by Gremlin. It was available only in a cocktail-table format. $50-$100.

BREAKOUT was one of Atari's biggest hits of the mid 1970s; the object of this 1976 game was to knock out the rows of bricks using an electronic ball that bounced off a paddle which moved from left to right along the bottom of the screen. A plastic overlay on the screen added color to the game. $200-$300.

This bootleg version of BREAKOUT was called SUPER CRASH and was sold only in Europe. The cabinet could be placed on a countertop or mounted on a wall. $100-$150.

Despite the claim on the sales brochure that "Flyball's animation and game play are so realistic, it's like playing the real thing," FLYBALL proved to be one of Atari's least successful video games. Two people could play FLYBALL simultaneously, with one pitching while the other was at bat. $100-$150.

Up to four players could compete at once on Midway's CHECKMATE (1976), a maze game which was available in both upright and cocktail table models. $150-$175.

Midway's hugely successful SEA WOLF (1976) was a video version of the company's electromechanical SEA RAIDER arcade game, produced in the early '70s. You had to fire underwater missiles at just the right moment to hit the passing ships. $200-$300.

38

SECRET BASE, produced in 1976, was the first Sega video game sold in the United States. The joystick controlled the plane's ascent and descent while the fire button dropped bombs on the enemy's hidden bases. $75-$100.

Sega's ROAD RACE (1976) offered the usual video driving thrills on an S-shaped roadway. $75-$100.

Midway's AMAZING MAZE, produced in 1976, offered over a million different maze patterns to keep the game challenging. $150-$175.

39

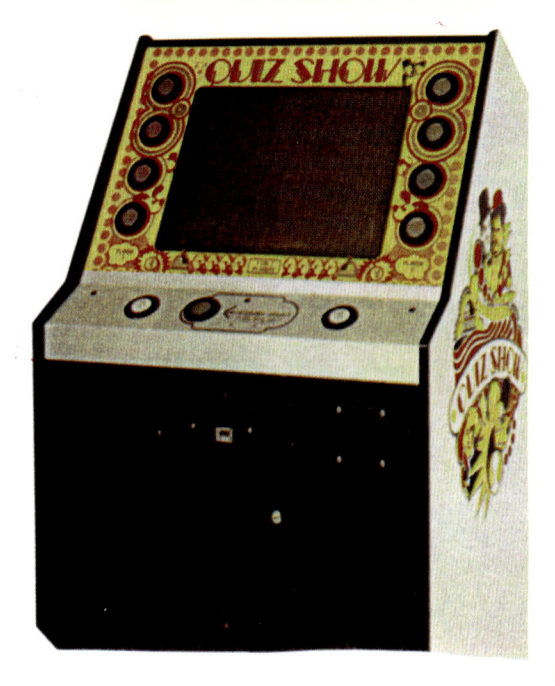

Laurel & Hardy and George Washington are among the personalities pictured on the cabinet of Atari's 1976 QUIZ SHOW. The game had 250 questions in four categories (sports, general knowledge, movies, and people), which was fine for players on location but repetitive as a home video game. QUIZ SHOW was the last game to carry the Kee Games name, although it was built in the Atari factory. $75-$150.

Hey! It's the Fonz on this 1976 video game from Sega. Despite the tie-in to *Happy Days*, the hottest TV show in America at the time, FONZ never attracted much of a following and was produced in very limited quantities. The low production, coupled with the continued popularity of *Happy Days*, makes this video game highly desirable today. $750-$1,000.

Many parents objected to the violent theme of Exidy's DEATH RACE (1976), which had an objective of hitting as many pedestrians as possible with your car. Exidy countered that the victims were really monsters rather than people so the violence was acceptable. $1,000-$1,200.

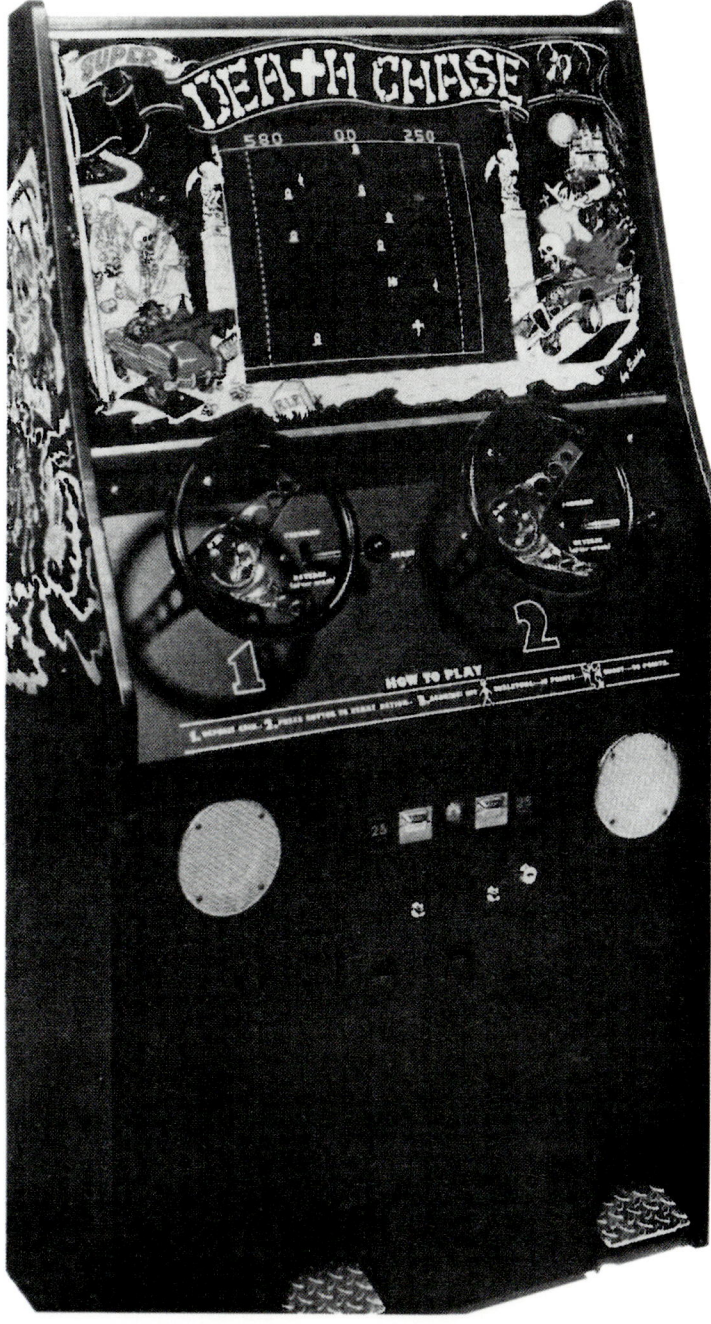

Exidy's SUPER DEATH CHASE was intended as a sequel to DEATH RACE, but the controversy surrounding the violent theme of DEATH RACE forced Exidy to pull the plug on SUPER DEATH CHASE after building only a sample run of the games. $2,000-$2,500.

Atari's STUNT CYCLE fared much better than Sega's FONZ, with game action better suited to Evel Knievel than to Fonzie. The idea was to jump your motorcycle over a row of buses without wiping out. $150-$250.

Chicago Coin's SUPER FLIPPER was a video game disguised as a pinball machine! This 1976 game had a video monitor mounted in a pinball cabinet with digital scoring in the backglass. You even shot the ball using a real pinball plunger! The game play failed to capture either video or pinball enthusiasts, and the machine is collectible today more for its novelty value than for its play appeal. $200-$350.

NIGHT DRIVER, produced by Atari in 1976, offered three player-selectable skill levels: expert, pro, and novice. It was also the first video driving game to have a dark background to simulate nighttime driving. $100-$150.

Elcon designed a line of restaurant table games so players could eat a meal and play the game at the same time. The concept never clicked. Pictured here is TANK BATTALION, Elcon's first offering. $100-$200.

An old-fashioned gangster shootout is the motif on Atari's 1976 COPS 'n ROBBERS. Along with high-speed shootouts, a beer truck appears on the screen from time to time to keep you sharp! $150-$200.

With its unusual cabinet design, Meadows' COBRA GUNSHIP got attention from players wherever it was operated. $50-$100.

43

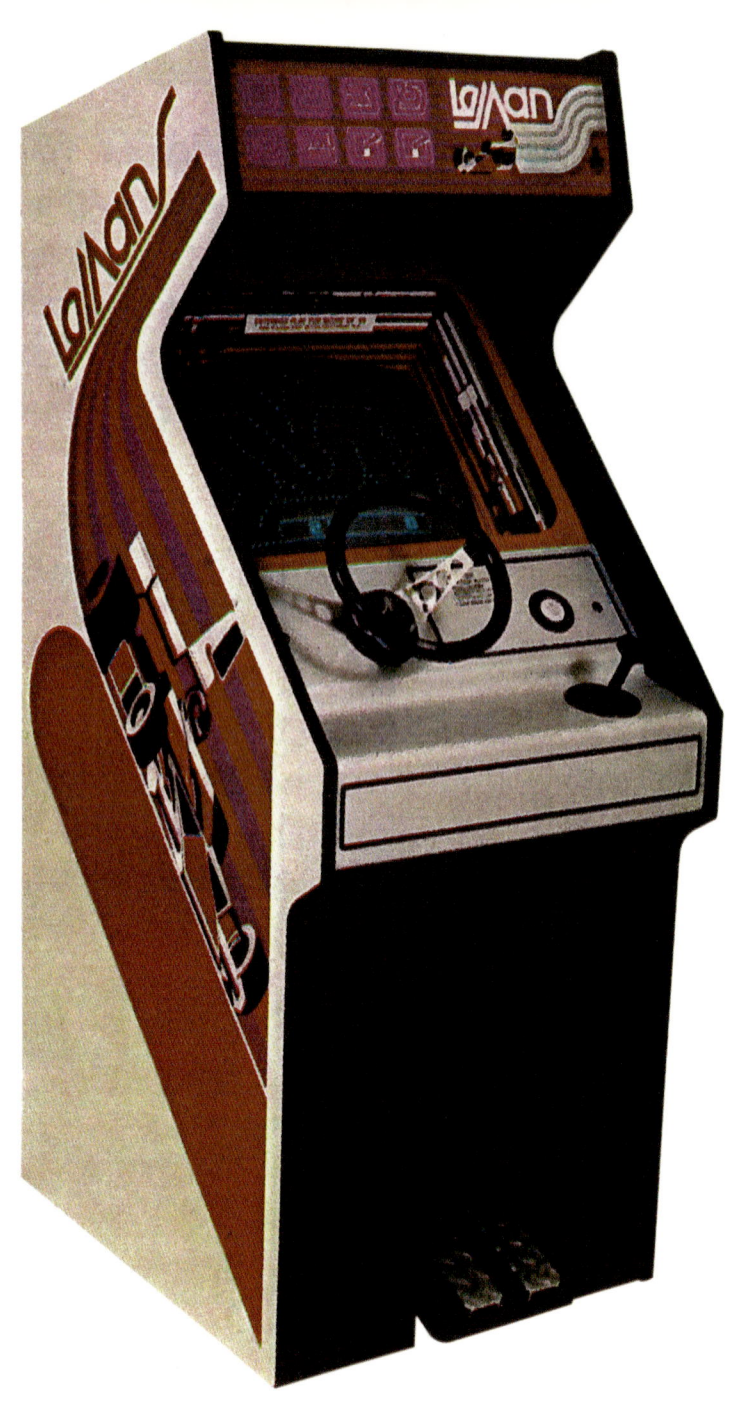

Nearly every one of the video driving games produced by Atari in the 1970s was a success, including LEMANS (1976), which offered ten different tracks with oil slicks and other road hazards. $100-$150.

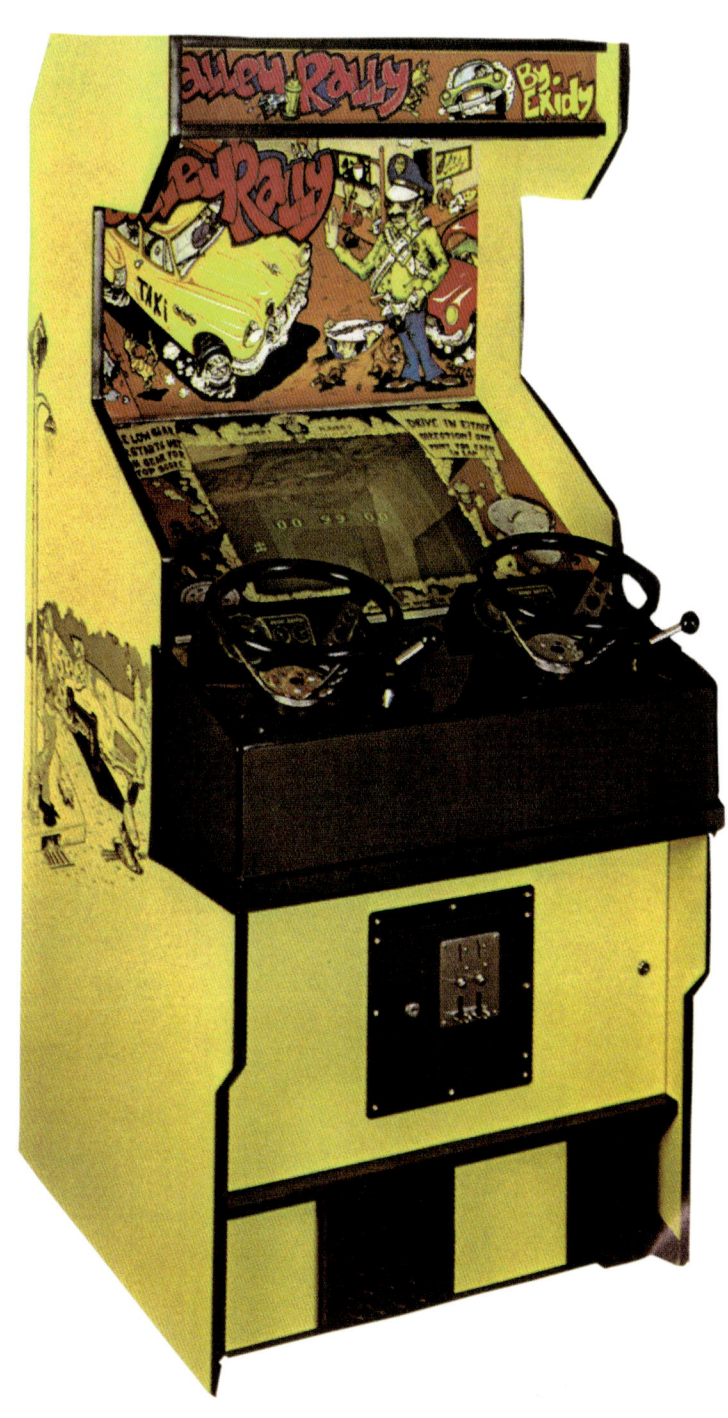

Exidy's ALLEY RALLY (1976) wasn't your typical video driving game. ALLEY RALLY was set on the seedy side streets of a big city and featured a variety of characters including drunks, taxi drivers, and hookers! $125-$200.

44

Part 2
INVADERS FROM SPACE
1977-1979

Video games had come a long way by the late 1970s. You could play sports like baseball (Midway's DOUBLE PLAY and Atari's FLYBALL), football (Atari's TWO-PLAYER FOOTBALL and Exidy's FOOTBALL), bowling (Meadows' MEADOWS LANES and Exidy's ROBOT BOWL), and even chess (Midway's CHECKMATE). You could race a car (Atari's NIGHT DRIVER, Midway's LAGUNA RACER, and Exidy's CAR POLO) or pilot a submarine (Gremlin's DEPTH CHARGE and Atari's DESTROYER). You could have a shootout with western outlaws, join the circus, or hunt big game. You could even pilot a space ship or take a space walk. It seemed that video games offered something for everyone.

But not everyone was playing video games anymore. In 1977, pinball went solid state, and suddenly everyone was lining up to play the new generation of pinball machines with digital scoring and electronic sounds. Even Atari, which had produced video games almost exclusively since the company was started, entered the pinball market in 1977.

Video technology had come a long way since the days of PONG, but the industry got back to its roots in 1977 with the release of SPACE WARS by Cinematronics. The game play on SPACE WARS was almost identical to COMPUTER SPACE, and this time, players were ready for the concept. SPACE WARS established Cinematronics as a major video game manufacturer.

SPACE WARS was one of the first video games to use a vector (or X-Y) monitor, which made the images on the screen look like line drawings and allowed for very high resolution. Most video games before (and after) SPACE WARS used a raster system, which displayed the images as tiny blocks that often only vaguely resembled what the image was meant to represent. Cinematronics had purchased the rights to the vector system from a small video game manufacturer called Vectorbeam, and over the next few years, the firm produced several more vector games.

But the video game industry received the boost that it had been looking for in the summer of 1978. On June 16, Taito introduced a game called SPACE INVADERS in Japan, and the video game world was changed forever. Space-themed games were nothing new; players had been piloting rockets and shooting at asteroids for years. But SPACE INVADERS introduced a new twist – the aliens fired back! Now you had to dodge the alien missiles while you were firing at them yourself! SPACE INVADERS demanded total concentration – let your mind wander for even a second and you would be vaporized. Each time you knocked off all 55 invaders, a fresh screen would appear with the aliens descending even faster. It was impossible to remain passive while playing SPACE INVADERS.

And SPACE INVADERS introduced something else new to video games – sound, or rather background sound. SPACE INVADERS had a kind of deep bass thumping

Ramtek's M-79 AMBUSH was so huge that you had to stand on the built-in step to see the monitor! The large size of this game makes it impractical for many collectors. $50-$75.

sound that resembled a heartbeat. At the start of the game, the beating would be slow, but the longer the game lasted, the faster the beating would get.

Finally, SPACE INVADERS was one of the first video games to reward a player's skill. Before SPACE INVADERS came along, most video games were played against the clock; that is, you would have a preset, operator-adjustable length of play time – 90 or 120 seconds, for example. On the other hand, you could keep your game on SPACE INVADERS going for as long as you could out-maneuver the aliens. First-time players often found that the game was over after less than half a minute, but SPACE INVADERS had an excellent learning curve that

Atari continued its string of driving game hits with SPRINT ONE (1976). $150-$200.

encouraged players to learn from their mistakes. SPACE INVADERS also awarded an extra base for reaching 1,000 points (the equivalent to an extra ball in pinball), and this award gave players something to strive for and to measure their skill against.

When Taito unveiled SPACE INVADERS in Japan on June 16, 1978, the Japanese players took to it immediately. After only a few weeks, SPACE INVADERS arcades began springing up in Japan with row after row of these games. By the end of the summer, the Japanese government declared that the country was running low on 100 yen coins because so many people were depositing their spare change in the machines. There was some doubt, however, as to whether American players would embrace SPACE INVADERS as warmly as Japanese players.

As part of its continuing licensing agreement with Taito, Midway had the rights to produce SPACE INVADERS in

Atari's DOMINOS was released in 1976. Send your opponent into the wall of dominos and watch the domino effect as the row of dominos topples across the screen. $150-$200.

of life, adults as well as children, men and women alike. It wasn't unusual to see doctors, lawyers, and other businessmen dressed in suits waiting in line to play SPACE INVADERS on their lunch hour. Suddenly, it became "fashionable" to play video games. Negative publicity soon followed, however, with stories of how youngsters were skipping school to play SPACE INVADERS and

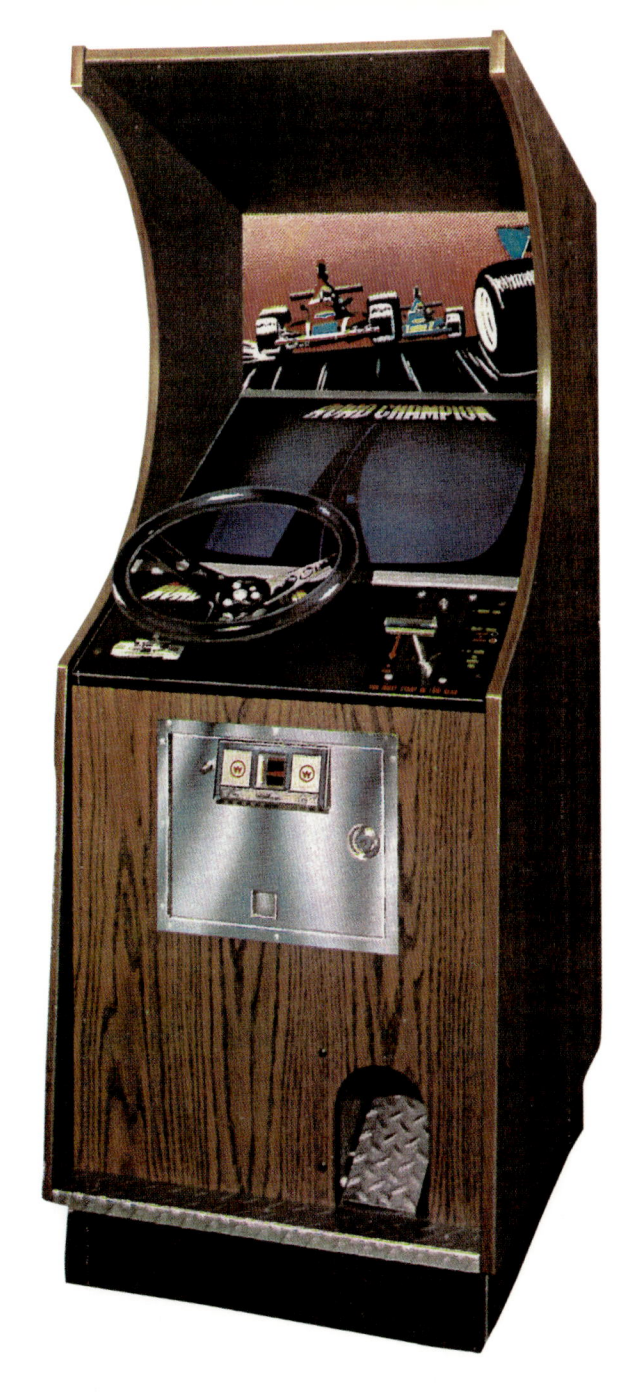

ROAD CHAMPION (1977) was Williams' first video game since PRO HOCKEY (1973); the company didn't produce another game until DEFENDER (1980). $100-$150.

the United States, and in October of 1978, Americans were introduced to the game in Midway's booth at the national coin-op games trade show. As stories of the game's popularity in Japan spread throughout the trade show, attendees lined up to play this landmark game. And Midway was sitting on a winner! Within the next year, more than 40,000 SPACE INVADERS machines were sold in the United States, making it the most successful video game in history. Although SPACE INVADERS never reached quite the level of popularity in the United States as it did in Japan, it wasn't unusual for U.S. arcades to have three or four of these games lined up together.

SPACE INVADERS attracted players from all walks

The game play on Gremlin's DEPTH CHARGE (1977) closely resembled Midway's SEA WOLF from the previous year. $75-$100.

Just as PONG had ushered in an era of paddle-style video games, SPACE INVADERS (along with ASTEROIDS and GALAXIAN) led the way as the outer space shoot-'em-up video games took over the arcades. After all, what game could ever hope to rival the popularity of SPACE INVADERS?

One of the most popular locations for video games was in bowling alleys, so it's only natural to find video bowling games like MEADOWS LANES, built by Meadows Games in 1977. $75-$100.

MIDWAY

Midway, the company that built such hit video games as SPACE INVADERS, PAC MAN, GALAGA, and MS. PAC MAN, has roots that go back more than fifteen years before the first video game was produced. Midway was founded in 1958 by Hank Ross and Iggy Wolverton; the company got its name because of its location near Chicago's Midway Airport. The firm's first game, RED BALL, was introduced in the fall of 1958 and was a novelty arcade game with eleven bouncing rubber balls inside a glass-enclosed play area. Throughout the 1960s and early '70s, Midway produced just about every type of arcade game imaginable – gun games, pinball machines, shuffle alleys, and more. The company quickly jumped on the video game bandwagon and introduced WINNER, its first video game, only a few weeks after PONG was unveiled.

Midway became the first company to license a video game from Japan when it acquired the rights to produce the highly successful GUNFIGHT video game from Taito. Midway's success with GUNFIGHT caught the attention of Bally, which had stayed out of the video market in the United States. In 1976, Bally bought Midway and wisely left the well-established Midway name on the company's video games. In fact, Bally controlled a large portion of the video game industry by the end of the 1970s since the firm owned a chain of coin-op game distributorships around the United States, as well as Aladdin's Castle, one of the large arcade chains in the country. By the early 1980s, the company's video games were produced under the name Bally Midway, but by the end of the decade, Williams Electronics had purchased the Bally Midway coin-op game division. Williams continued producing video games and novelty redemption machines under the Midway name until Williams closed its amusement game division in 1999.

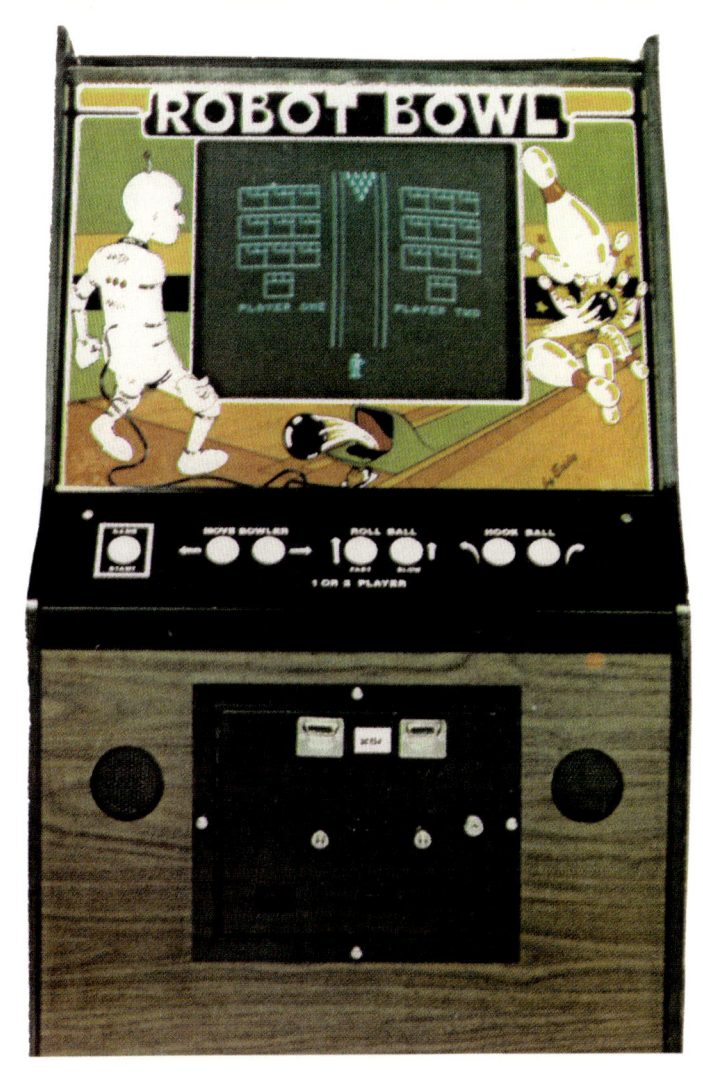

Ever seen a robot bowl? You would if you played Exidy's ROBOT BOWL (1977). $125-$175.

Up to four players could play Atari's SPRINT 4 (1977). $300-$500.

The cocktail version of Exidy's ROBOT BOWL lacked the clever cartoonish graphics that made the upright version of the game so appealing. $75-$125.

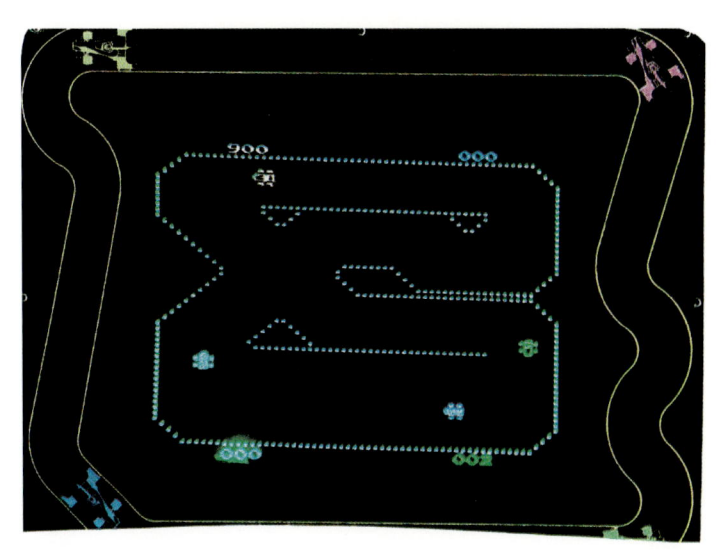

SPRINT 4 screen shot.

Exidy's 1977 CAR POLO definitely wasn't your average driving game. Rather than racing around a track, you played polo, bumping the ball into the goal by hitting it with your car! This game was only released in the large, four-player cabinet design pictured on the sales flyer. Game shown in this period ad is $250-$350.

You would find yourself with a red light and a penalty message if you jumped the starting gun on Atari's DRAG RACE (1977). $100-$150.

SUPER BREAKOUT, the 1977 sequel to Atari's popular BREAKOUT video game, never attained the popularity of its predecessor. $100-$150.

Atari's SUPERBUG (1977) was one of the first video games which could be adjusted to display information in English, French, German, and Spanish. $100-$150.

52

Warner Brothers didn't care for the name ROAD RUNNER on Midway's 1977 video rifle game; the film studio thought that the name might be misleading to players who would be expecting the see the cartoon Road Runner character, and Midway voluntarily renamed the machine DESERT GUN. $300-$400.

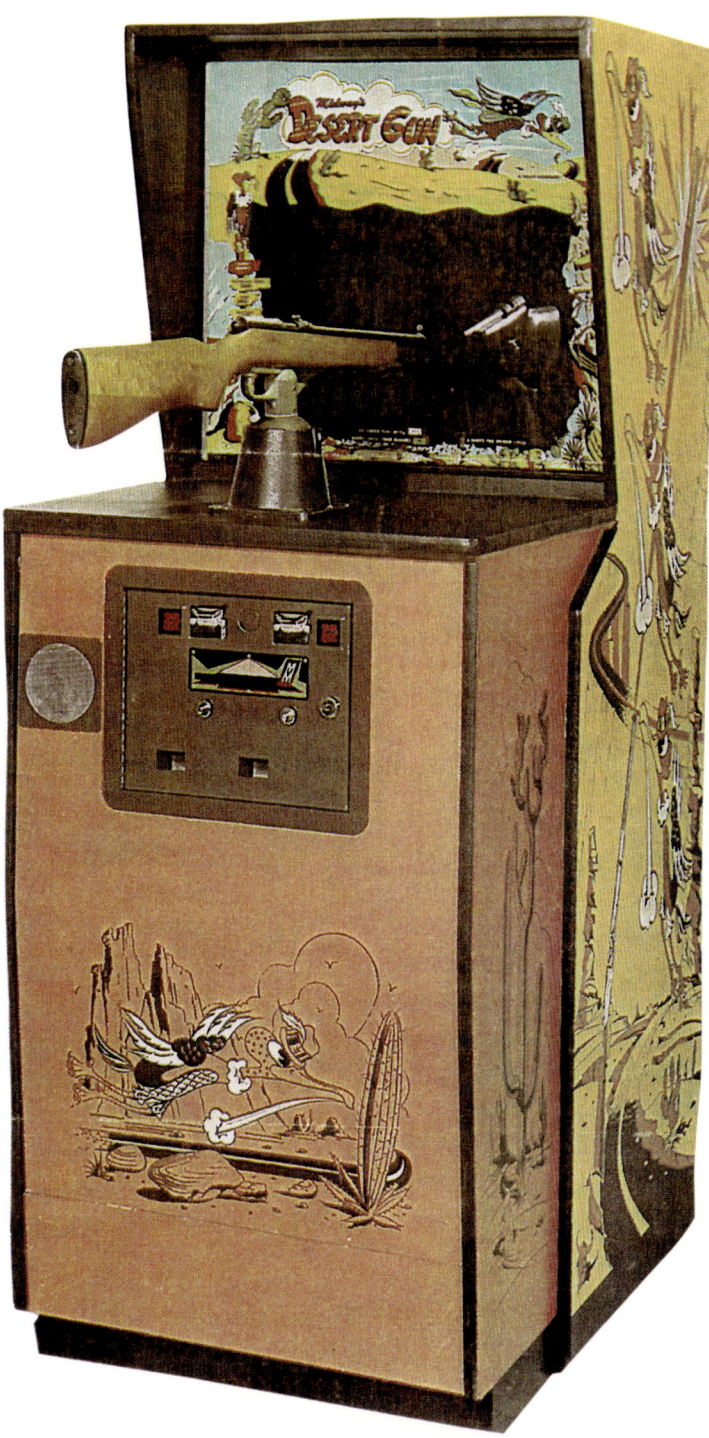

Notice how the cute little road runner speeding along the mountainous terrain on ROAD RUNNER has been changed to an unshaven buzzard flying just above the road on DESERT GUN. The artwork was changed on both the front of the cabinet and on the monitor glass. $200-$300.

53

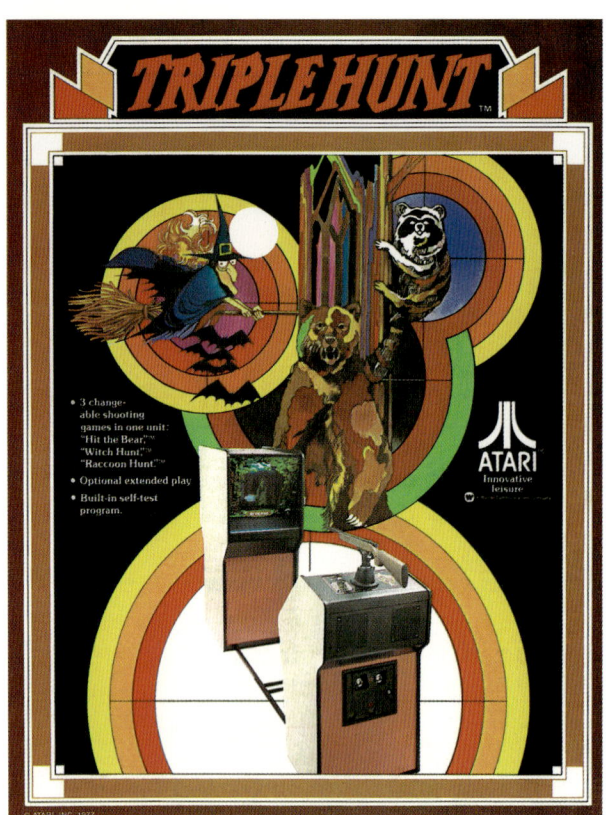

Atari's TRIPLE HUNT rifle game came in two large sections which had to be set up five to ten feet apart. You could select from three different games (Hit the Bear, Witch Hunt, and Raccoon Hunt) on this 1977 machine. Game shown in this period ad is $200-$300.

If you have a billiards theme in your rec room, then POOLSHARK is perfect for you. Try to sink all fifteen balls in thirty seconds without scratching. This 1977 Atari game had the monitor mounted horizontally inside the cabinet to create the illusion of playing on a billiard table. $100-$150.

Atari's SPRINT 8 was the largest video game ever built until that time. Because this game was so expensive and required so much floor space, production on SPRINT 8 was very limited and these games are extremely difficult to find today. Game shown in this period ad is $500-$800.

Midway's DOUBLE PLAY (1977) could be played by either one or two players, and offered double plays and errors. $100-$150.

The better your skill at shooting the wild animals in Gremlin's 1977 SAFARI, the more aggressive the animals become. $75-$125.

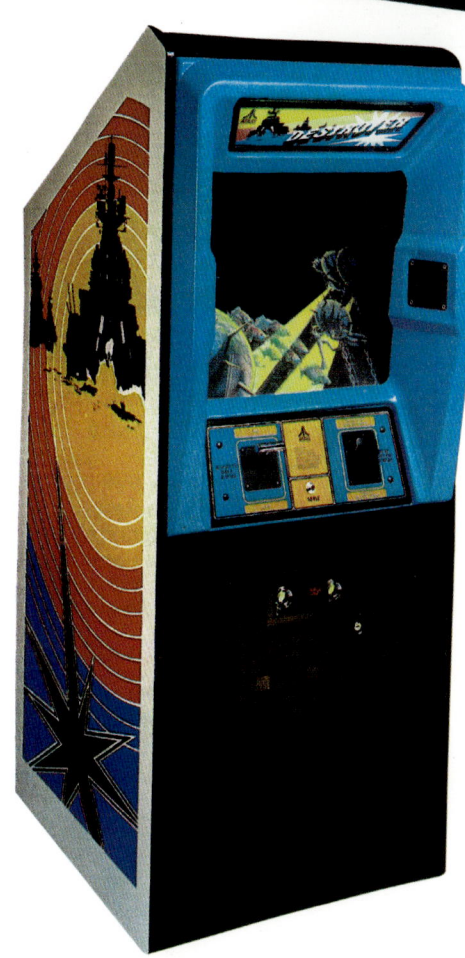

Like Gremlin's DEPTH CHARGE, Atari's DE-STROYER (1977) was loosely based on Midway's popular SEA WOLF video game. $100-$150.

55

CANYON BOMBER (1977) had a World War I motif, with blimps and biplanes dropping bombs into the canyons below. $100-$150.

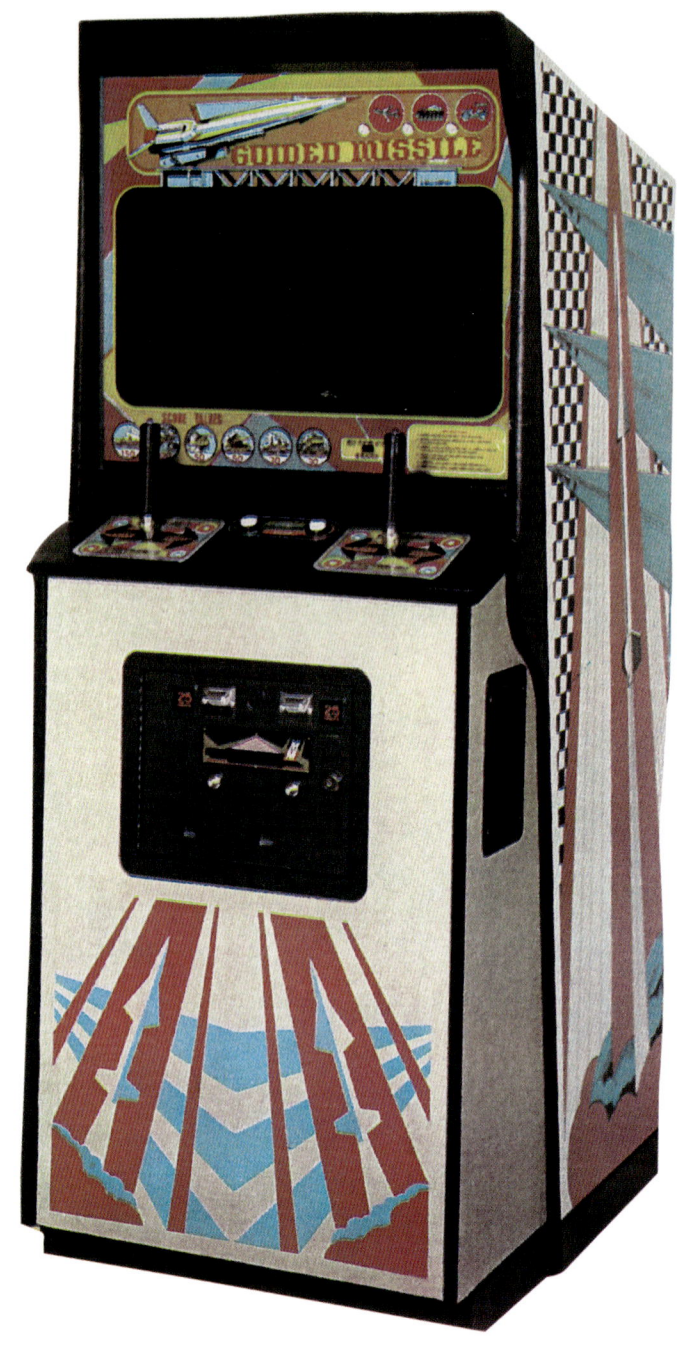

Players were starting to grow weary of rocket-firing games like Midway's GUIDED MISSILE by 1977. $100-$125.

Guide your spaceship to enemy planets and fire your proton torpedoes to destroy the aliens in Atari's 1977 STARSHIP 1, one of the first outer space shoot-'em-up video games. The attention-grabbing cabinet always caught players' attention. $150-$200.

56

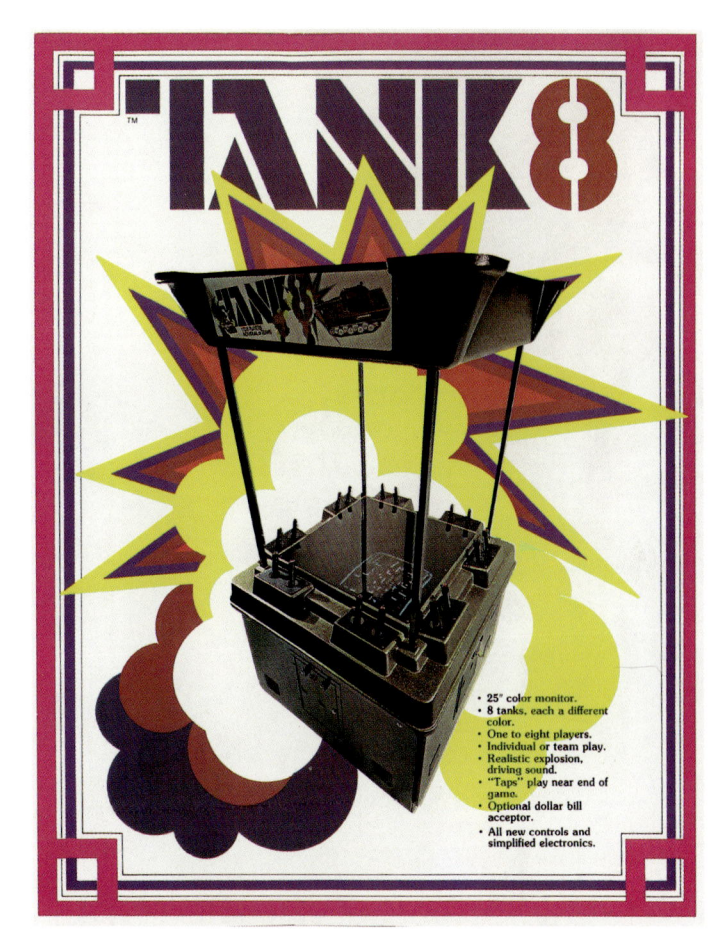

Atari sold very few TANK 8 games because of the amount of space required to operate them. You could team up with other players for team play on this 1977 machine. Game shown in this period ad is $500-$800.

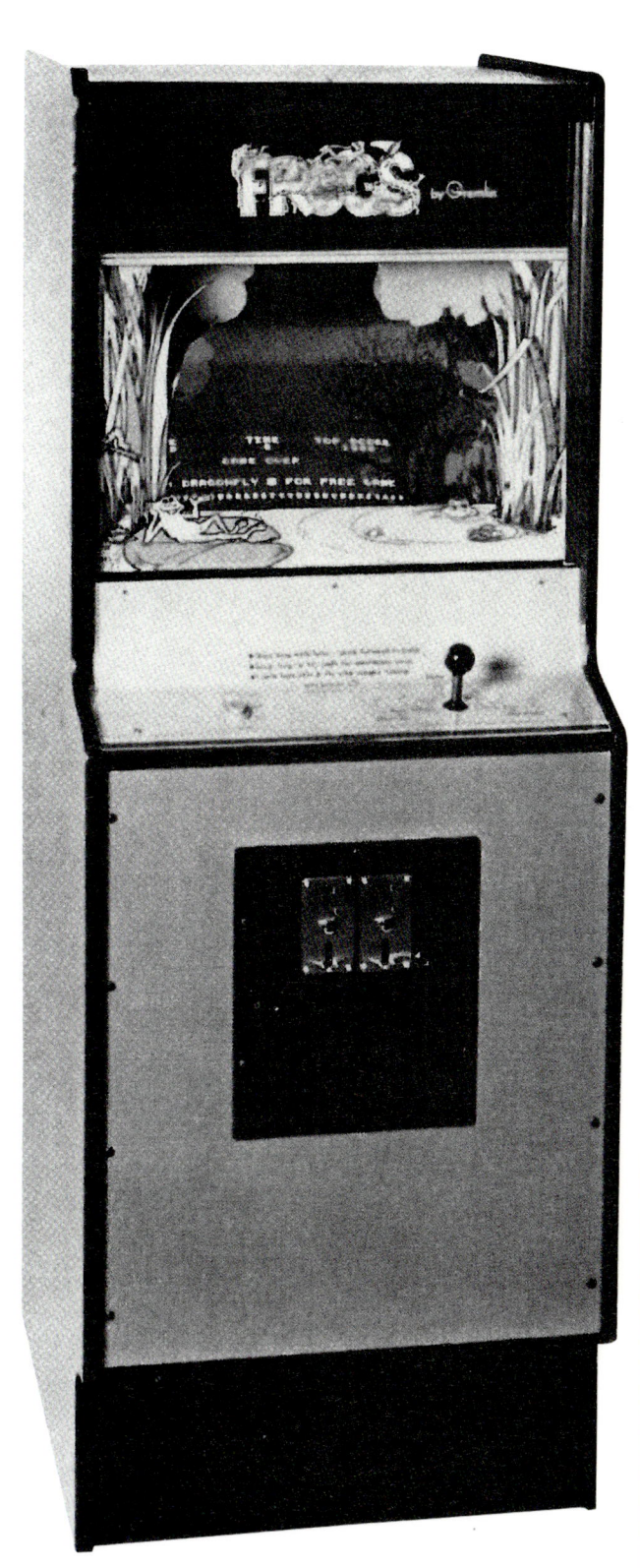

Don't confuse Gremlin's FROGS with Sega's FROGGER. You had to control the frog's tongue to grab as many insects as possible in this 1977 game. $150-$200.

TANK 8 screen shot.

57

Gremlin was a bit optimistic when it called HUSTLE "clearly the greatest single-player video game ever created" in its sales literature. The idea of the game was to use the four direction buttons on the control panel to steer your "arrow" around the screen while avoiding enemy arrows. $75-$100.

Ramtek's BARRICADE (1977) was nearly identical to Gremlin's HUSTLE, although up to four players could compete simultaneously on BARRICADE, while HUSTLE was designed for only one or two players. $75-$100.

Not much new on Midway's 1977 M-4 combat video game. $75-$100.

Midway's 1977 LAGUNA RACER was an updated version of the firm's 1975 WHEELS. $75-$100.

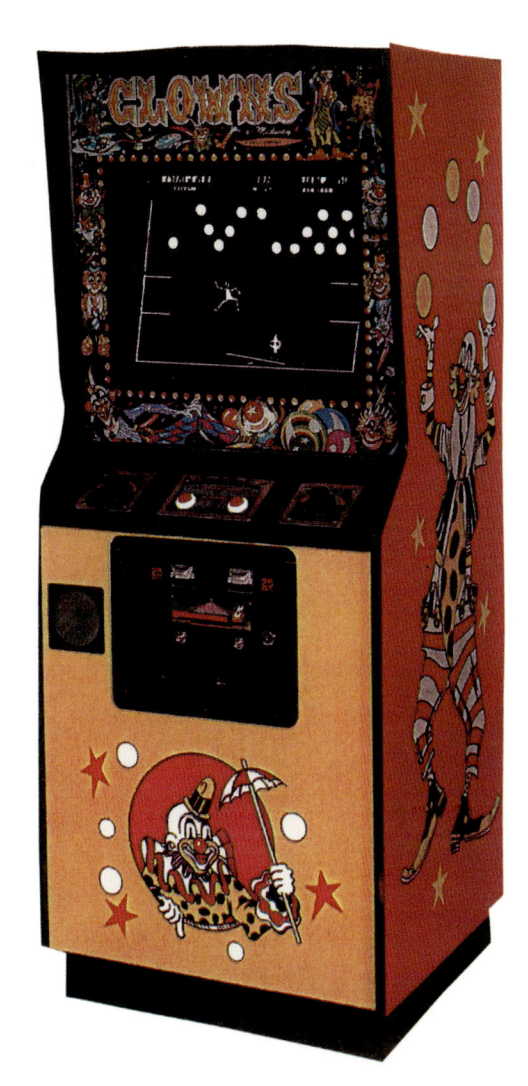

If you liked Exidy's CIRCUS, then you'll probably like Midway's CLOWNS. Same idea – bounce your clown off the springboard to pop the balloons at the top of the screen. $125-$175.

Midway's CLOWNS used the same cocktail-table design as GUNFIGHT, with both players sitting side by side rather than at opposite ends of the table. $75-$100.

59

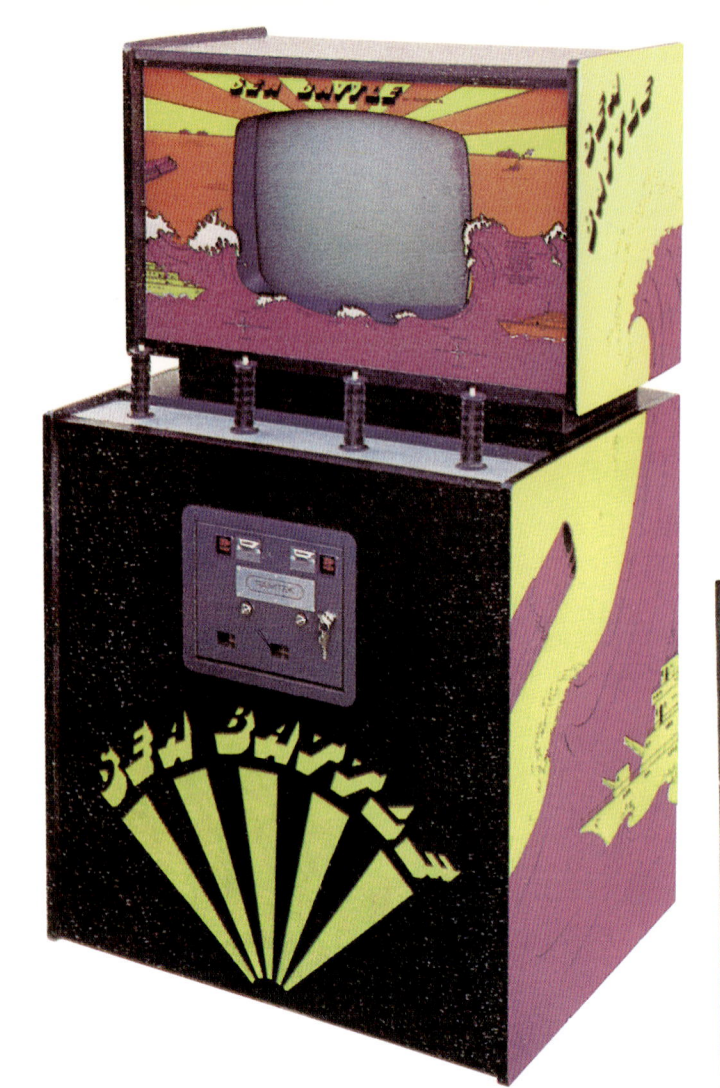

Ramtek's 1977 SEA BATTLE took up lots of space but didn't bring in many quarters for video game operators. Parts and service for games made by companies like Ramtek can be difficult for many collectors to find. $50-$75.

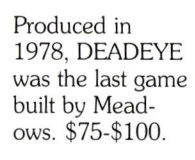

Produced in 1978, DEADEYE was the last game built by Meadows. $75-$100.

SPACE WARS proved to be a surprise hit for Cinematronics in 1977, and helped establish the company as a major video game manufacturer. The game play was a cross between Nutting's COMPUTER SPACE and Atari's ASTEROIDS. $500-$600.

Originally called MIDNIGHT RACER, Midway's 1977 280-ZZZAP was one of the first video games to have a "High Score of the Day" feature. $100-$150.

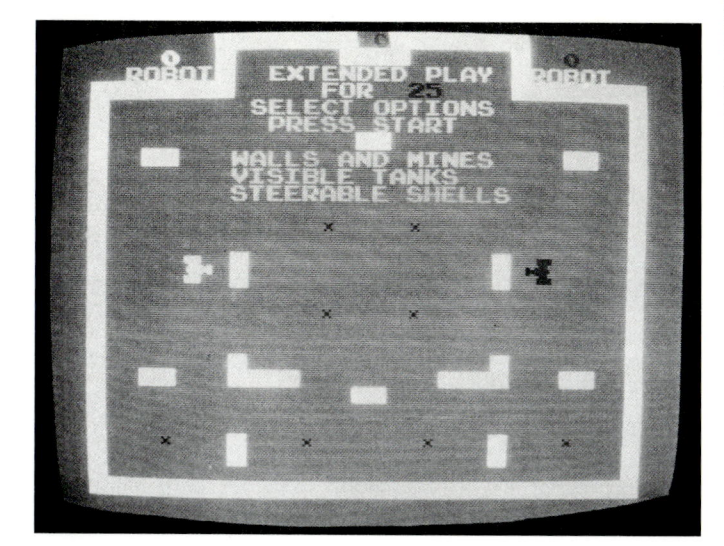

After TANK, TANK 4, and TANK 8, Atari's 1977 ULTRA TANK was the last entry in the series. This game featured invisible tanks, rebounding shells, and a robot tank. $100-$150.

ULTRA TANK screen shot.

Midway's DOG PATCH (1977) didn't feature L'il Abner, but this game have "the Wild Goose 50 Point Bonus Target" and "Handsome 'Down-Home' Cabinet Graphics," according to the sales brochure. $100-$150.

61

Look at the artwork on Exidy's 1977 FOOTBALL – it's soccer! Although Exidy never became one of the top video game manufacturers in the United States, the company's games sold fairly well in the United Kingdom and throughout Europe where the American game of soccer is called football. $100-$150.

Here's the two-player version of Atari's FOOTBALL, sometimes called "X & O FOOTBALL" because the game used those letters to mark the offensive and defensive action. Released in 1977, it was the first of Atari's popular sports-themed video games, and was found in virtually every arcade in the mid 1970s. $200-$250.

Notice the Xs and Os in the center of the gridiron in this screen shot from Atari's FOOTBALL.

62

Outer space-themed games like Midway's SPACE WALK (1977) were starting to become popular with players in the mid 1970s. SPACE WALK could be played by either one or two players. $100-$150.

Produced as a sequel to SEA WOLF, Midway's 1977 SEA WOLF II had two periscopes so two could play at the same time. $100-$150.

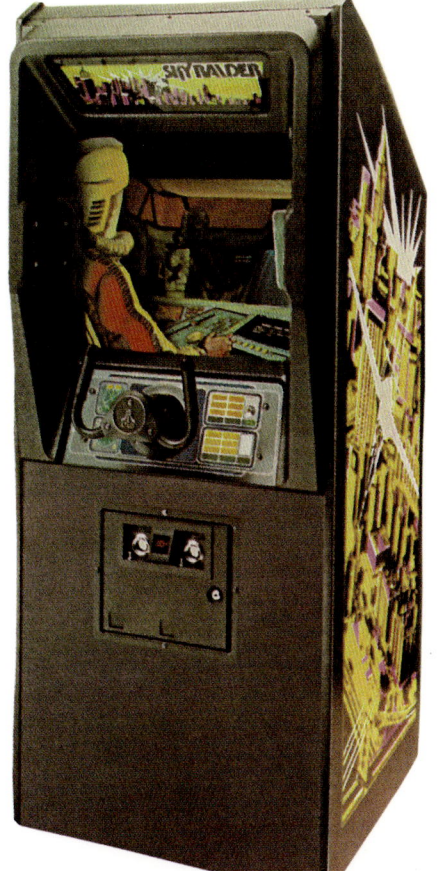

As with most video games that were produced before SPACE INVADERS, players had a set amount of game time (operator adjustable to 60, 80, 100, or 120 seconds) on Atari's 1977 SKY RAIDER rather than a set number of "lives" or "bases." $100-$150.

Close up of SEA WOLF II's twin periscopes.

63

Look at the giant ripcord controls on the front panel of Atari's SKYDIVER (1977). Miss your jump, and a video ambulance drives on the screen to attend to the hapless diver. $150-$200.

Maneuver your space ship through the mine field and blast the enemy mines. If you beat the clock and exploded all of the mines quickly, you would win a free game. Gremlin's BLASTO (1977) was one of the last video games to award free games. $75-$100.

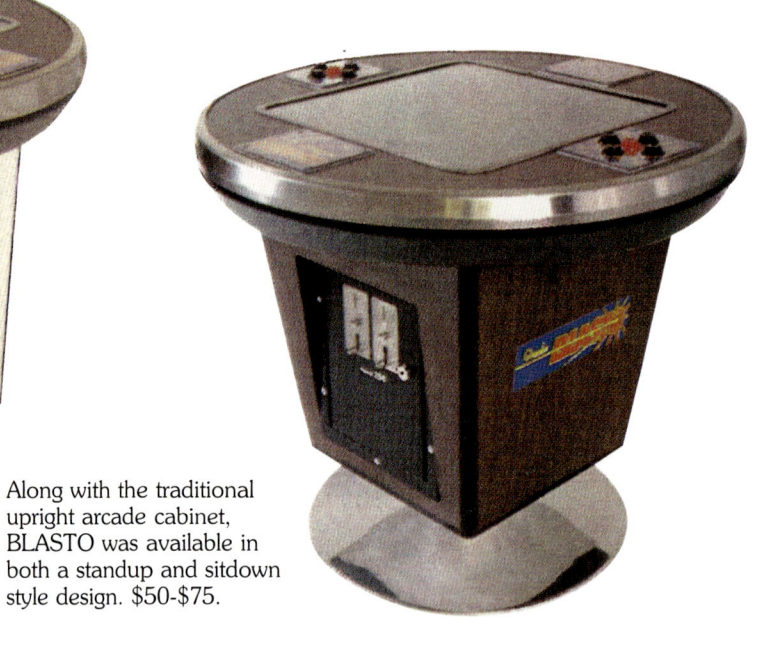

Along with the traditional upright arcade cabinet, BLASTO was available in both a standup and sitdown style design. $50-$75.

64

Atari's AVA-LANCHE was a cross between PONG and BREAKOUT. Use the row of paddles arranged vertically at the bottom half of the screen to catch the avalanche of rocks falling from the top. $100-$150.

Atari's SMOKEY JOE (1978) was a single-player version of FIRETRUCK. Although the game was priced slightly less than FIRETRUCK, SMOKEY JOE lacked the unique cabinet design and two-player cooperative play that made FIRETRUCK such a hit. $150-$200.

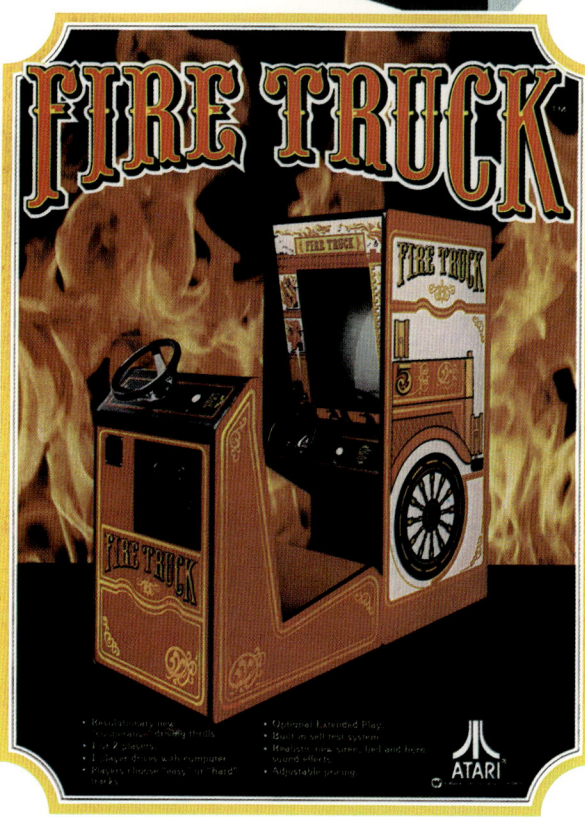

DARK INVADER (1978) was Ramtek's final video game. $75-$100.

Two people would play Atari's FIRETRUCK (1978) together, with one operating the front of the truck and the other operating the back. A single player could choose to operate either section. Notice the unusual cabinet which had one player standing behind the other! Game shown in this period ad is $250-$300.

65

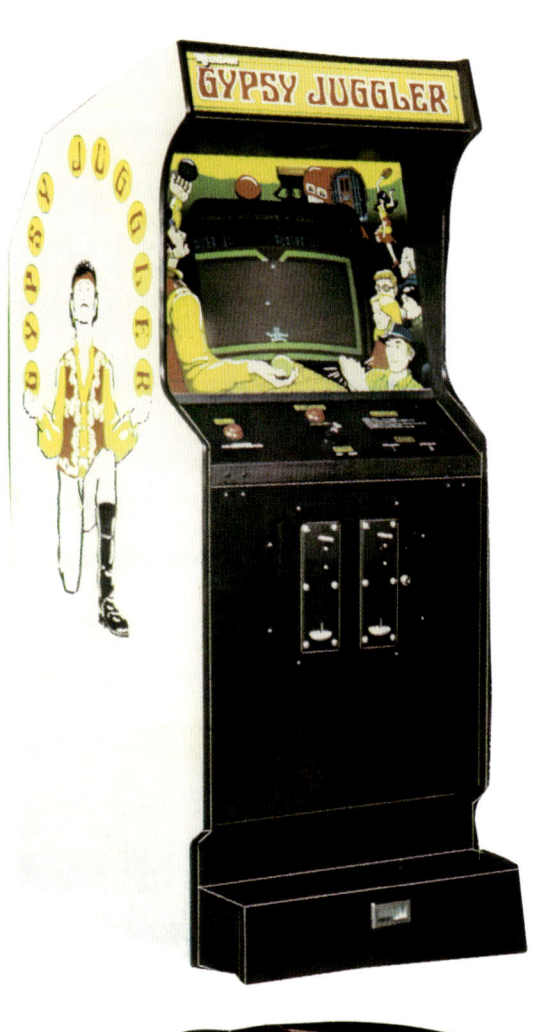

Toss the balls and catch them for big points in Meadows' 1978 GYPSY JUGGLER. $75-$100.

Check out the fourteen buttons on the control panel of Atari's 1978 ORBIT, the most buttons on any video game control panel. $100-$150.

Exidy's STARFIRE (1978) was available in this elaborate cockpit model as well as in an upright cabinet. It was hard to miss this game in any arcade! $350-$500.

66

Does the puck control look familiar? Midway's SHUFFLEBOARD (1978) used the same brown and white marbleized ball as coin-op ball bowling machines. $100-$150.

You could win an extra inning by hitting to left, center, and right field and spelling M-I-D-W-A-Y! Midway's EXTRA INNING was produced in 1978. $100-$150.

Atari's TOURNAMENT TABLE (1978) had one of the most generic names ever given to any video game. Offered only in a cocktail table format, you could play twelve different games on TOURNAMENT TABLE, including Breakout, Quadrapong, Basketball, and Volleyball. $75-$100.

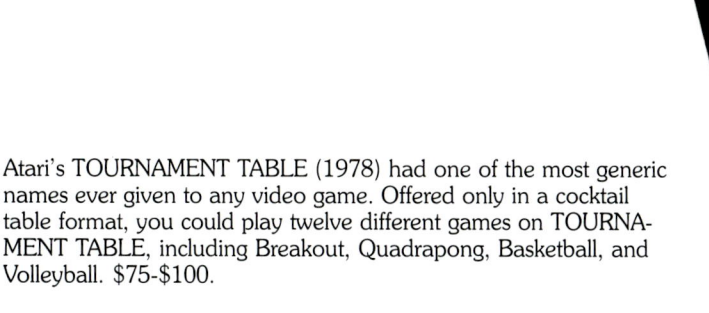

67

Midway's SPACE INVADERS took over arcades in 1978, and the video game world has never been the same. After the introduction of SPACE INVADERS, video games would never again be thought of as filler games or relegated to the back corners of game rooms. $250-$450.

You used a plastic lever to move your laser base from side to side on the cocktail table version of Midway's SPACE INVADERS, rather than the button controls found on the upright games. $300-$500.

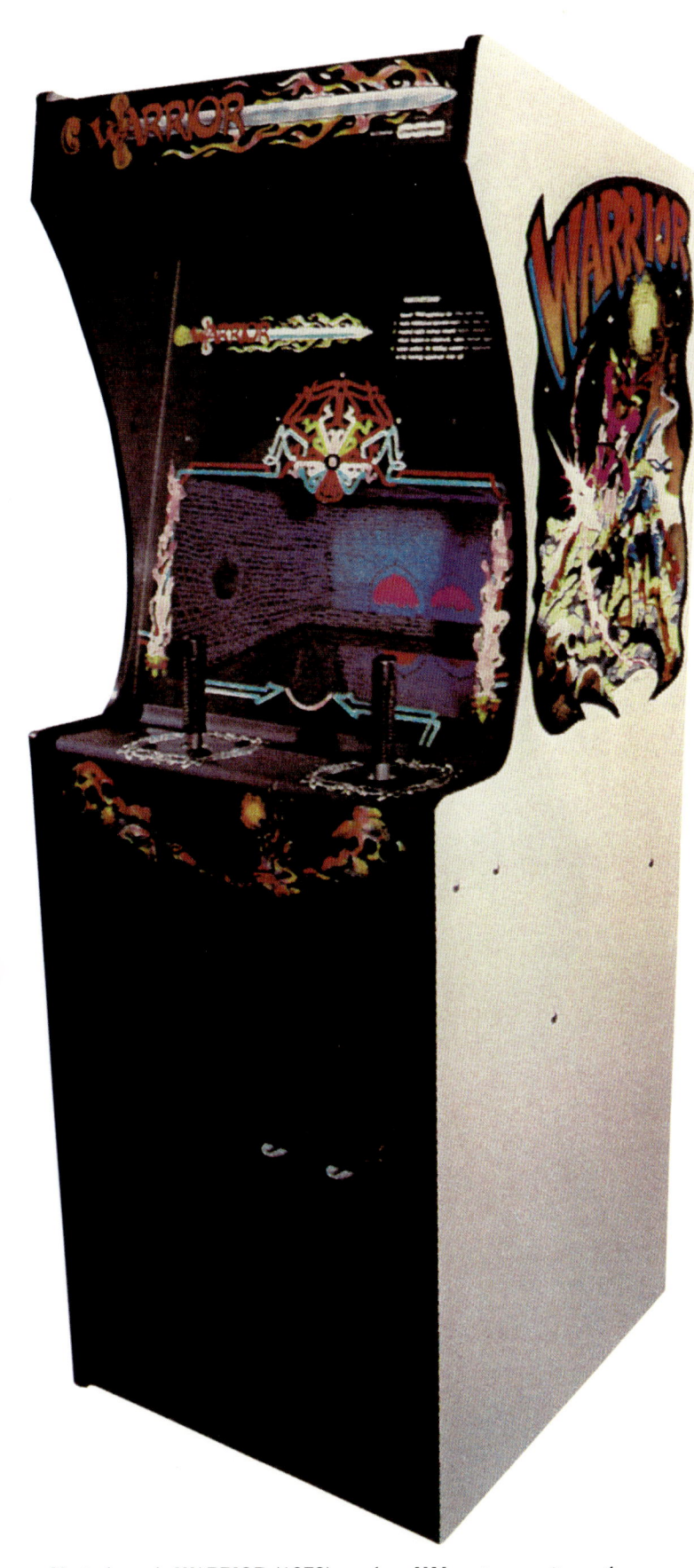

Vectorbeam's WARRIOR (1979) used an X-Y vector monitor rather than the raster monitor found in most other video games. The sword and sorcery theme, along with the usual graphics and original play action, make this game a favorite of collectors – and the low production on this machine keeps the price high. $1,000-$1,200.

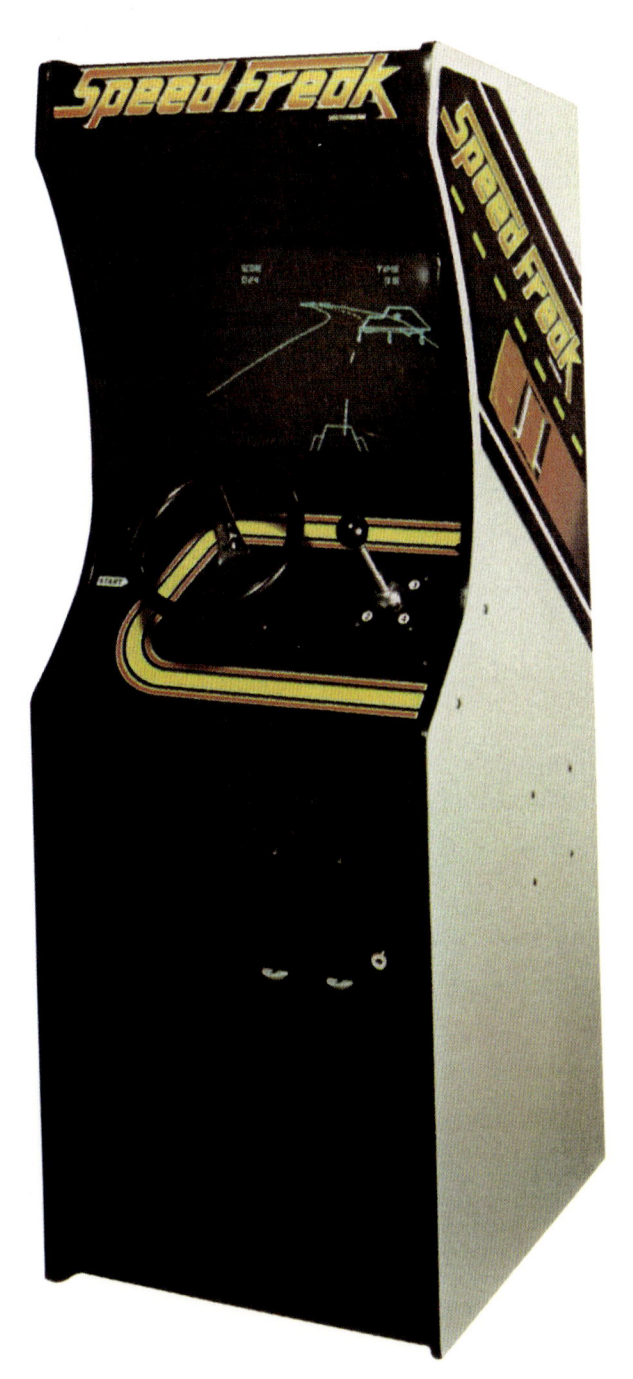

Shortly after Vectorbeam produced SPEED FREAK in 1979, the company was purchased by Cinematronics. $400-$500.

TAILGUNNER (1979) had been in development at Vectorbeam when Cinematronics purchased the company; the game was released under the Cinematronics name. $200-$300.

A screen shot from Cinematronics' TAILGUNNER shows the line drawings used to represent the images in X-Y vector video games.

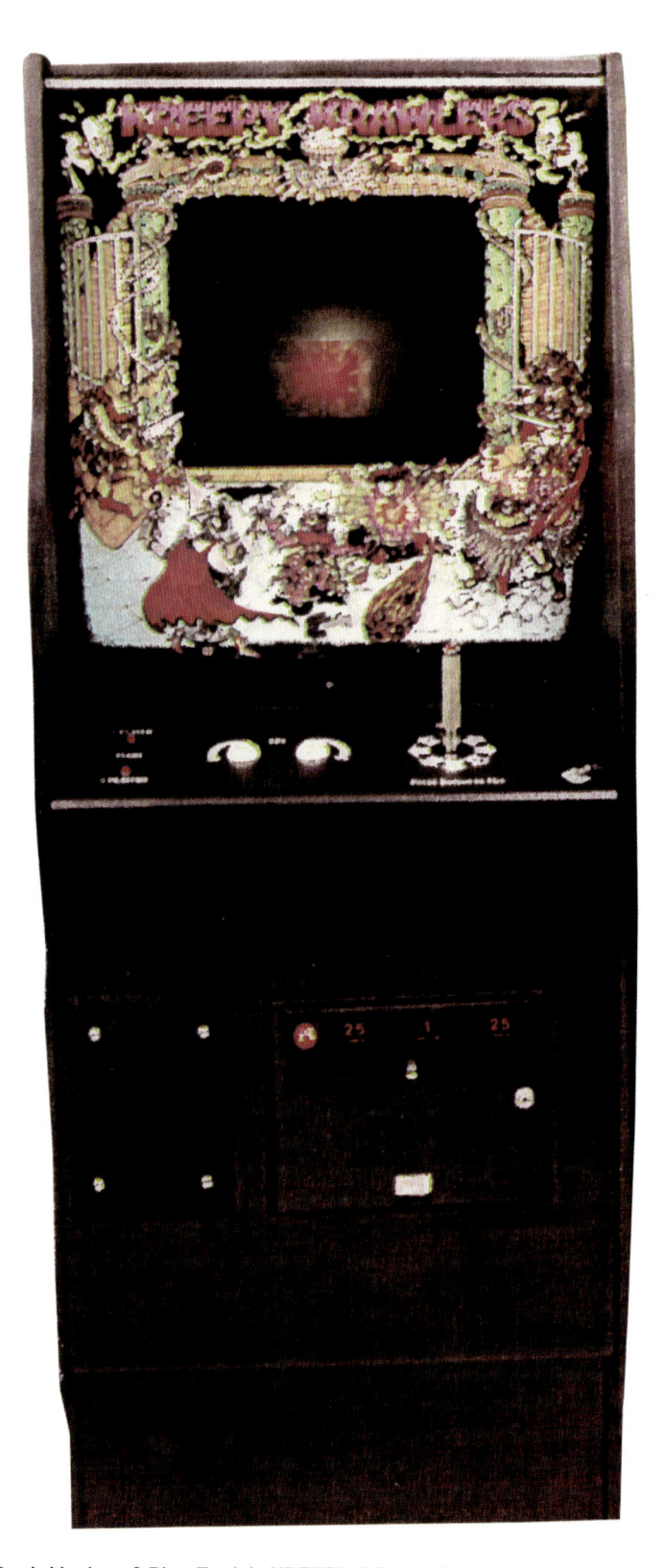

Don't like bugs? Play Exidy's KREEPY KRAWLERS (1979) and squish as many of the insects as you can. $100-$150.

Score points as you pick up passengers waiting along the side of the tracks on Exidy's SIDE TRAK (1979). If you like trains, then this game might be perfect for you. $100-$150.

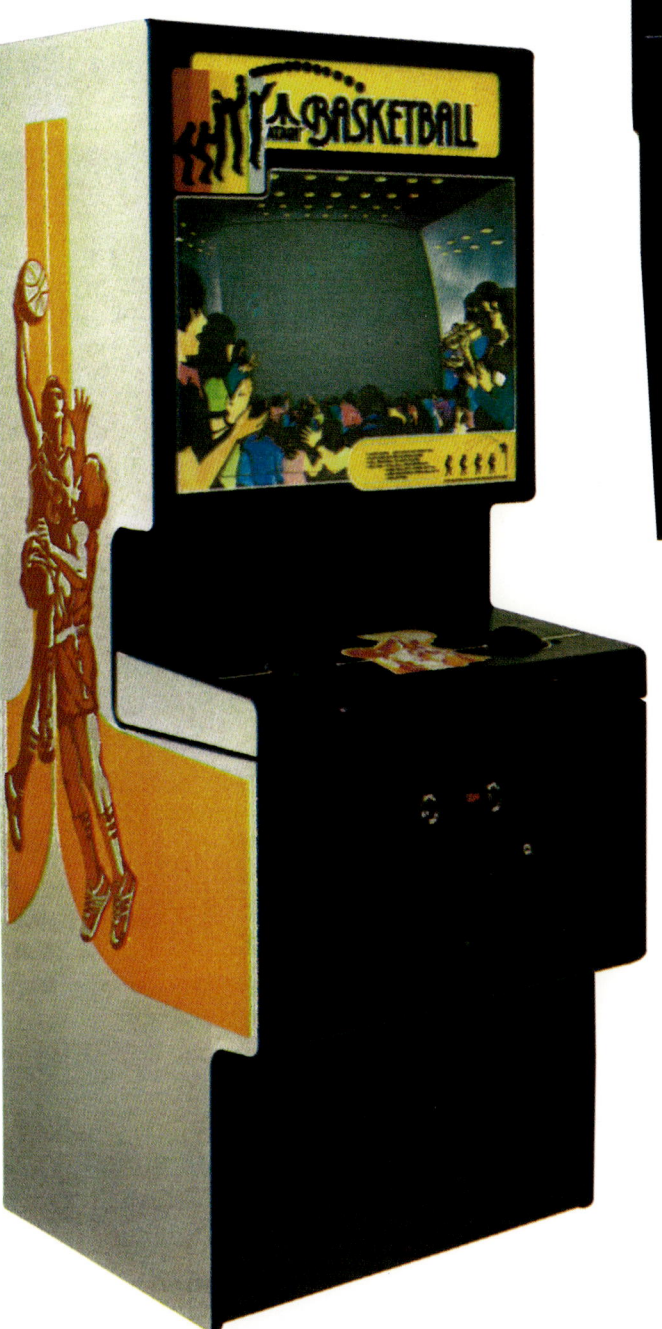

Atari's BASEBALL (1979) tried to duplicate the success of Atari's two-player FOOTBALL game, but the game was largely overlooked by players. $150-$200.

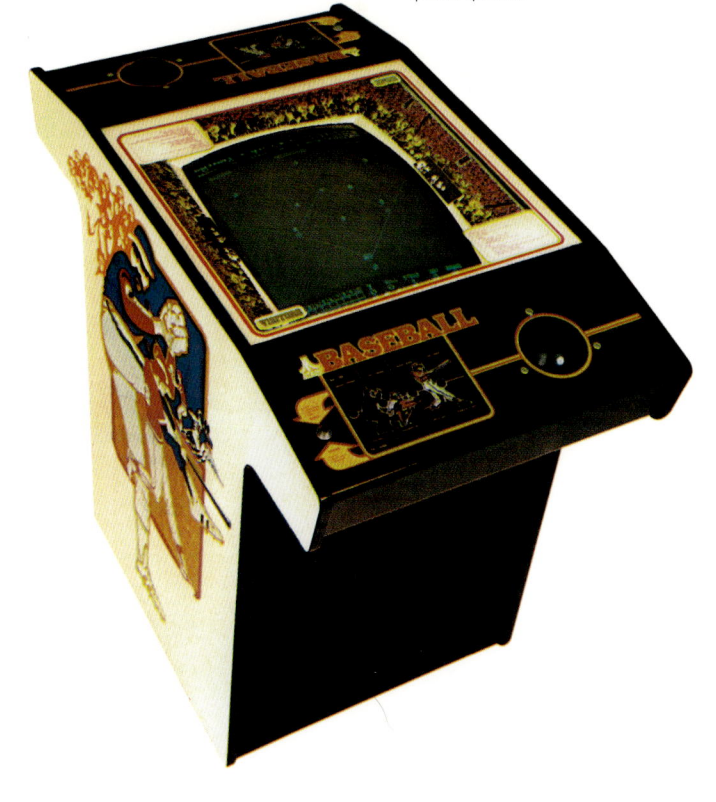

Play along to the tune of "Sweet Georgia Brown" on Atari's BASKETBALL, one of the most popular video games of the late '70s. A colorful cardboard cutout around the monitor made it look like you were watching a basketball game from one of the upper rows in an arena in this 1977 video game. $250-$350.

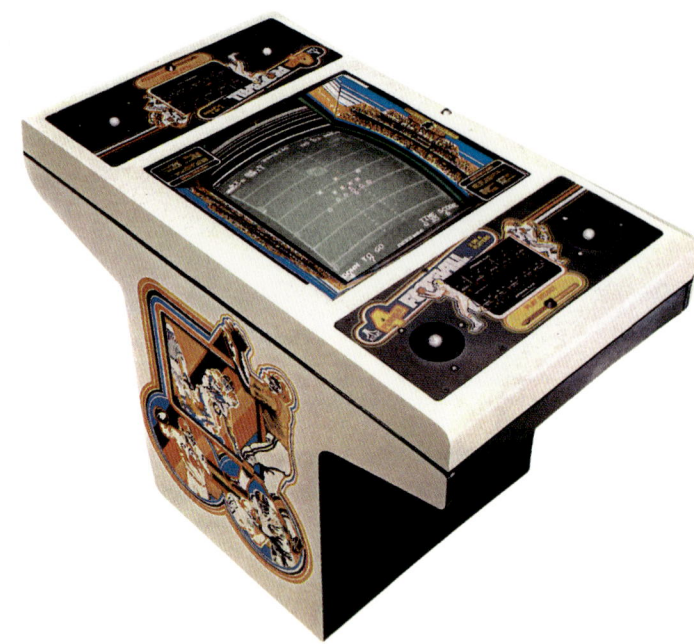

Atari introduced a four-player version of its popular FOOTBALL in the fall of 1979. The game play was nearly identical to the play on the two-player version of the game. $150-$200.

Atari's SUBS (1979) had two separate video screens. Each player would view the undersea action from his own perspective, unable to see his opponent's position. The extra monitor increased the retail price of the machine, and many operators didn't want to purchase a submarine game at a time when players seemed to prefer outer space video games. $100-$150.

What's left after FOOTBALL, BASKETBALL, and BASEBALL? Atari introduced SOCCER in the summer of 1979. Up to four players could compete simultaneously. Not surprisingly, the game fared better in Europe than in the United States. $150-$200.

Cinematronics' 1979 SUNDANCE didn't have an old west theme. Set in outer space, you opened space hatches to catch the bouncing suns in this X-Y vector game. $300-$400.

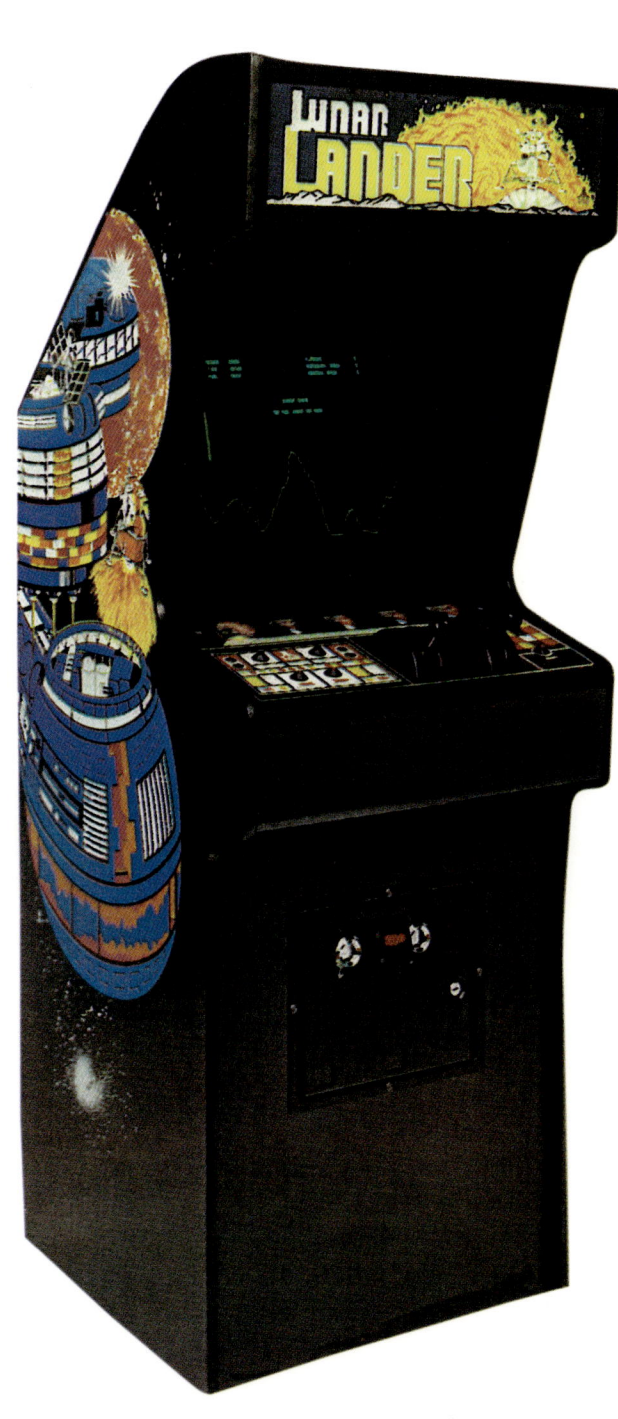

LUNAR LANDER used an X-Y vector display to simulate a moon landing. This 1979 video game from Atari let you chose one of four skill levels: training, cadet, prime, or command. $500-$600.

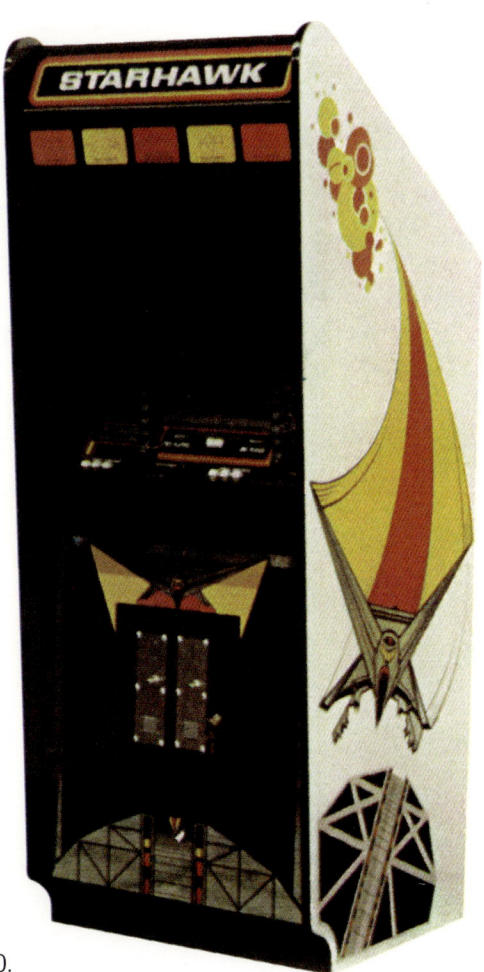

STARHAWK (1979) was another X-Y vector outer space shoot-'em-up from Cinematronics. $300-$400.

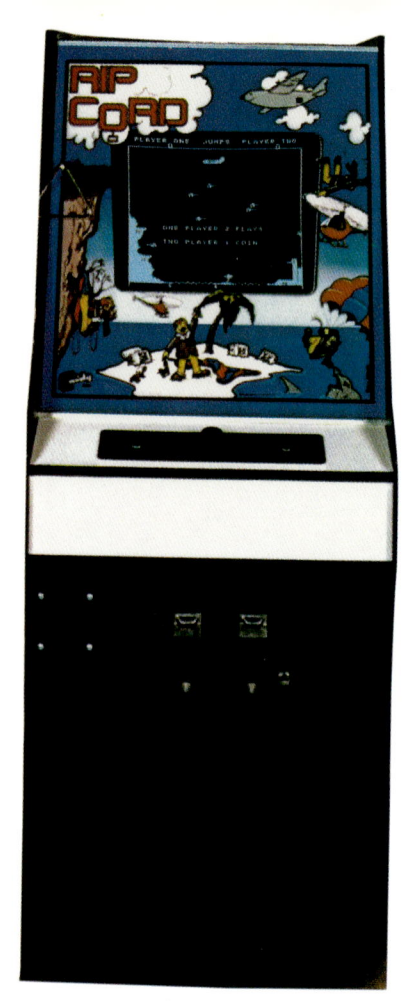

Like Atari's SKYDIVER, Exidy's RIP CORD (1979) featured parachuting action with a ring control on the front panel. $100-$150.

CRASH was a combination of a driving game and a maze game. The idea was to drive over all of the dots in the maze-like track. $100-$150.

BLUE SHARK (1979) was the first video game produced by Midway following the spectacular success of SPACE INVADERS. The game was largely overlooked in the wake of its predecessor. $100-$125.

Atari was looking for a blockbuster video game to rival Midway's SPACE INVADERS – and the company had it with ASTEROIDS. Released in 1979, ASTEROIDS became Atari's biggest hit, with over 50,000 ASTEROIDS games produced. $400-$750.

Introduced in the fall of 1979, Midway's SUPER SPEED RACE was the first video game to display the top five scores in the digital displays to the left of the screen. $250-$350.

SUBMARINE was actually an electromechanical arcade game, rather than a video game. Midway hoped that players who enjoyed SEA WOLF a couple of years earlier would enjoy the novelty of this EM machine which Midway had licensed from Namco in 1979. $100-$150.

Midway's BOWLING ALLEY (1979) used the same large marbleized bowling ball found in coin-op ball bowling machines, and even featured a choice of regulation or flash scoring like traditional arcade bowling machines. $125-$175.

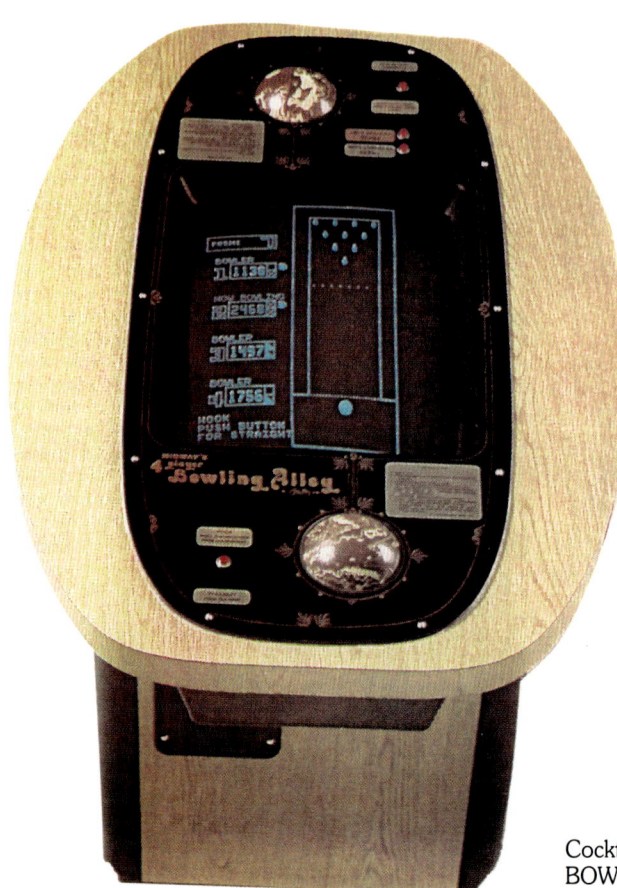

One of Midway's final air combat games was PHANTOM II, released in 1979. $100-$150.

Cocktail table model of Midway's BOWLING ALLEY. $175-$250.

76

Gremlin released several games in a countertop format, including INVINCO, a SPACE INVADERS clone. Pictured here is the countertop version of HEAD ON. $200-$250.

Atari's VIDEO PINBALL was probably the most popular coin-op video simulation of pinball ever produced. The playfield's disco theme and artwork reflected popular music of that time. $300-$400.

The monitor on this submarine hunt game was divided electronically, and the cabinet was designed with a partition so that one player couldn't see what the other was doing. FIRE ONE (1979) could be played by either one or two players, in either a submerged or surface mode. $125-$175.

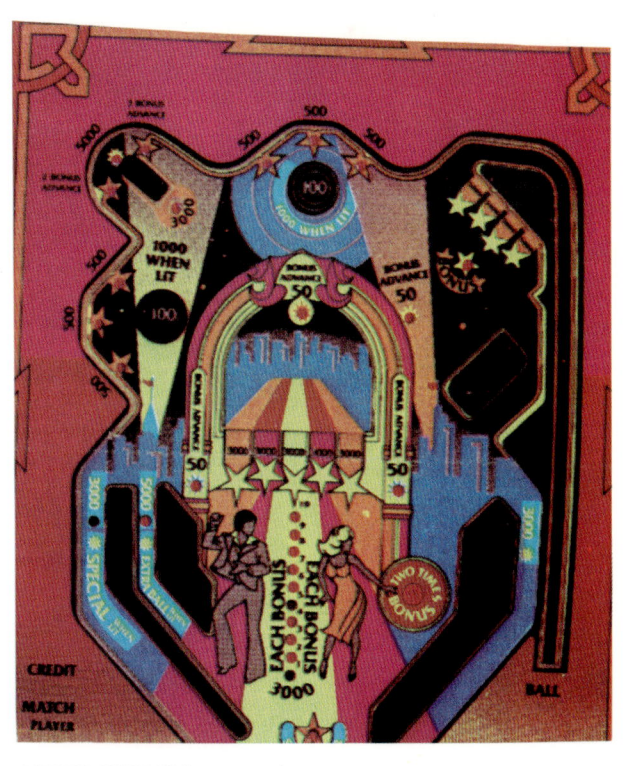

VIDEO PINBALL screen shot.

77

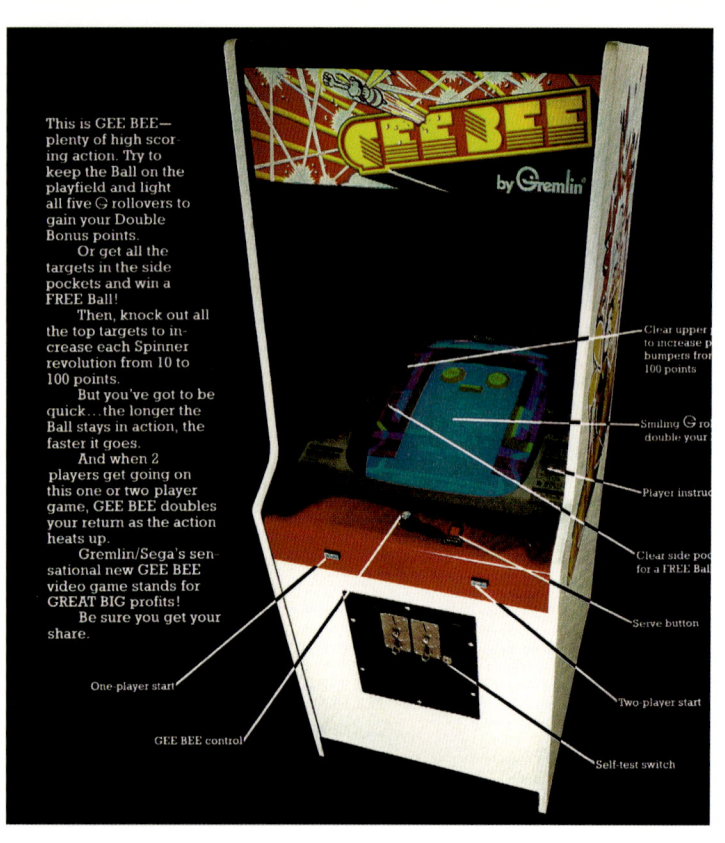

This is GEE BEE—plenty of high scoring action. Try to keep the Ball on the playfield and light all five G rollovers to gain your Double Bonus points.

Or get all the targets in the side pockets and win a FREE Ball!

Then, knock out all the top targets to increase each Spinner revolution from 10 to 100 points.

But you've got to be quick...the longer the Ball stays in action, the faster it goes.

And when 2 players get going on this one or two player game, GEE BEE doubles your return as the action heats up.

Gremlin/Sega's sensational new GEE BEE video game stands for GREAT BIG profits!

Be sure you get your share.

- One-player start
- GEE BEE control
- Clear upper to increase bumpers from 100 points
- Smiling G ro double your
- Player instru
- Clear side poc for a FREE Bal
- Serve button
- Two-player start
- Self-test switch

You'd never know it from the name, but Gremlin's 1979 GEE BEE was a video pinball game complete with rollovers, bumpers, and a spinner. Game shown in this period ad is $150-$200.

Midway licensed the rights to produced GALAXIAN in the United States from Namco, and the game was an instant hit. GALAXIAN (1979) was one of the first games with a full-color monitor. $250-$350

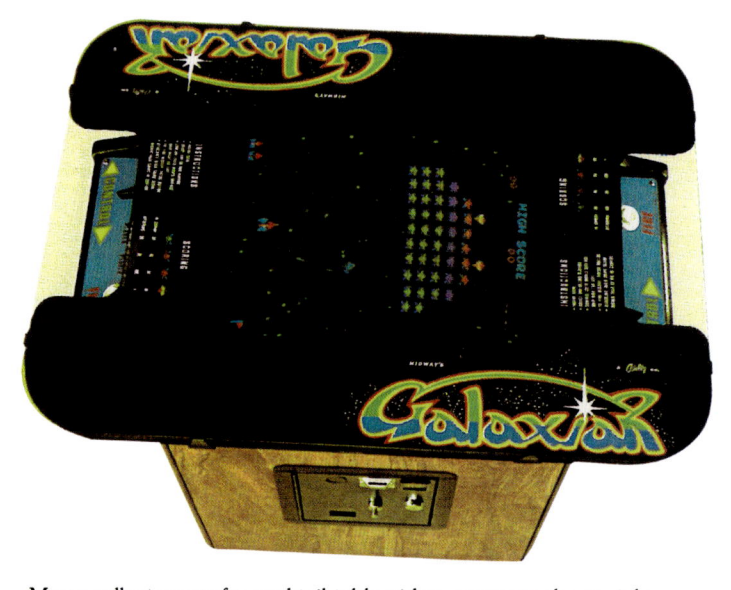

Namco introduced GALAXIAN to players in 1979. $350-500.

Many collectors prefer cocktail table video games to the upright counterparts. $300-$400.

78

Part 3
THE PAC MAN YEARS
1980-1982

After SPACE INVADERS, what do you do for an encore? SPACE INVADERS DELUXE, of course. Released in the beginning of 1980, Midway's SPACE INVADERS DELUXE was similar to the original SPACE INVADERS game, with a few new twists. For one thing, starting with the second screen, some of the aliens would split into two smaller aliens when hit, rather than disintegrate! And from time to time, a saucer would fly across the screen, dropping new aliens to replace those already destroyed. And SPACE INVADERS DELUXE even had a secret bonus feature for skilled players: If the last alien destroyed in any screen was the one at the bottom of the far left column, you would receive a 1000 point bonus and be treated to the "rainbow effect" as the entire screen lit up. This trick was rather difficult to accomplish, and is not mentioned anywhere in the game's instructions.

Based on the popularity of SPACE INVADERS, ASTEROIDS, GALAXIAN, and even SPACE INVADERS DELUXE, video game manufacturers continued making outer space shoot'em-up games. Midway's SPACE ENCOUNTERS and SPACE ZAP, Centuri's EAGLE, and Cinematronics' STAR CASTLE were just some of the games players had to choose from in 1980.

Driving games were always perennial arcade favorites, and one of the most popular video driving games ever made came out in 1980. The detailed graphics and the cockpit cabinet of Sega/Gremlin's MONACO GP made this one of the most realistic video driving games ever produced until that time.

Just as Midway had released SPACE INVADERS DELUXE as a sequel to the original SPACE INVADERS, Atari's ASTEROIDS DELUXE appeared in the summer of 1980 with a few features not found in the original ASTEROIDS. Unlike SPACE INVADERS DELUXE, though, ASTEROIDS DELUXE never approached the popularity of the original ASTEROIDS.

A couple of new manufacturers entered the scene in 1980, including Data East, a Japanese company which had carved out a niche in Japan a few years earlier. Data East introduced the Deco Cassette system, which allowed operators to convert one Data East game to another simply by changing a game cassette inside the cabinet. The first two Deco Cassette games introduced by Data East were BURGERTIME and BUMP 'N JUMP, both of which were licensed by Midway and released the following year in dedicated form.

Pinball had started declining in popularity by 1980, and the booming video game market was just too tempting for the pinball manufacturers to resist. By the end of the year, Williams Electronics unveiled DEFENDER, the company's first video game in five years. With its pods, mutants, and baiters, DEFENDER was one of the biggest video game hits of the year, and the first in a long line of video hits from Williams.

Stern Electronics also released its first video game in 1980. ASTRO INVADER featured the usual outer space shoot-'em-up action, but the company's next video, BERZERK, really clicked with players. BERZERK was a maze game which let you use a joystick with a fire button to shoot the attacking robots while you made your way from one end of the maze to the other.

Even Gottlieb, the most conservative pinball manufacturer, began producing video games in the fall of 1980. NO MAN'S LAND, the company's first effort, was licensed from Japan and was similar to the old TANK video game from several years earlier.

But of all the video games released in 1980, none can compare in popularity and longevity to the undisputed king of video games – PAC MAN. Unveiled at the national coin-op games trade show in the fall of 1980, Midway's PAC MAN was licensed from Namco, the same Japanese company that had produced GALAXIAN the previous year. The game had been a moderate success in Japan while Namco was producing it under the name PUCK MAN, based on the main character of the game who was shaped like a puck or disc. Midway executives thought that the name PUCK MAN would be too tempting a target for vandals wanting to deface the graphics on the cabinet, and the name was changed to PAC MAN for the U.S. market.

When it was first shown at the trade show, most video game operators dismissed PAC MAN as too cute to become popular. After all, video games were played primarily by teenage boys who wanted outer space shoot-'em-ups or macho war-themed games. Maze games were nothing new, thought most operators, and although PAC MAN might make a decent filler piece for a large arcade, its $2,450 price tag was just too expensive.

Were they ever wrong! PAC MAN was an overnight sensation, a game that appealed to women and children along with teens. PAC MAN was easy to understand yet difficult to master because it became more challenging the longer you played.

DELUXE SPACE INVADERS was released both as an upright game and in a cocktail table format. $350-$450.

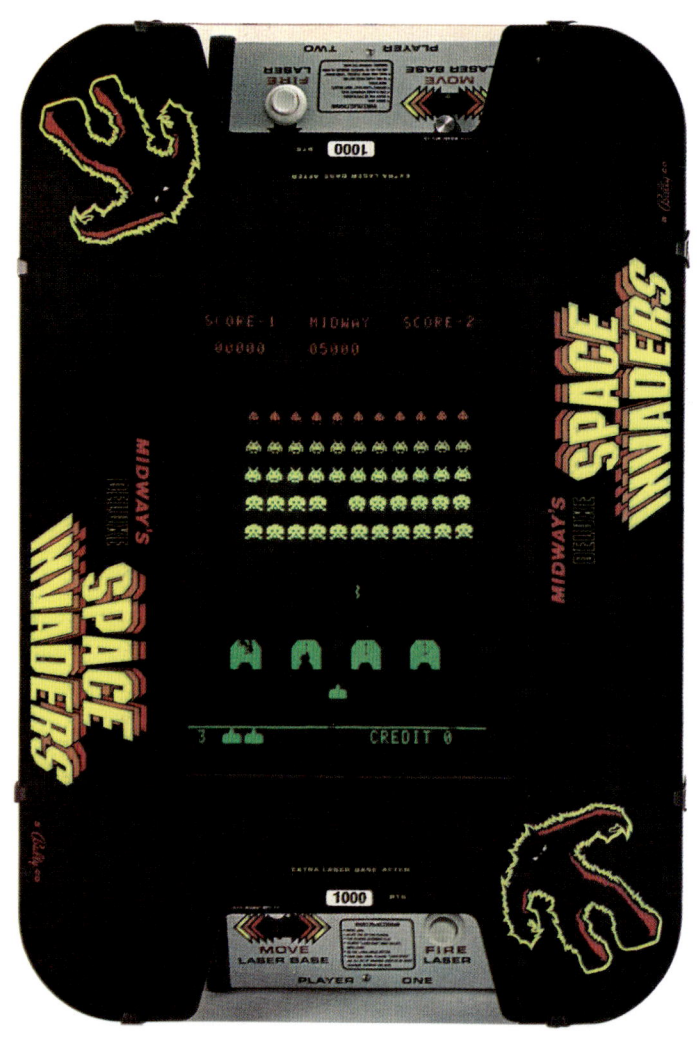

What do you do for an encore after SPACE INVADERS? DELUXE SPACE INVADERS, of course, which was almost as popular as the original game. The machine was also released under the name SPACE INVADERS II. $300-$450.

Top view of Midway's DELUXE SPACE INVADERS cocktail table.

80

The game play was deceptively simple. Just move your yellow Pac Man around the maze, gobbling up dots while avoiding the monsters chasing you. Eat one of the large power pellets found in the corners, and for a few seconds, you could turn the tables on the monsters and eat them for extra points. The game became a national phenomenon, with tournaments held in just about every major U.S. city. Hardcore players began to suffer from "Pac Man Elbow," a condition caused by spending too much time moving the joystick back and forth without a break.

Midway built more than 96,000 PAC MAN machines, but the company still couldn't keep up with the demand for the game. To fill the void, video game operators bought bootleg versions of the game with names like GOBBLEMAN and HANGLY-MAN. One of the most unusual versions had a Popeye head floating around the maze gobbling up cans of spinach instead of dots! By virtue of its impact on the video game industry, PAC MAN is often considered the ultimate video game by collectors.

Illegal imports became an issue for video game manufacturers in the early 1980s. Midway owned the rights to manufacture and distribute PAC MAN in the United States, while Namco was producing the game for the Japanese market. PAC MAN was an instant hit, and Midway couldn't produce the machines fast enough. Some video game operators, anxious to cash in on PAC MAN's popularity, began importing PAC MAN boards which Namco had produced for use in Japan, then installed these boards in their older video games which weren't making money. It didn't matter to players in the U.S. whether they were playing a Midway PAC MAN or a Namco PUCK MAN machine, but it made a big difference to Midway, which aggressively enforced its exclusive U.S. rights to the game. Midway had these illegal PUCK MAN games confiscated, and many video game operators suffered major financial losses as a result.

Bootleg video games also posed problems for video game manufacturers. It was fairly easy for someone with the right equipment to copy the data on the circuit board and produce homemade versions of popular games. Many of these knockoffs had some minor variations from the original game, such as the colors of some of the characters. And these bootleg games frequently had names similar (but not identical) to the original. For example, bootlegged versions of Nintendo's DONKEY KONG video game were sold as KRAZY KONG.

But despite the imports, bootlegs, and knockoffs, players of every age, race, gender, and demographic group lined up to drop their quarters into PAC MAN and other hot games. PAC MAN's popularity among women led video game manufacturers to come up with new video game ideas besides outer space shoot-'em ups to keep the female players' interest. With its cute theme, Sega's FROGGER drew in female players who enjoyed helping to get the frog across the road without getting crushed by a car. Nichibutsu's CRAZY CLIMBER, Universal's LADY BUG, and Exidy's MOUSE TRAP were also popular with women.

Atari's CENTIPEDE proved particularly popular among women. Released in 1981, CENTIPEDE let you blast away at spiders, snails, and, of course, centipedes. The game was easy to understand and featured unique sounds keyed to the game action.

Midway's 1981 sequel to GALAXIAN, GALAGA, proved even more popular than its predecessor. GALAGA featured play action that was more aggressive than GALAXIAN, but you were rewarded with a "Challenging Stage" from time to time which let you shoot at the aliens without their firing back at you. More than twenty years after its release, you can still find GALAGA machines earning money in arcades.

Midway released another PAC MAN game in 1981 – sort of. PAC MAN PLUS was an update kit (what Midway called an enhancement kit) that could be installed on PAC MAN to spice up the game. PAC MAN PLUS offered the same maze pattern as the original game, but the monsters became invisible from time to time, which made the game difficult to master. And instead of fruit like cherries and bananas, your Pac Man gobbled up bottles of Coca-Cola in the maze! With all of the unauthorized bootlegs and conversion kits that were on the market, PAC MAN PLUS was the only factory-authorized kit which operators could use to legally convert the game.

But not every video game offered cute graphics and harmless fun – at least according to critics who blasted Pacific Novelty's 1981 SHARK ATTACK. The game was graphic (according to the sales brochure, "Screams of pain are heard as shark munches on divers") and generated a public outcry similar to the protests which had been aimed at DEATH RACE a few years earlier. Pacific Novelty licensed SHARK ATTACK to Game Plan, which also produced the game under the name DEEP DEATH, but the game faded quickly from view.

However, SHARK ATTACK was only the catalyst for the growing uneasiness among some parents over the harmful effects – both physical and social – of video games. There was little dispute among medical practitioners that playing the same video game for eight or ten hours a day would lead to repetitive motion injuries. But a number of psychologists claimed that teens who spent hours each day playing ASTEROIDS, PAC MAN, and other games were not developing adequate social skills. Even worse, many children were reportedly skipping school to hang out in the arcade or convenience store playing video games.

Cities across the United States passed ordinances designed to keep the problem of "video delinquency" (as it was called) from growing worse, including banning school-age players from arcades before 3 p.m. Some towns went so far as to ban video games entirely.

When it became apparent that these measures were ineffective, many cities decided to follow the adage, "If

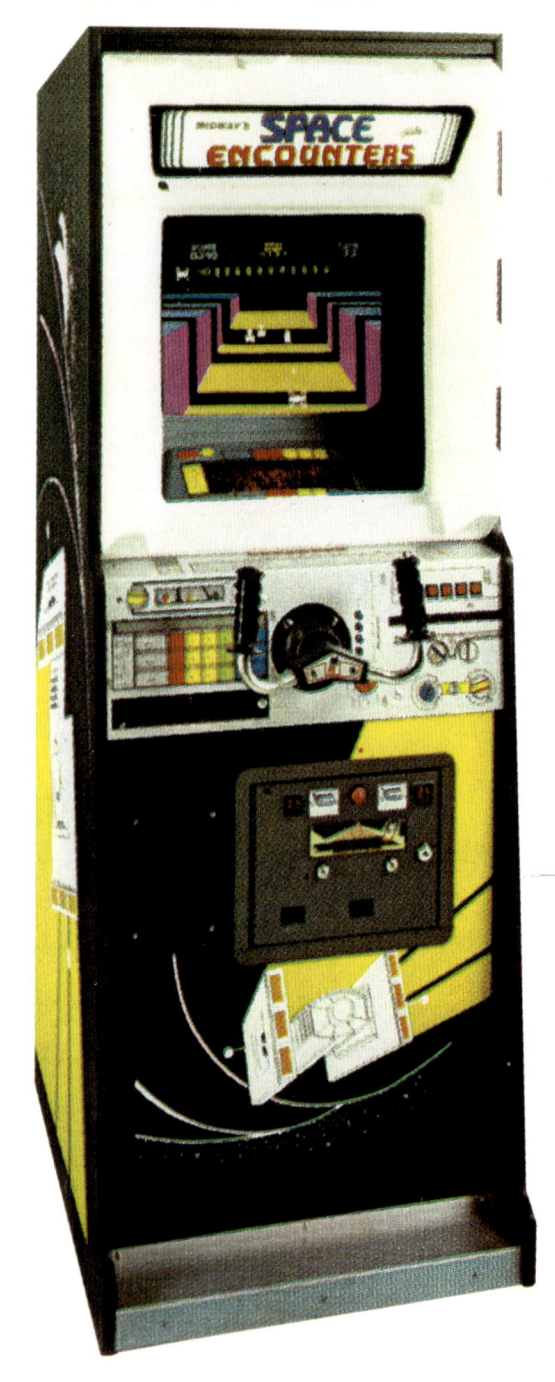

Pilot your ship through the "space channel" while shooting at aliens on Midway's 1980 SPACE ENCOUNTERS. $100-$150.

you can't beat 'em, join 'em." Instead of banning video games, a number of cities decide to make money off the games by taxing them. Video game operators were forced to apply for operating permits from city hall, and then pay a licensing fee for each game operated in the city – sometimes as much as $200 per game per year. This way, city officials could profit from the popularity of the games while at the same time preventing a proliferation of games from sprouting up on every street.

By 1982, video games had grown into a national phenomenon, grossing more revenue than the movie industry that year. There was even a nationally televised game show called *Starcade* broadcast on the TBS cable channel which provided a daily showcase for the latest games. Two teenaged players would answer questions about video games (for example, "How many dots are in a PAC MAN maze?"), and the first to answer the question

SPACE ENCOUNTERS was the first Midway game released in a Mini-Myte cabinet style. Notice the joystick control on this game, which is different from the handlebar controls used on the upright arcade game. $150-$200.

Not much strategy involved in Midway's 1980 SPACE ZAP – just aim your cannon in one of four directions from the center of the screen and fire at the attacking aliens which come at you from all directions. Game shown in this period ad is $100-$150.

correctly would have the opportunity to play one of five video games. At the end of the show, the highest-scoring contestant would try to win the grand prize of a new video game by beating the average score of all the audience members on that game. The show was broadcast Monday through Friday at 5:30 p.m., just about the time that the teenage viewers would be arriving home from school.

Interest in video games was reaching epidemic proportions, fueled by a number of hit games that were released in 1982. Mylstar (formerly known as Gottlieb) finally came up with a blockbuster game with Q*BERT, a cute game featuring a round orange character who hopped around a pyramid. The game had all the charm of PAC MAN, and became Mylstar's best-selling video game.

Another hit game (to the surprise of many people) was Nintendo's DONKEY KONG. The idea was to guide poor little Mario past the flaming barrels and other obstacles in his way as he tried to rescue a beautiful woman from the grinning ape holding her prisoner. The game featured several different play modes to keep players challenged.

Nintendo's POPEYE, released later in 1982, was another hit game for the company. Even players who weren't fans of the Popeye cartoons seemed to enjoy trying to save Olive Oyl from Brutus' clutches. Of course, the Popeye character could gobble up cans of spinach during the game to make it easier for him to overpower Brutus.

In answer to the question, "How do you top PAC MAN?" Midway introduced MS. PAC MAN. This 1982 video game featured new mazes, floating fruit, and car

Centuri was a new video game manufacturer which bought out the assets of Allied Leisure Industries in 1980. One of the company's first games was EAGLE. $150-$200.

83

Centuri's EAGLE was available in a mini upright cabinet for locations which didn't have the space for a full-size upright arcade game. $200-$300.

apples and keys! The game was moderately successful, but never came close to the popularity of the original game.

But the Pac family wasn't done growing yet. In October of 1982, the newest member of the PAC MAN family was born – BABY PAC MAN. This game was a hybrid, a combination video game and pinball machine. The video portion of the game was remarkably similar to the original PAC MAN video game, and sending your Pac Man into one of the two tunnels at the bottom of the screen shifted the action to the pinball playfield below. Some players weren't comfortable with the flipper controls, which were on the control panel rather than on the sides of the cabinet where flipper buttons have traditionally been located. Still, the game was a hit with both video and pinball players, although Midway's follow-up game, GRANNY AND THE GATORS, didn't fare quite as well.

Hot on the success of CENTIPEDE, Atari introduced MILLIPEDE in 1982. Instead of bullets, you fired arrows at the attacking insects, and could even detonate DDT bombs to stop the bugs! MILLIPEDE never quite attained the popularity of CENTIPEDE, but still gained a respectable following among video game players.

toon interludes between screens, and was also licensed from Namco. While players could memorize patterns and eventually learn to beat the original PAC MAN, MS. PAC MAN had monsters that moved randomly around the maze, making it impossible to play for hours at a stretch. MS. PAC MAN became one of the most popular video games ever made, with a production run of over 70,000 machines. Like GALAGA, MS. PAC MAN games had an incredibly long arcade life, with many of them still earning well on location after more than twenty years.

MS. PAC MAN was joined by SUPER PAC MAN later that year. Eating a power pellet super-sized your Pac Man and made him temporarily able to walk through walls! Instead of a maze filled with dots, SUPER PAC MAN ate

Cinematronics' STAR CASTLE (1980) was designed by programmer Wynn Bailey and originally called RING WAR. The name was changed to STAR CASTLE to better reflect the game's outer space setting. $150-$250

Another big hit for Atari was POLE POSITION, one of the most popular video driving games ever made. With graphics that changed perspective as your position on the roadway shifted, POLE POSITION was a top earner on location for several years. Other popular driving games unveiled in 1982 were Taito's GRAND CHAMPION and Sega's TURBO.

Sega's biggest hit of 1982, though, was PENGO, a cartoonish game that featured a cute little penguin trying to assemble an igloo by sliding blocks of ice around the screen. Sega had high hopes for SUBROC 3-D, but the stunning graphics weren't enough to draw players to this game. Stern's DARK PLANET also featured 3-D graphics, but like SUBROC 3-D, DARK PLANET was largely overlooked by players. Sega's ZAXXON also had 3-D graphics, but the exciting game play helped make this game a top earner.

There were plenty of outer space shoot-'em-up video games to choose from in 1982, including Sega's BUCK ROGERS, which was available in both upright and cockpit models. Williams' SINISTAR, Taito's SPACE DUNGEON, and Cinematronics' WAR OF THE WORLDS were just a few of the other space-themed video games grabbing quarters.

But the most visible science-fiction themed video game was released by Midway in 1982 and based on the Disney film *Tron*. Midway's TRON video game featured sounds and graphics based on the movie, and was instantly recognizable to anyone familiar with the film. TRON was one of the most popular video games of the 1980s, and is still highly sought after by both video game enthusiasts and sci-fi fans today.

One of the most surprising success stories of 1982 was MR. DO, made by Universal, a Japanese manufacturer. With its cute clownlike theme, MR. DO attracted both male and female players. But MR. DO was the first successful video game sold strictly as a conversion kit rather than as a complete game. Until MR. DO's release, no hit game had ever been available in kit form. From a player's perspective, there was nothing special about MR. DO – but for a video game operator, MR. DO represented an inexpensive answer to the problem of rapidly escalating prices on new machines.

While conversion kits helped operators transform their older video games into newer, more profitable machines, these conversions have caused lots of headaches for collectors. Although Midway produced nearly 100,000 PAC MAN machines, for example, there's no way of knowing for certain how many of those games are still around and how many have been converted into other machines. Some collectors estimate that only about 5 percent to 10 percent of the total production run of a machine survives more than ten years, and when you consider that the production run of an average video game was usually between 2,000 and 3,000 units, it's easy to see why some video games can be so difficult to find today.

But video game operators bought games based on their ability to bring in quarters, not for their future collectibility. And conversion kits offered operators an inexpensive way to breathe new life into old machines for about half the cost of buying a new game.

Video games were certainly riding high following the introduction of PAC MAN in 1980. The only problem is that the higher you fly, the harder you hit the ground when you fall.

Exidy's BANDIDO (1980) had a cute western theme, complete with a wanted poster of the bad guy above the monitor. $125-$200.

TAITO

Taito will probably always be remembered as the company which created SPACE INVADERS, but the company actually goes back to 1953. That's when Michael Kogan emigrated to Japan from Russia and established Taito as an arcade game operating company. By the late 1960s, Taito had established a manufacturing and distributing branch called Taito Trading Co. Ltd., and began producing novelty arcade games like CANNON BALL and FANTASY. By the time the company introduced its most popular game, a submarine hunt game called PERISCOPE DELUXE in the early '70s, Taito's machines were being sold throughout Europe and sometimes even exported to the United States.

When PONG was released, Taito became the Atari distributor for the Japanese market, and before long, the company was manufacturing its own video games. The firm's GUNFIGHT was the first microprocessor-controlled video game, and was also the first Japanese-designed video game licensed to a U.S. manufacturer. Three years later, Taito released SPACE INVADERS and never looked back. The company had a string of video game hits in the late 1970s and early '80s, including STRATOVOX (the first talking video game), QIX, JUNGLE KING, and ELEVATOR ACTION. Taito's ICE COLD BEER was a novelty arcade game designed for taverns, and one of the few non-video games produced by the company. ARKANOID and OPERATION WOLF were two more video game hits from the late 1980s, but as the video game market declined near the end of the decade, Taito began producing redemption games and novelty arcade games before ending production in the 1990s.

Targs, the Wummel, and the Spectar Smuggler are three of the characters that you'll find in TARG (1980), one of Exidy's biggest hits. Game shown in this period ad is $150-$200.

TARG was the first video game licensed from one U.S. game manufacturer to another. Exidy created the game and produced the upright version, while Centuri licensed the rights to produce the cocktail table model from Exidy. $200-$250.

MISSILE COMMAND (1980) was a big hit for Atari. You used a rolling trackball control and fired at airborne enemies to defend your cities. MISSILE COMMAND was also released in a cockpit cabinet, although production was very limited on the cockpit design. $200-$350.

Sega's CARNIVAL (1980) was a hit among women as well as men with its cute carnival shooting gallery motif. Shoot the ducks and clay pipes, but shoot fast because the ducks come to life and eat your supply of bullets if you're too slow! A catchy background tune is played throughout the game. $200-$250.

Even though MONACO GP (1980) had the Sega name on it, the game was still manufactured in the Gremlin plant. One of the most elaborate video driving games produced to date, you felt like you were really inside a car when you stepped inside MONACO GP's cockpit cabinet. $300-$400.

Cinematronics' RIP OFF (1980) – another outer space shoot and dodge game with an X-Y vector monitor. $250-$300.

Centuri licensed the rights to build the cocktail table version of RIP OFF from Cinematronics, which had designed the game. $250-$300.

Atari's MONTE CARLO came with three coin chutes; the center chute was designed for the Susan B. Anthony dollar coin. $100-$150.

Midway's EXTRA BASES (1980) was produced in what the company called a "business" cocktail table model for more upscale locations. The game was designed to appeal to older players who weren't interested in space-themed games. $100-$150.

GALAXY WARS was the first video game produced by Universal, a Japanese firm, to be sold in the United States. $100-$150.

HEAD-ON 2 was one of the final video games designed by Gremlin's engineering staff before Sega acquired the company. The game was released in 1980. $100-$125.

Released in 1980 about a year after the original, Atari's ASTEROIDS DELUXE had player-controlled shields and a colorful backdrop above the monitor. $200-$350.

The screen action on ASTEROIDS DELUXE was superimposed over a colorful backdrop.

ASTEROIDS DELUXE was available in this cabaret cabinet, as well as in upright and cocktail table models. $300-$400.

Gremlin/Sega's 1980 ASTRO FIGHTER offered several different mini games (or phases) which had to be completed before you reached the final stage and had the chance to destroy the Master. If you failed to destroy all of your opponents in any stage, you had to begin that stage all over again on your next rocket. $150-$200.

NO MAN'S LAND (1980), Gottlieb's first video game, was licensed from Universal in Japan and was similar to Kee Games' TANK from 1974. $100-$150.

Gremlin/Sega's 1980 CAR HUNT was a maze-driving game similar to the company's HEAD ON. $100-$150.

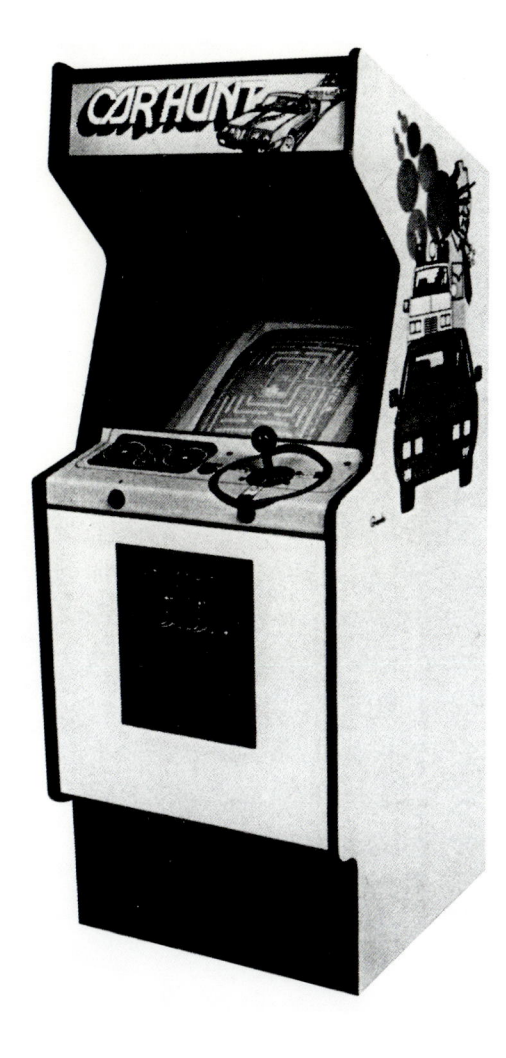

COSMIC GUERILLA (1980) was the first of Universal's line of "Cosmic" video games. $125-$175.

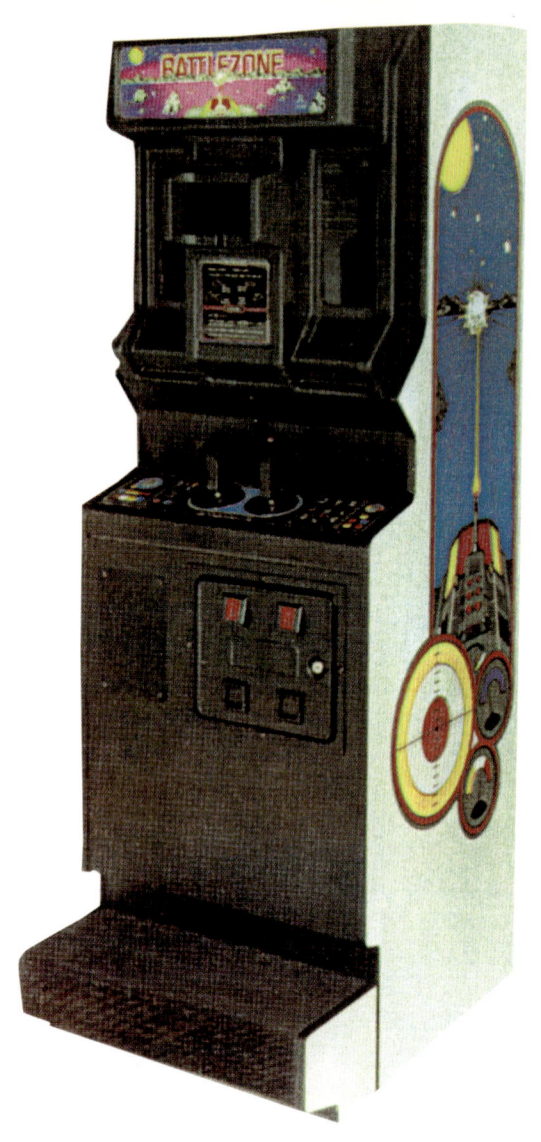

Atari's BATTLEZONE (1980) was an outer space tank competition complete with great sound including "The 1812 Overture." The cabinet stood over 74 inches tall! The U.S. army reportedly purchased many of these machines to train its combat soldiers. $300-$400.

BATTLEZONE was also available in a cabaret cabinet. $400-$500.

BATTLEZONE screen shot.

Universal's 1980 CHEEKY MOUSE awarded points for hitting mice with a hammer. Clobber all the mice before they can get the cheese to their mousehole. $150-$175.

"Help Me!" "Lucky" "Very Good" and "We'll Be Back" were some of the phrases uttered by Taito's STRATOVOX (1980), the first talking video game. $200-$300.

Here's a great theme for a video game: Shoot the giant grubs dropping from the space ship before they hit the ground and turn into larva. The larva will turn into a cocoon, and eventually into an Ultramoth! That's the game play on MAGICAL SPOT, produced in 1980 by Universal. $150-$175.

Taito's POLARIS was a sea-to-air combat game. One of the first video games produced by Taito and sold in the U.S. $100-$150.

Stern's second video game was also its most popular. Guide your robot through the maze with the joystick while firing at the enemy robots. Released on November 12, 1980, BERZERK even had a mechanical sounding voice to taunt you during the game. Stern produced 14, 437 upright games, but only 222 cocktail models. $200-$250.

Stern Electronics entered the video game field with ASTRO INVADER, released on June 25, 1980. You controlled a laser base at the bottom of the screen, and moved the base to the left and right while firing at the descending aliens. Stern built 4, 401 upright models and 499 cocktail models. $150-$200.

BUMP 'N JUMP was one of the first games in Data East's Deco Cassette lineup of convertible games. You could change from one Data East game to another in just a few minutes. $150-$200.

Game Plan's first video game, TORA TORA, featured torpedo bombs and anti-aircraft guns. $100-$150.

Data East offered BURGERTIME as part of its Deco Cassette system. BURGERTIME was also available from Midway as a dedicated video game the following year. $150-$200.

95

Notice the artwork on Namco's PUCK-MAN (1980), the original version of PAC-MAN. Namco's version of the game was never sold in the United States. $1,000-$1,500.

DEFENDER trade magazine ad.

Unveiled at the 1980 national coin-op games trade show, Williams' DEFENDER was the first video game produced by the firm in three years – and it became one of the most popular video games of all time. $400-$700.

96

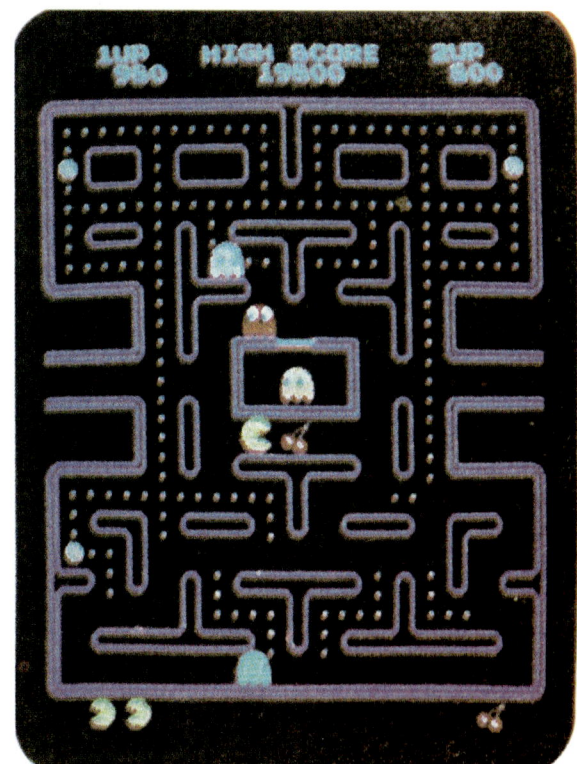

PAC MAN screen shot.

PAC MAN, the most popular video game ever made. Midway produced more than 96,000 of these machines. Game shown in this period ad is $500-$800.

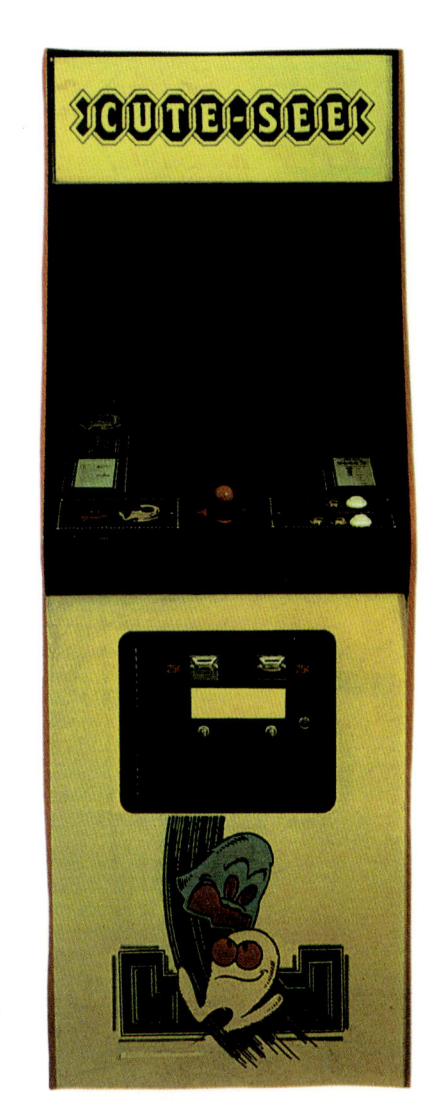

CUTE-SEE (1983) was one of the many conversion kits that were marketed when earnings on PAC MAN started to drop. $250-$350.

97

Williams' STARGATE (1981) was a sequel to the company's popular DEFENDER video game. The DEFENDER name even appears at the top center of the game's header. $350-$450.

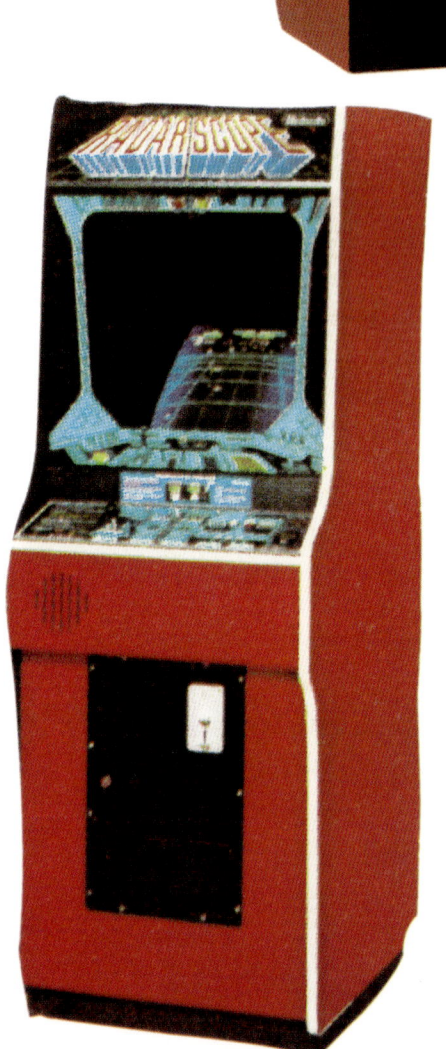

RADARSCOPE (1981) was one of the first video games sold in the United States by Nintendo, a Japanese company which was founded in the 1880s as a playing card manufacturer. Poor sales of RADARSCOPE forced the company to end production sooner than expected, and the bright red cabinets were reused on the early models of the firm's next game – DONKEY KONG. $150-$200.

Help the frog to get across the street without getting squished by a car. Sega's FROGGER (1981) was one of the firm's most popular games; it appealed to all ages and genders. FROGGER was even featured in an episode of TV's *Seinfeld* as one character tries to get the game across the street in the same manner as the frog in the game. $250-$400.

Drive your car through the maze while avoiding the other cars that are speeding around. RALLY-X had a scrolling screen so you could see only one small portion of the maze, but there was also a radar scope on the screen so you could keep track of the enemy cars. Produced by Midway in 1981, this game was designed by Namco. Game shown in this period ad is $250-$350.

Universal's COSMIC ZERO (1981). Although Universal's video games sold poorly in the United States, they were moderately popular throughout Europe and Asia. $100-$150.

Centuri's PHOENIX (1981) had giant eggs hatching in outer space and turning into predatory birds! The game was available in both a cabaret model and an upright cabinet. $200-$300.

Move the paintbrush around the maze to paint the entire screen, but watch out for the goldfish and the cat which can get in your way. Williams' MAKE TRAX (1981) was a cute maze game designed to appeal to players who enjoyed PAC MAN. $150-$250.

You're the mouse, running through the maze to find the cheese while avoiding the cats. You can even gather up dog bones and turn into a ferocious dog for a short time. Exidy's MOUSETRAP was produced in 1981. $100-$150.

Released in 1981, GORF was Midway's first talking game and featured five different outer space challenges, including modes similar to SPACE INVADERS and GALAXIAN. $250-$350.

100

Midway's WIZARD OF WOR (1981) had a "Dungeons & Dragons" theme. Set in a series of mazelike dungeons, you had to move your character through each screen while avoiding the bad guys. $250-$400.

Trade ad for the cockpit version of RED BARON. Game shown in this period ad is $300-$400.

Atari introduced RED BARON, a World War I biplane flying game using an X-Y vector monitor, in 1981. $250-$300.

101

Scale the building to save the girl by grabbing onto the window sills while avoiding the flower pots thrown down at you from above. CRAZY CLIMBER (1981) was one of the few video games licensed to two different U.S. manufacturers for simultaneous production. Nichibutsu's version is pictured here. $150-$200.

Like Nichibutsu, Taito also produced CRAZY CLIMBER. Although the cabinet styles were different, both games were identical. $200-$250.

Taito also produced CRAZY CLIMBER in this cabaret-style cabinet. $250-$300.

102

Centuri's PLEIADES (1981), licensed from Japanese manufacturer Tehkan, was a standard outer space shoot-'em-up video game. $125-$175.

You'll combat meteors, spiders, dragonflies, and other outer space creatures in Taito's 1981 ZARZON. You must complete each of the five waves before you can finally engage the evil Zarzon in battle. $150-$200.

The front of this cabaret-style cabinet reads: "The original Taito SPACE INVADERS." By the time Taito began selling this model in the U.S. in 1981, SPACE INVADERS had already become a classic. $300-$400.

COLONY 7 offers you lots of options with your futuristic weaponry. If necessary, you can hit your Mega Blaster (which will destroy everything in the blasting radius) or if the situation is desperate, use your Eradicator, which will wipe out everything on the screen. And if it's hopeless, drop in another quarter, which will give you extended weaponry! Produced by Taito in 1981. $150-$200.

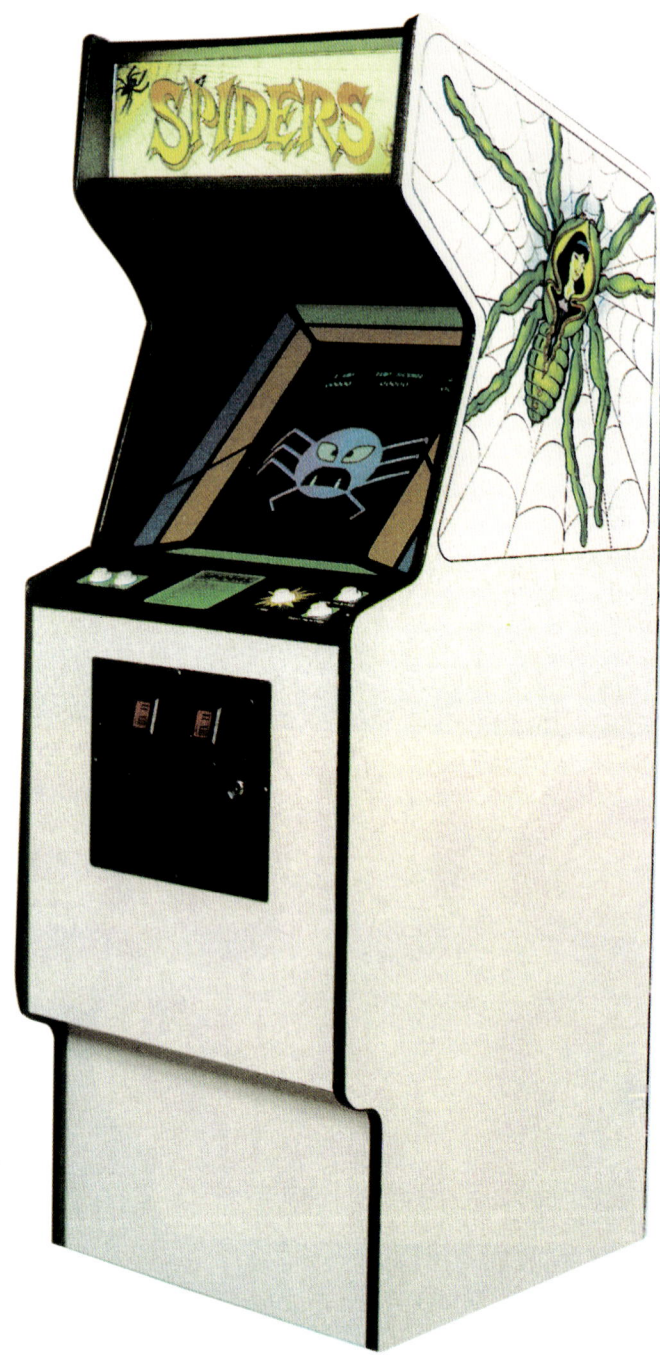

If you were looking for other insects to shoot besides centipedes, then try SPIDERS, produced by Venture Line in 1981. A giant purple spider with long fangs appeared on the screen at the beginning of *every* game. $100-$150.

OMEGA RACE (1981) was the only game ever produced by Midway with an X-Y vector monitor. It was also the only game produced in four different cabinet styles: upright, mini, cocktail table, and cockpit. $250-$300 (upright, mini, cocktail); $400-$500 (cockpit).

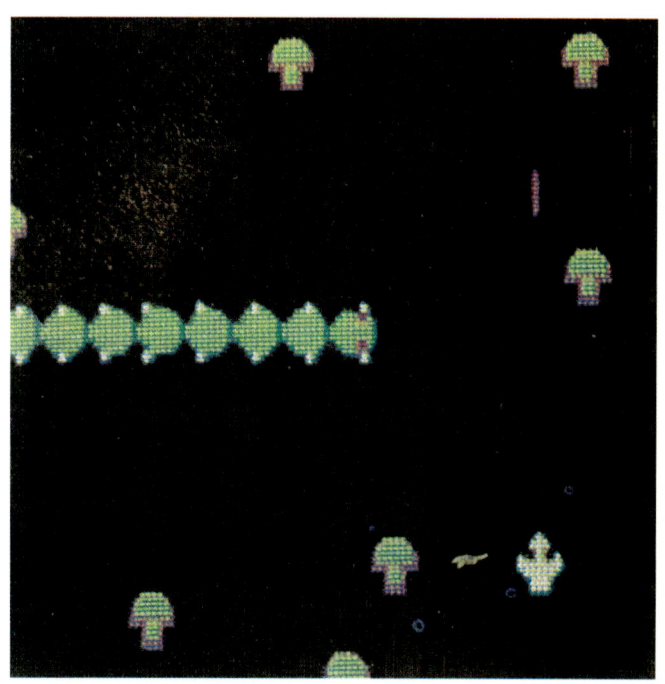

CENTIPEDE screen shot.

Shoot the centipede – and the mushrooms, scorpions, and spiders – before the centipede reaches your gun at the bottom of the screen. Released in 1981, CENTIPEDE quickly became one of Atari's most popular video games. $500-$750.

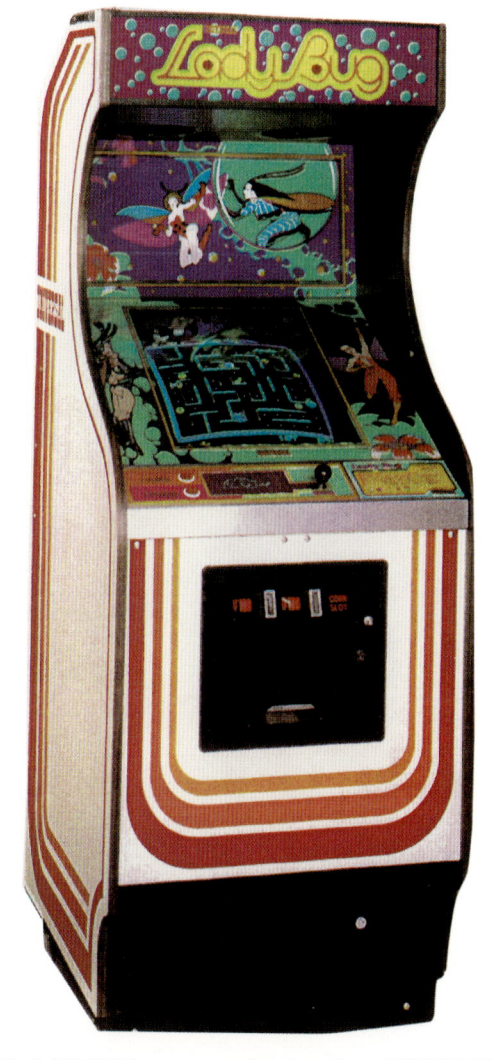

Universal's LADYBUG was more low-key than CENTIPEDE or SPIDERS. LADYBUG was a maze game similar to PAC MAN. $100-$150.

Ladybugs chasing turtles? That's the storyline in Stern's TURTLES (1981), a maze game that included a bug bomb which you could activate to wipe out everything on the screen. $150-$200.

Taito licensed MOON SHUTTLE (1981) from Nichibutsu. This outer space shoot-'em-up video game never attracted many players. $100-$150.

QIX (pronounced kicks) was unveiled by Taito in 1981. The idea was to draw your way around the screen while avoiding the obstacles and enemies. $400-$500.

ASTRO BLASTER (1981) was Gremlin/Sega's first talking video game. $125-$200.

ASTRO BLASTER screen shot.

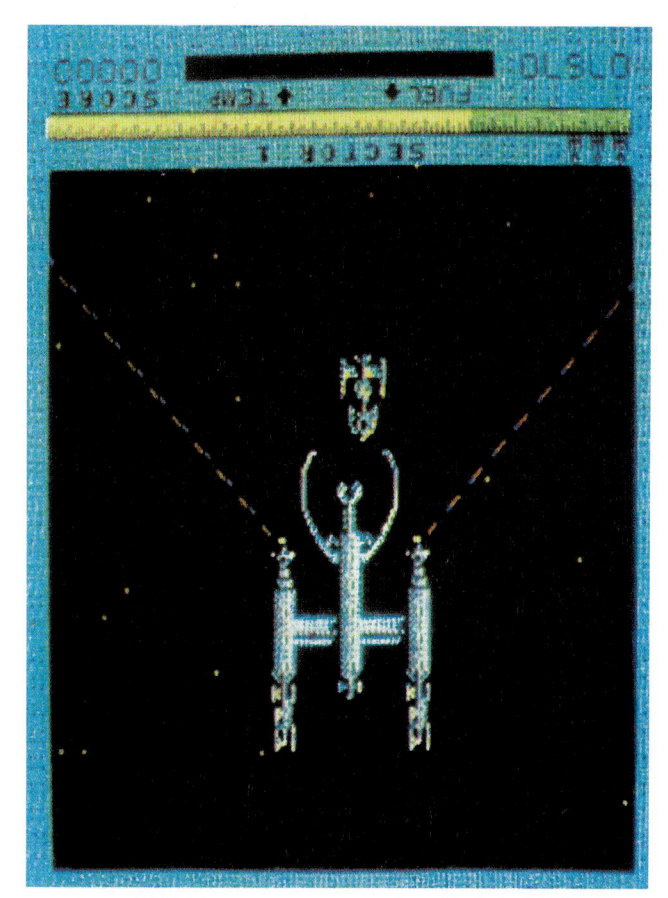

Produced in 1981, Atari's TEMPEST used a color vector monitor and featured 99 different challenges, getting progressively more difficult as the game went on. Skilled players could warp ahead to the more challenging phases of the game. $400-$500.

ELIMINATOR was the last game to carry the Gremlin name. $200-$300.

INTRUDER (1981) was one of the few video games produced by Game Plan. The machine featured a colorful cabinet but there was nothing new in the game play. $100-$150.

Atari's WARLORDS (1981) was available in both an upright cabinet and a cocktail table format. $250-$350.

Unlike the company's first video game (NO MAN'S LAND, which was licensed from a Japanese manufacturer), Gottlieb's NEW YORK NEW YORK was designed in-house at the firm's Chicago facility. $150-$200.

Gottlieb's 1981 CAVEMAN was part pinball machine, part video game. The upper portion of the backbox hung out over the playfield to cut down on overhead glare which might make it difficult to view the video game at the top of the playfield. $400-$500.

Because the head of the engineering department at Game Plan was left-handed, most of Game Plan's machines were designed so that they could be played by either left- or right-handed players. The joystick was in the center of the control panel on KILLER COMET (1981), with two identical sets of buttons on each side of the control panel. $100-$150.

109

GALAGA screen shot.

More than two decades after its release, Midway's GALAGA (1981) can still be found taking in quarters in arcades. The game is now attracting a second generation of players. $400-$750.

Game Plan's first talking video game was KING AND BAL-LOON (1981). $100-$150.

110

Chances are you probably think that Rock-Ola made only jukeboxes. The company made a few video games in the early 1980s, and the firm's first game was WARP WARP (1981). $100-$150.

Game Plan's DEEP DEATH (1981) created a stir of controversy across the country for its violent theme of sharks devouring divers. Here's the twist – you're the shark, out to gobble up the hapless divers, rather than being the diver trying to escape from sharks. $400-$500.

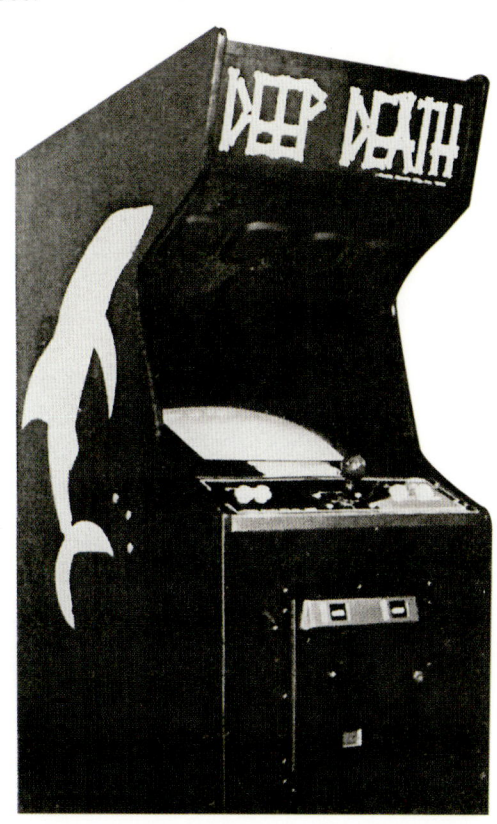

Sega introduced SPACE FIREBIRD in 1981 under license from Nintendo, which produced the game for the European market. $100-$150.

DEEP DEATH was renamed SHARK ATTACK after critics objected to the morbid sound of the word "death" in the name. Both Pacific Novelty and Game Plan produced the game. Shown here is Pacific Novelty's version. $400-$500.

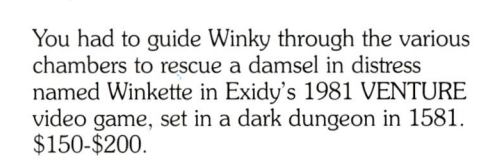

You had to guide Winky through the various chambers to rescue a damsel in distress named Winkette in Exidy's 1981 VENTURE video game, set in a dark dungeon in 1581. $150-$200.

Game Plan also sold SHARK ATTACK in a cocktail-table cabinet. $500-$600.

Trade ad for Game Plan's SHARK ATTACK. Game shown in this period ad is $400-$500.

Stern's 1981 STRATEGY X is a World War II-style combat game with rotating cannons, attacking jeeps, and shooting tanks. $150-$200.

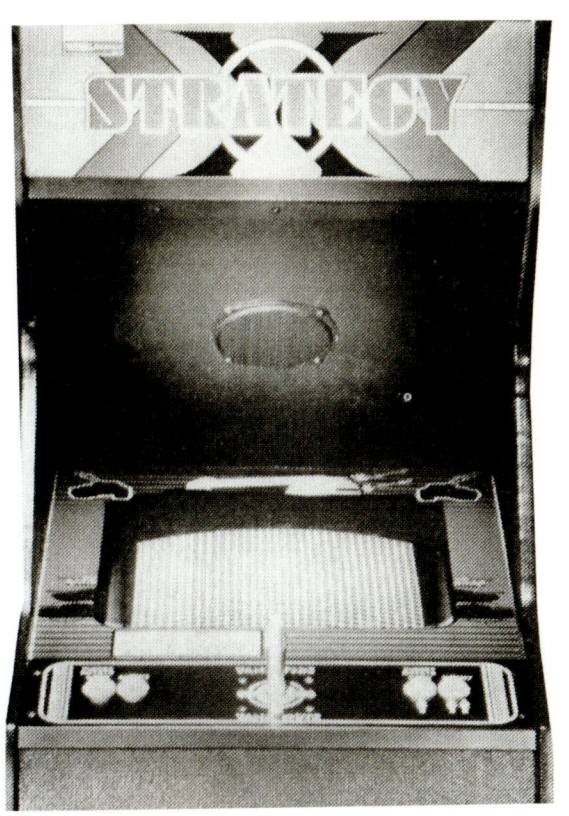

SHARK ATTACK

TAKE A DIVER TO LUNCH

Sharks munch a bunch for lunch in exciting new shark/diver challenge!

- 19" Color Monitor with seawater bachground.
- It's Shark vs Divers.
- Divers appear in squadrons of four.
- Screams of pain are heard as shark munches on divers.
- Bonus after shark eliminates 7 squadrons.
- Personal involvement... high scoring player initials high score to date.

KEEP YOUR EYE ON GPI

GPi Game Plan, inc.
1515 Fullerton Ave. Addison, IL 60101
Phone: 312/628-8200 Telex: 20-6098

Produced under license by Pacific Novelty Manufacturing, Inc.

Stern's JUNGLER, produced in 1981, was a cute maze game with attacking bugs and insects. $150-$200.

Although Konami designed and sold SCRAMBLE in Europe, Stern bought the rights to produce this game in the United States. Stern produced 13,486 SCRAMBLE upright games starting on March 16, 1981, and 1,650 of the cocktail models beginning on April 27. $200-$250.

COSMIC AVENGER (1981) was the second of Universal's "Cosmic" series of video games. $100-$150.

005 was advertised as the first of Sega's Convert-A-Game series. This 1981 video game was designed so that it could be easily changed into another game in minutes. Game shown in this period ad is $150-$200.

Game Plan was still looking for a hit with ENIGMA II (1981), but didn't find it here. $100-$150.

Use the paint roller to paint your way around the maze while avoiding the kitten, the mouse, the bird, and even a runaway tire! This 1981 maze game called CRUSH ROLLER was produced by Exidy. $100-$150.

CRUSH ROLLER screen shot.

Game Plan's MEGATACK (1981) had two distinct modes. In the first, you battled against monsters and giant pods. If you made it through this mode, then you faced the fiendish space rings. $100-$150.

Original concept artwork for Midway's EARTH FRIEND MISSION video game. The game was slated for production in 1981, but the project was killed at the last minute. Original artwork such as this rarely leaves the manufacturer and is extremely difficult to come by. $2,500-$3,500.

Released in 1981, Cinematronics SOLAR QUEST used an X-Y vector monitor and offered 500 play levels to keep the game challenging. $200-$300.

ARMOR ATTACK (1981), made by Cinematronics, was a tank combat game that did rather well in arcades. $100-$200.

116

Stern's horizontally scrolling SUPER COBRA (1981) had sidewinder missiles and flying saucers attack your helicopter from the front, while rockets and moving tanks fired from below. $150-$200.

Players loved to maneuver Q*BERT, a small orange ball with feet and a large trunk, around the pyramid. Mylstar produced two different headers on this 1981 game – one with the name of the machine and the other with symbols like "@!#?@!" (often referred to as the swearing header). Mylstar's best-selling video game. $300-$400.

Is it Kaos or Chaos? Only Game Plan's 1981 video game (and Maxwell Smart of Control) spelled it KAOS. No relation to the *Get Smart* TV series. $100-$150.

117

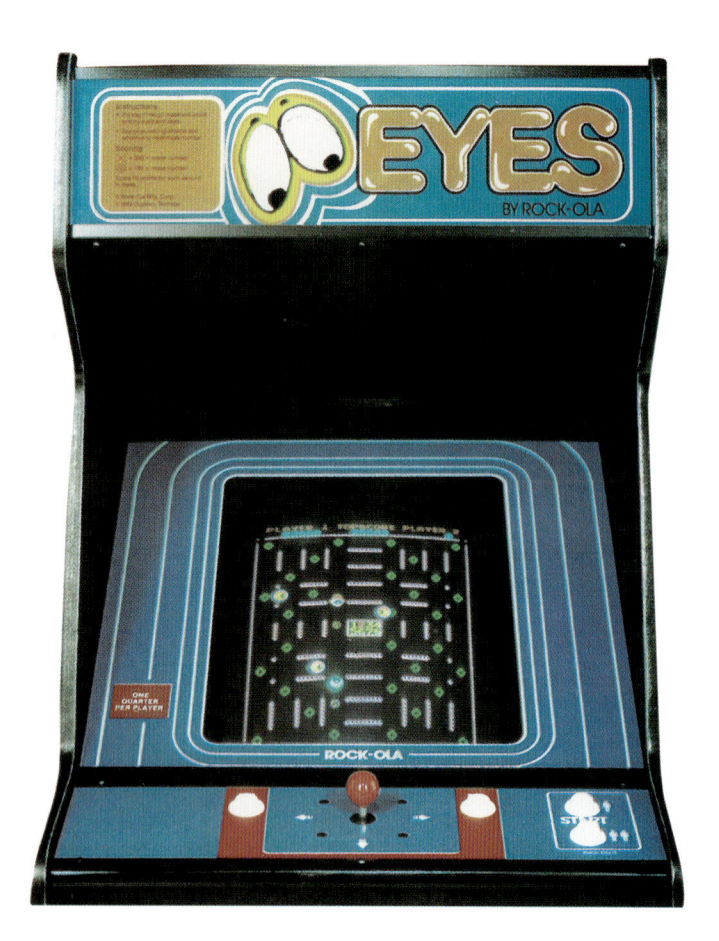

Rock-Ola's EYES (1981) had moving eyeballs that followed you around the screen! $150-$200.

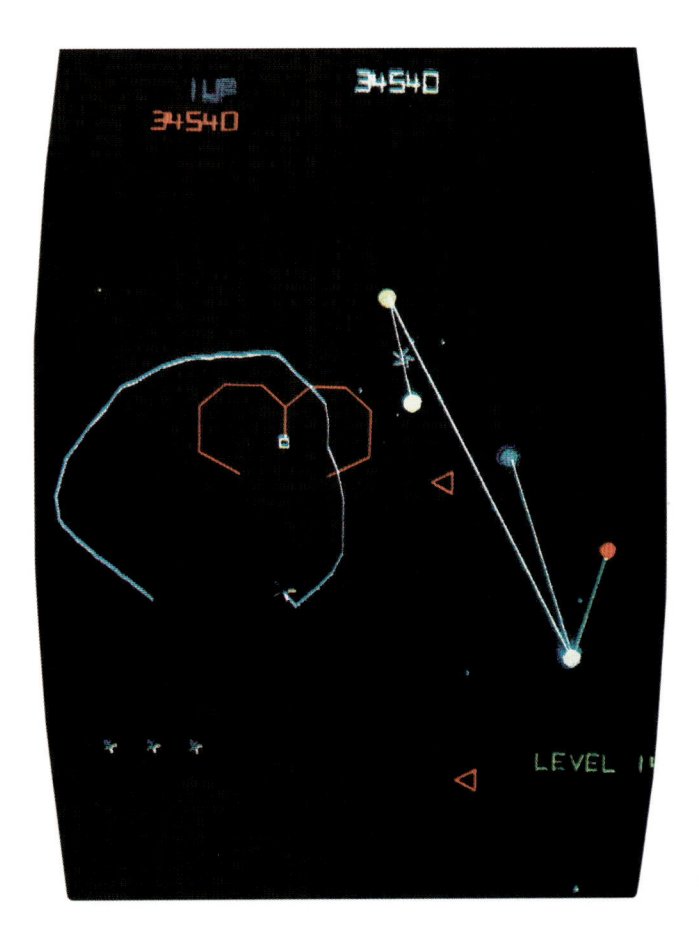

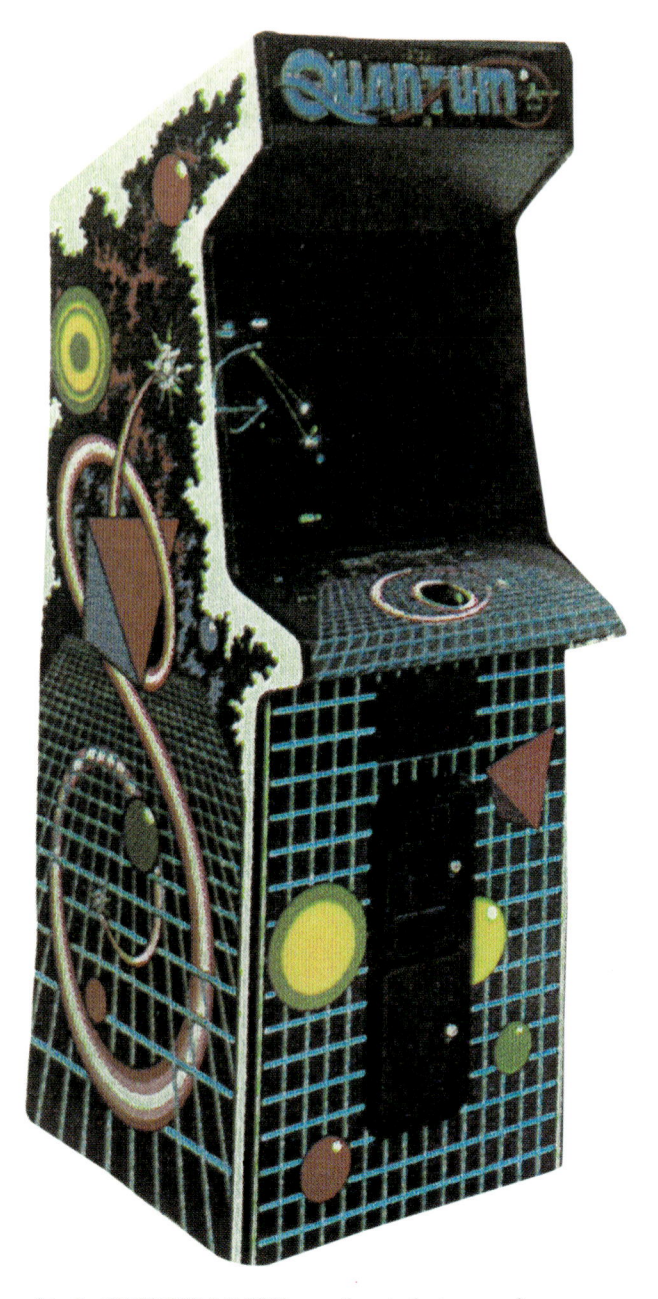

Atari's QUANTUM (1981) was the perfect game for nuclear physicists! Move the probe around the screen to capture particles like electrons, photons, positrons, pulsars, and triphons. The game was far too complicated for most players, but the X-Y graphics and the deep strategy required to play well have made this one of the most sought-after games among collectors. $1,000-$1,750.

QUANTUM screen shot.

LIBERATOR (1982) introduced the "Atari Force," a team of futuristic superheroes led by Commander Champion. The game was intended as the first of a series of Atari Force video games, but only this initial game was produced. $150-$200.

Visit the Eyeball Room, the Sickle Room, the Caterpillar Room, and the Cyclotron Room but watch out for the butterflies, faces, and hoppers! Stern's TAZZMANIA was produced in 1982 and included a Smart Bomb which could destroy everything in a pinch. $150-$200.

Exidy's 1982 VICTORY was an outer space shoot-'em-up game which featured a three-channel soundtrack, reverberating tones, and speech. Exidy also produced a conversion kit which would transform VICTORY into a new game called VICTOR BANANA. $100-$150.

No, there was never a game called PEPPER – only PEPPER II, a 1982 game from Exidy which featured cute devils and angels. $150-$200.

Well, blow me down! Nintendo's POPEYE, released in 1982, featured all of the familiar characters from the cartoons: Olive Oyl, Brutus, Sweet Pea, Wimpy, the Sea Hag, and, of course, Popeye himself. Despite the mediocre game play, the game remains collectible because of its name. $300-$500.

POPEYE screen shot.

Nintendo's best-selling video game was DONKEY KONG (1982), which let you guide hapless little Mario past flaming barrels and up treacherous ladders to rescue his princess from a giant ape. Most DONKEY KONG video games were sold in a light blue cabinet, although the early games were released in a bright red cabinet which is slightly more desirable for collectors. $400-$600 (blue cabinet); $500-$700 (red cabinet).

Sega's MONSTER BASH (1982) was part of the firm's Convert-A-Game system; the game was also made in dedicated form. $200-$300.

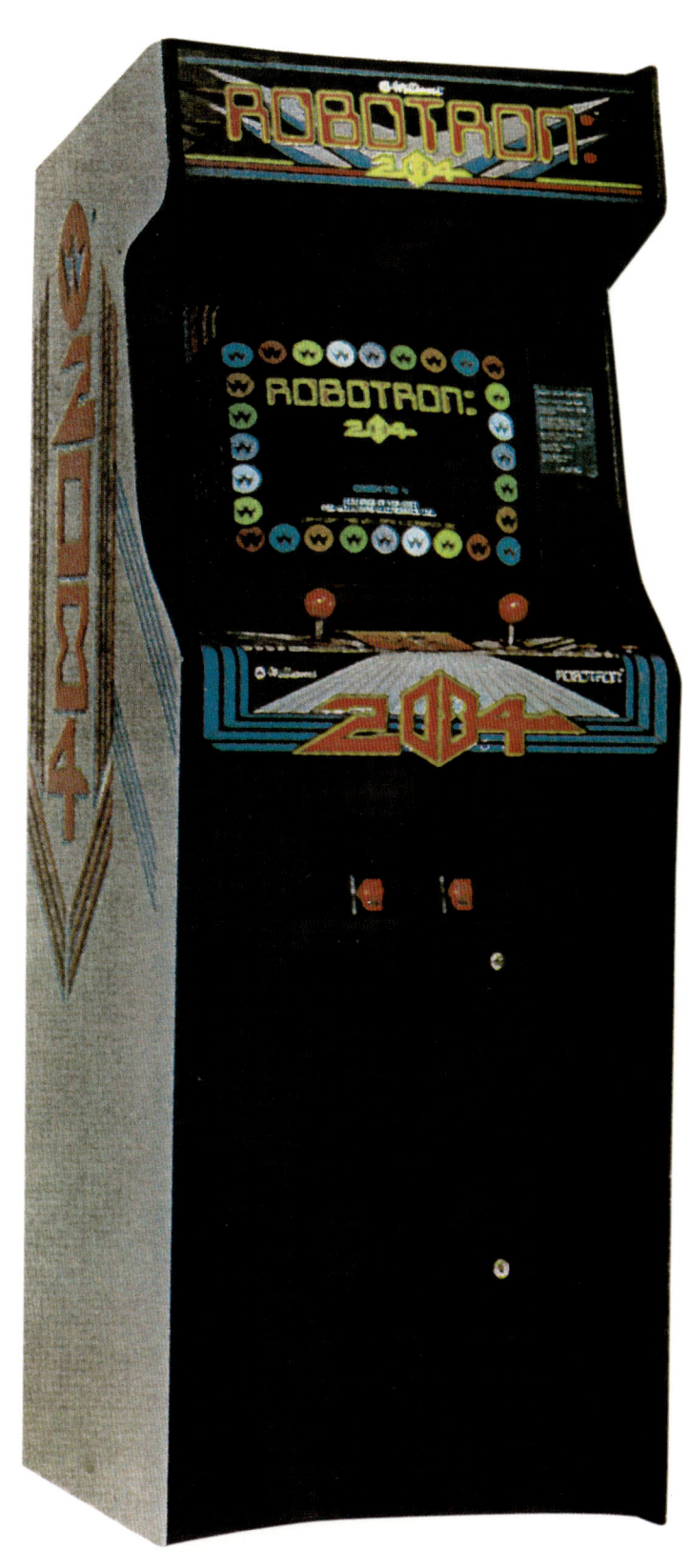

Set in the year 2084, Williams' ROBOTRON (1982) was an intense game with color graphics and a robotic voice. Move your robot around the screen while fighting off the attacking robots. $500-$850.

Unlike most other flying games, Venture's LOOPING (1981) wasn't an aerial combat game. Instead, the idea was to fly the plane though loops and perform other aerial stunts. $100-$150.

FRENZY, the sequel to Stern's popular BERZERK video game, had robotic skeletons and eyeballs chasing you! It was produced in 1982. $200-$250.

Instead of horses, the medieval knights on Williams' JOUST rode into battle on ostriches! Great one- or two-player game which included hatching ostrich eggs! $400-$600.

INTRODUCING...
THE NEW FEMME FATALE OF THE GAME WORLD

MS. PAC-MAN

The amazing Ms. Pac-Man offers all the fun of Midway's famous Pac-Man™ with four new mazes, added bonus fruit symbols that float freely through the maze, two new side exits that give four chances for get away and a unique cartoon series.

Produced by Midway Mfg. Co. under agreement with Namco Ltd.

MIDWAY
A BALLY COMPANY
VIDEO IS OUR GAME

Midway's MS. PAC MAN (1982) was almost as popular as the original PAC MAN. The monsters were smarter in MS. PAC MAN than in the original game, though, making it impossible to memorize patterns and play for hours at a time. Game shown in this period ad is $500-$800.

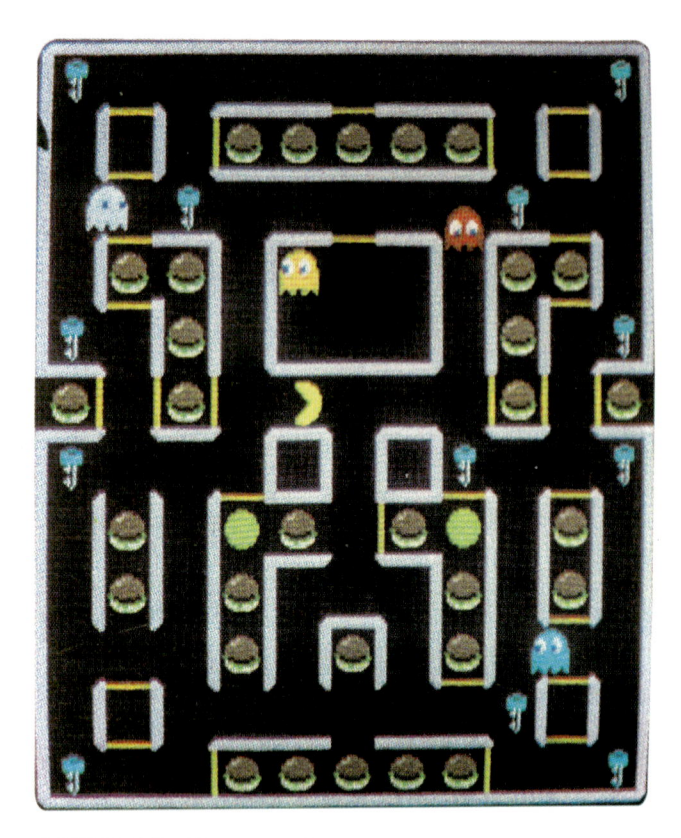

SUPER PAC MAN screen shot. Notice that the dots have been replaced by hamburgers.

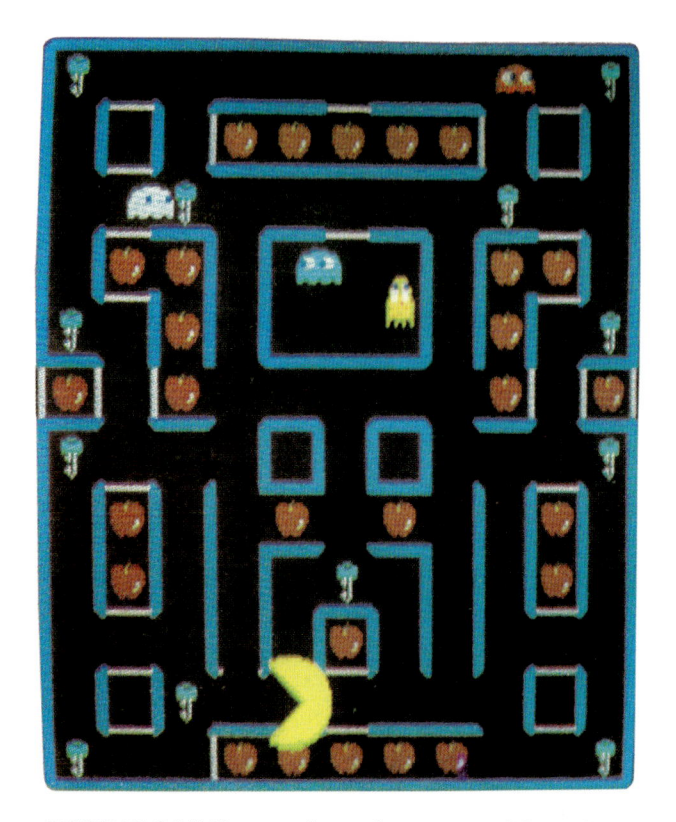

SUPER PAC MAN screen shot with a supersized Super Pac Man.

A new super hero is born – Midway's SUPER PAC MAN. Produced in 1982, the maze in SUPER PAC MAN had sealed entrances that could only be opened if you gobbled the nearby keys, and the dots were replaced by hamburgers and apples. Eating a power pellet would make Super Pac Man invincible – and quite large – for a short time. $200-$350.

Is it a video game or a pinball machine? It's two games in one. You started in the video maze at the beginning of the game, and could play the pinball game by guiding your Pac Man down one of the corridors at the bottom of the screen. You had to be good at both the video and the pinball games to score well on Midway's 1982 BABY PAC MAN game. $600-$1,000.

Centuri's D-DAY (1982) put you in the action at the famous World War II battle. $125-$200.

SATAN'S HOLLOW screen shot. Notice the devil's head at the top of the column.

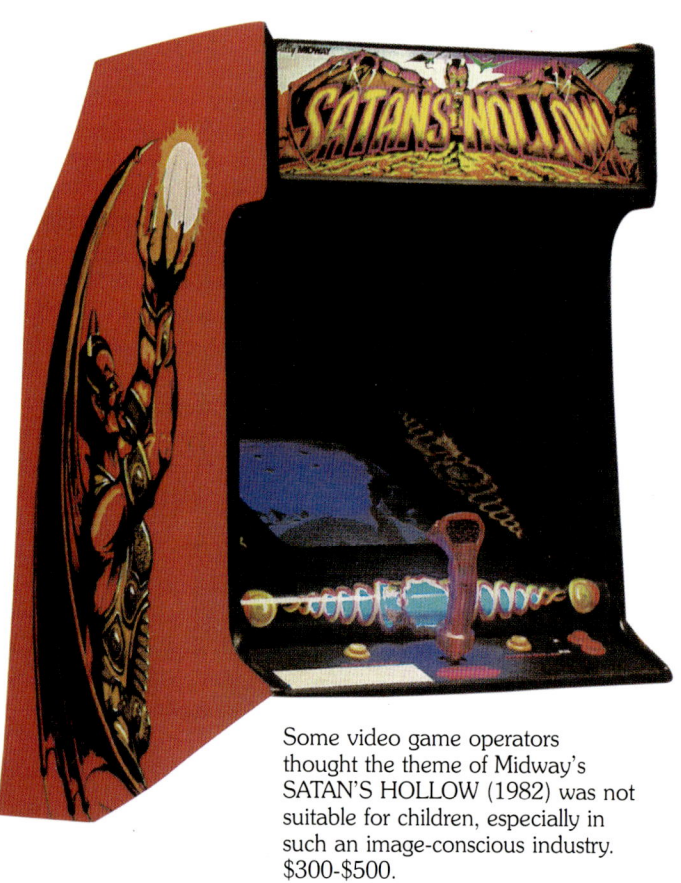

Some video game operators thought the theme of Midway's SATAN'S HOLLOW (1982) was not suitable for children, especially in such an image-conscious industry. $300-$500.

SATAN'S HOLLOW screen shot.

126

You could detonate DDT bombs to wipe out the attacking insects in Atari's MILLIPEDE (1982), the sequel to the company's CENTIPEDE video game. $300-$400.

MILLIPEDE screen shot.

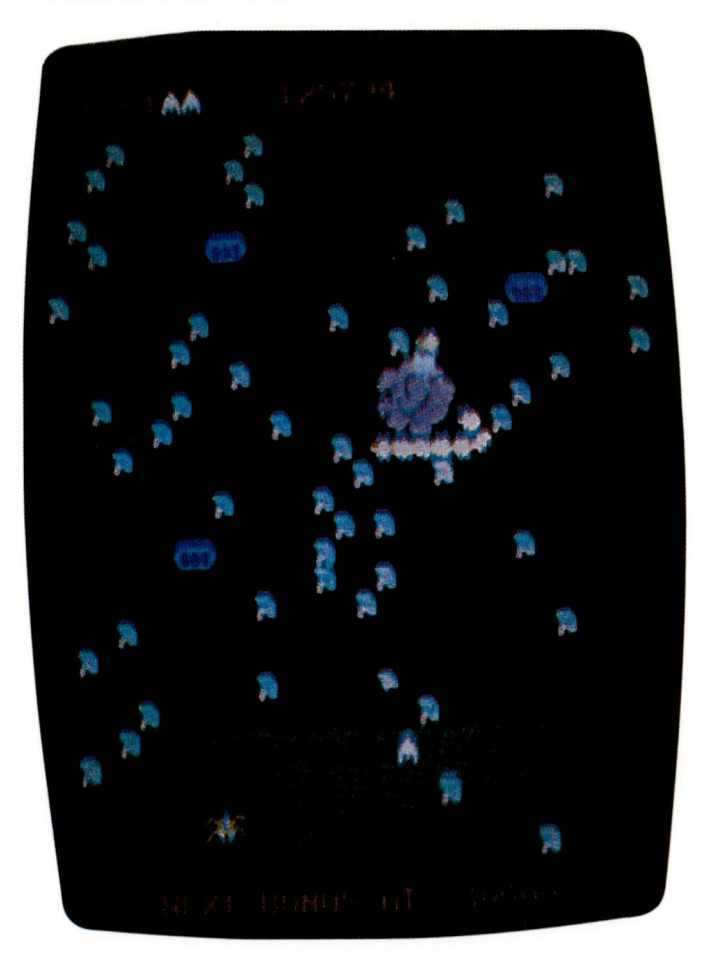

Atari's 1982 SPACE DUEL was a one- or two-player shootout in space with X-Y vector graphics. $400-$500.

You control Dig Dug, the hero of this game, and have to eliminate the bad guys by tunneling underneath them until the ground caves in – or you can pump them up until they explode! Atari produced DIG DUG in 1982. $300-$400.

Dig Dug stands ready to inflate his enemies with his pump in Atari's DIG DUG.

Pooka from DIG DUG.

Fygar from DIG DUG.

128

DIG DUG screen shot.

Hang gliding was the theme in Atari's FAST FREDDIE, produced in 1982. $200-$300.

Atari's POLE POSITION (1982) was one of the best-selling video driving games ever made. You could enter your initials in the high score table if you were one of the top 300 highest scoring players on the machine. $300-$400.

129

Unlike POLE POSITION, which was set on a speedway, Sega's TURBO video driving game had you driving down urban streets at top speed with skyscrapers on either side of the road. Same cockpit cabinet styling as Sega's MONACO GP. $300-$500.

Race your car through downtown streets on TURBO.

TURBO was also available in a mini cabinet design. $200-$300.

130

Sega's BUCK ROGERS, PLANET OF ZOOM (1982) was based on the popular comic strip and TV series. The game's main appeal was to diehard "Buck Rogers" fans. $150-$200.

Released at about the same time as POLE POSITION, Taito's GRAND CHAMPION was overlooked by players and rarely found on location. $200-$300.

Sega also produced a cockpit version of BUCK ROGERS, PLANET OF ZOOM. $300-$400.

Help the penguin build his igloo by pushing the ice blocks around the screen while avoiding the evil Sno-Bees. That's the plot of Sega's PENGO (1982). $200-$250.

Stern's DARK PLANET (1982) used the same 3-D technology as Sega's SUBROC 3-D. Even with the incredible graphics, DARK PLANET was just another outer space shoot-'em-up. $200-$300.

Even the fantastic 3-D graphics didn't draw players to Sega's SUBROC 3-D. The game was available in both an upright and a cockpit model, and was released in 1982 at about the same time as several 3-D films were playing in theaters. $200-$300.

It's difficult to find the cockpit version of SINISTAR in good condition after two decades. The cabinet included lots of molded plastic parts (such as the two gold thrusters on the front), which are usually found broken or cracked – or even missing – today. $750-$1,000.

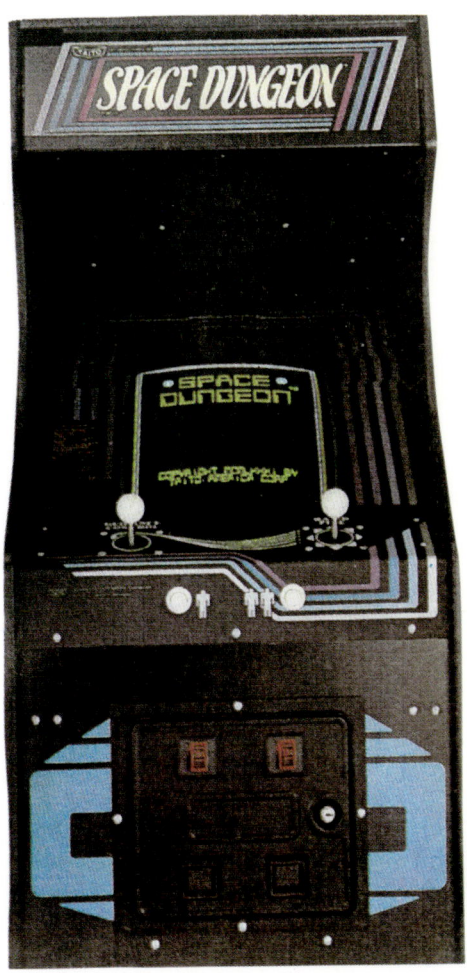

Williams' SINISTAR (1982) joined the list of hot Williams video games with its clever graphics and innovative game play. $400-$600.

Taito's SPACE DUNGEON (1982) was certainly a generic looking game – and it offered the usual generic outer space shoot-'em-up action. $100-$150.

133

Cinematronics' WAR OF THE WORLDS (1982) was based on the classic H.G. Wells' novel. $250-$350.

JACK THE GIANTKILLER screen shot.

It's not exactly Jack and the Beanstalk, but it's close. Plant the magic beans then climb the beanstalk to rescue the princess from the evil giant in Cinematronics' JACK THE GIANTKILLER (1982). Cinematronics offered this marketing suggestion to video game operators: "Feature photos of players who Rescue the Princess in the game location." $150-$200.

MOON PATROL (1982) was still another top-earning video game from Williams. $400-$500.

If you liked Atari's CENTIPEDE, then you would probably like SLITHER (1982), one of the few video games produced by GDI/Destron. $100-$150.

Stern's LOST TOMB was a conversion game which could be installed only in other Stern video games such as THE END, SCRAMBLE, SUPER COBRA, MOON WAR, TURTLES, ARMORED CAR, JUNGLER, STRATEGY X, and AMIDAR. Stern even offered operators a $50 rebate if they returned the old boards from the converted game to Stern. $100-$150.

It's difficult to forget an unusual name like OLI BOO CHU. This 1982 game from Thomas Automatics takes its names from the game's characters (Oli, Boo, and Chu). Game shown in this period ad is $125-$175.

Stern's BAGMAN (1982) had great cartoon graphics on the header and on the sides of the cabinet. The game was licensed from S.A. Valadon in France. $150-$250.

135

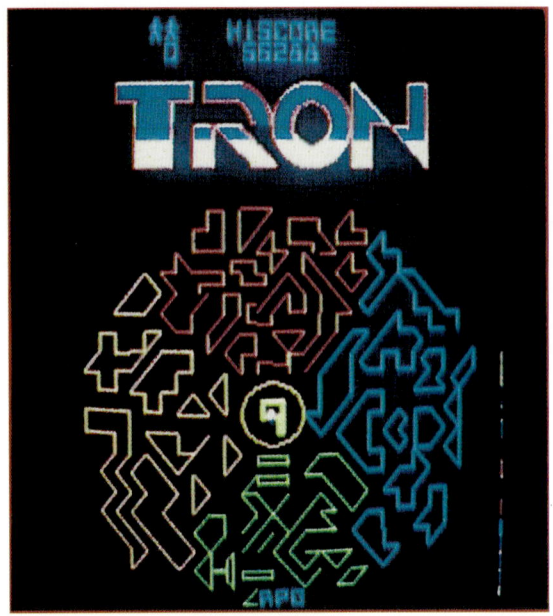

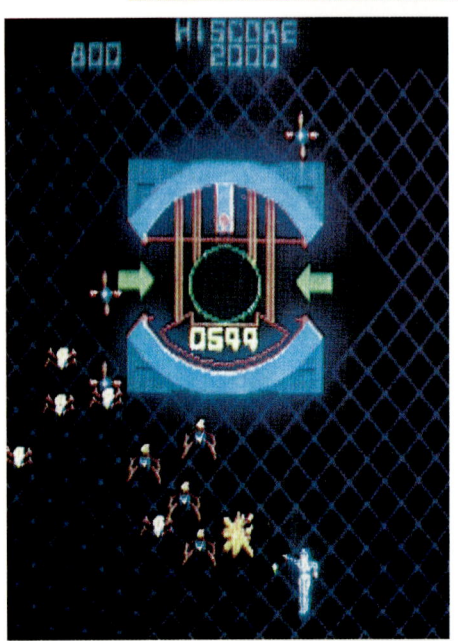

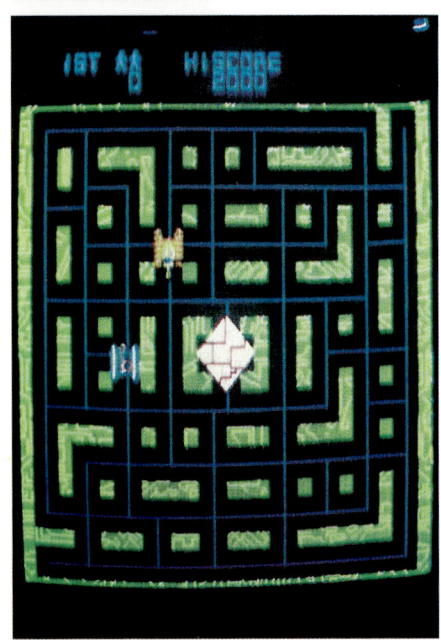

TRON screen shots.

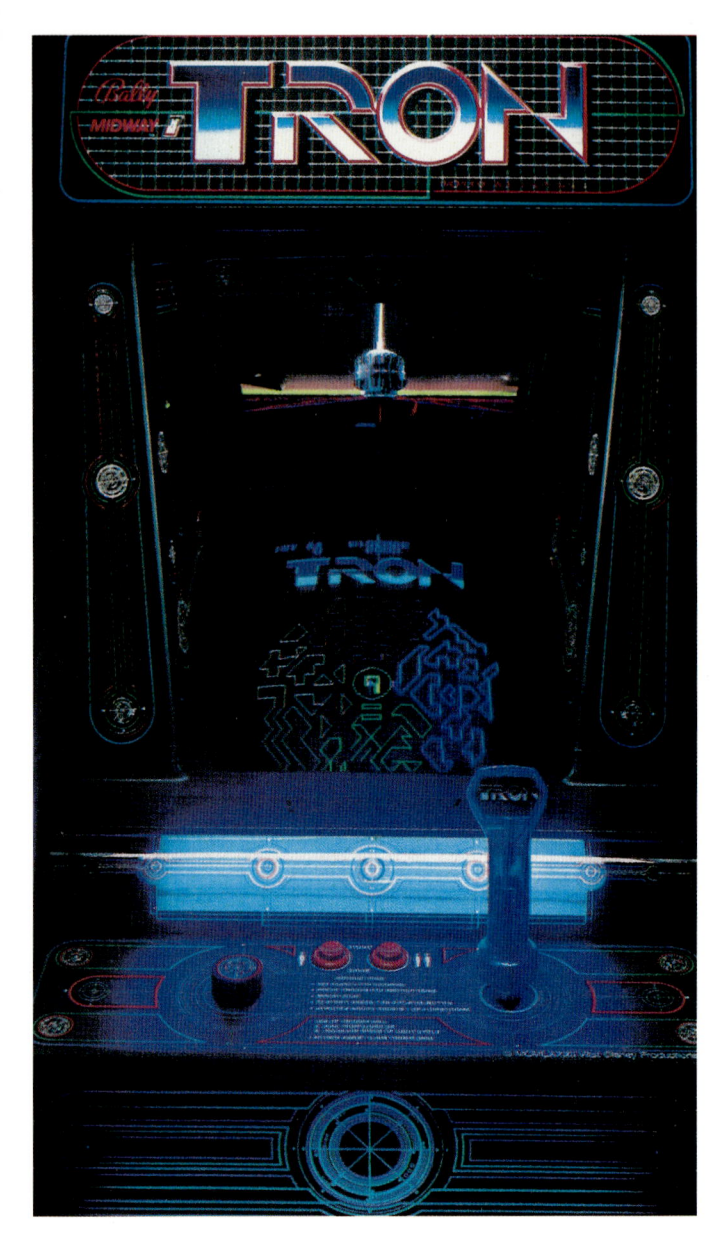

Disney's blockbuster hit film *Tron* was the inspiration for this 1982 Midway video game. The game featured music from the movie soundtrack and a unique blue joystick control, and was sold in both upright and cocktail table styles. $500-$1,000.

You could "Walk the Dog" on Taito's THE ELECTRIC YO-YO (1982) – if you can find one of these low-production games. $300-$400.

Midway released a giant wall poster in 1982 picturing the headers from the company's most popular video games over the last four years. Posters like this are often difficult to find because they were distributed at national trade shows, and most showgoers disposed of these large bulky posters when they left the exhibit hall floor rather than hauling them home on an airplane. Reproductions of this poster are now being sold. $20-$30 (original poster).

Taito's KRAM was in production for less than three weeks when it was released in the summer of 1982. $150-$200.

You floated through the sky in a hot air balloon in Rock-Ola's FANTASY video game. $125-$200.

A kangaroo with boxing gloves? That's what you'll find on Atari's 1982 KANGAROO. You scored points by punching out monkeys, apple cores, and apes, and could also score points for rescuing the baby kangaroo. $200-$300.

KANGAROO screen shot.

WILD WESTERN screen shot.

Protect the train from outlaws by firing your eight-way joystick in all directions on Taito's WILD WESTERN (1982). Although the header looks generic, WILD WESTERN was sold only as a dedicated video game, not a conversion. $100-$150.

Midway's BOSCONIAN (1982) featured a "Vocalized Command System" with phrases like "Blast Off," "Alarm! Alarm!" and "Battle Stations!" to correspond with the screen action. $200-$300.

139

Centuri's THE PIT (1982) offered extraterrestrial excitement as you dug tunnels under the surface of an alien planet in search of treasure. $100-$150.

BEEZER, by Intrepid Marketing, was a 1982 update kit designed to convert Midway's GALAXIAN. Along with new program chips, operators got a new header and cabinet decals with the kit. $150-$200.

Centuri introduced SWIMMER in 1982. You have to dodge snapping turtles, crabs, water spiders, and piranhas as you swim upstream (or is it downstream?) to face the vicious giant crab at the end of each round. $100-$150.

TANK BATTALION (1982) was one of the last video games produced by Game Plan. Blast through the brick walls with your tank and then go after the enemy tanks on the other side. $100-$150.

BOXING BUGS

- The proven Wells-Gardner color X-Y Monitor System #6101 brings quality full color action to the screen.
- Expanded 32 K memory allows full animation of characters on the screen.
- Surveys indicate bonus rounds offer strong player incentives for replay.
- Evaluate adjustable features with the built-in play audit information.
- One bonus cannon is awarded with operator adjustable bonus levels.
- Players follow their progress as they advance through boxing weight classes.
- In the attract mode, high scoring players watch their intitials rise to become the champ.

CINEMATRONICS Inc.   1841 Friendship Dr. • El Cajon, CA 92020 • (714) 562-7000 • (800) 854-2666

From a bug that jumps to one that boxes. Cinematronics' 1982 BOXING BUGS featured insects slugging it out. BOXING BUGS was one of the few non-space themed video games to use an X-Y vector monitor. Game shown in this period ad is $200-$300.

You drive a Volkswagen Beetle (yes, a "bug") from scene to scene while collecting moneybags from clouds, rooftops, and even underwater in Rock-Ola's JUMP BUG (1982). $150-$200.

Sega's TAC/SCAN was offered as part of the company's Convert-A-Game system and could be used to update earlier Sega games like SPACE FURY, ELIMINATOR, and ZEKTOR. TAC/SCAN included more than 1,300 space sound variations in its programming. $200-$300.

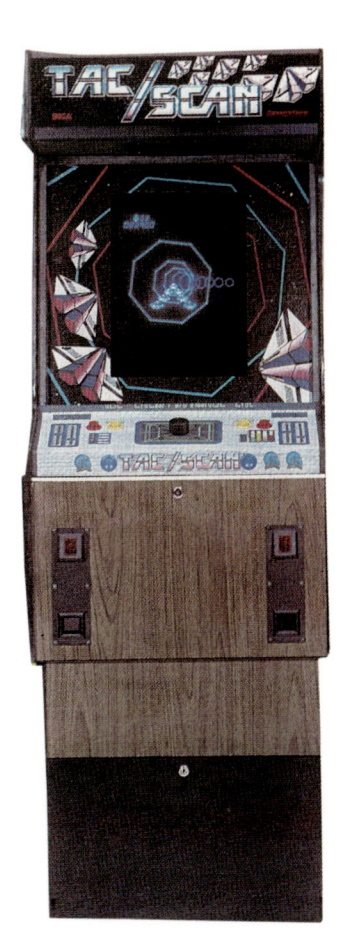

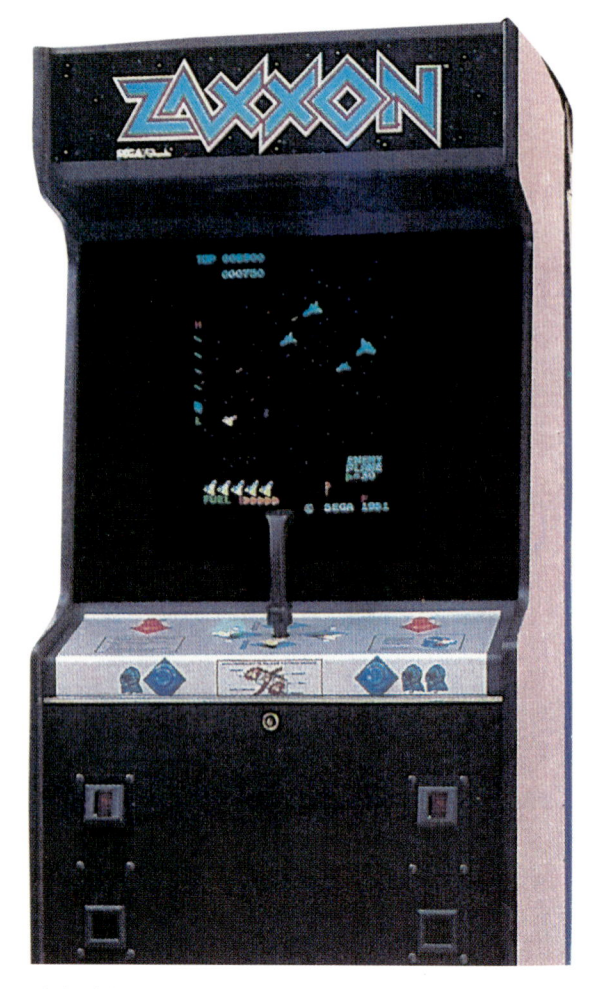

Colorful graphics that changed perspective as you soar through the air made Sega's ZAXXON one of the most popular video games of 1982. You actually had to bank your plane up and down to avoid flying into the 3-D objects around you. $250-$350.

Midway's SOLAR FOX (1982) was another outer space shoot-'em-up video game. You viewed the game through an unusual monitor glass with bright green and neon pink colors. $125-$200.

Original hand-drawn artwork for Midway's MOTHERSHIP, a video game which never made it into production. Such original artwork is extremely rare. $2,500-$3,500.

GRAVITAR screen shot.

Atari's GRAVITAR (1982) was an X-Y vector outer space bombing game. $350-$500.

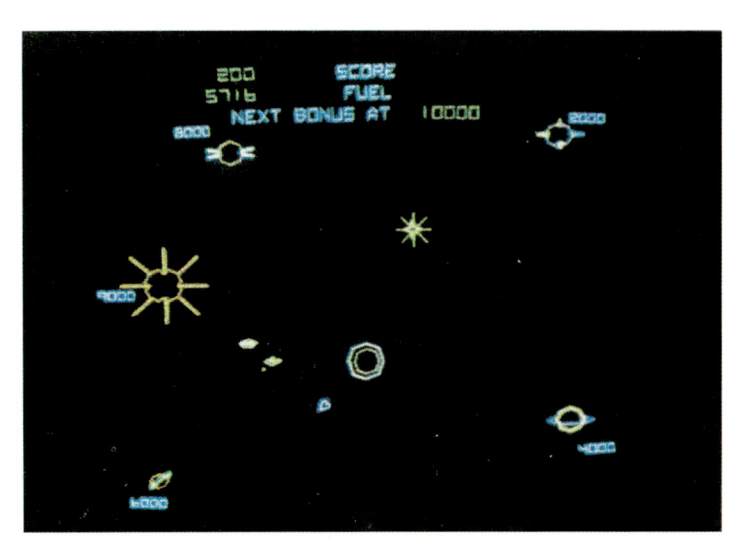

LIL' HUSTLER (1982) was made by Dynamo, a company best known for its line of table soccer (foosball) games. The game was licensed from Konami, and was Dynamo's only video game. $125-$175.

You have to be a bad boy to score big on Cinematronics' NAUGHTY BOY. Guide the boy through forests, fields, and mazes – and don't forget to knock down the flags and throw rocks at your enemies along the way in this 1982 game. $125-$175.

The big bad wolves are after the three little pigs in POOYAN, produced by Stern in 1982. You're the Mama Pig defending your baby pigs from the rows of wolves that are dropping down from the sky! $150-$250.

You'll hear "I've Been Workin' on the Railroad" when you play Centuri's 1982 LOCO MOTION. Lay down the train tracks in a straight line for big points. $100-$150.

Midway's 1982 DOMINO MAN had an *eye*-catching cabinet with huge dominos attached to the front. $150-$200.

You're the chef preparing a juicy burger in Midway's 1982 BURGERTIME. All you have to do is walk over all of the ingredients to drop them into the buns at the bottom of the screen while you avoid Mr. Pickle, Mr. Egg, and Mr. Hot Dog. You can always throw pepper at them to stun them temporarily! Game shown in this period ad is $300-$450.

Bally/MIDWAY

BurgerTime

...The Tastiest New Entrée On The Video Menu!

The specialty of the house! Help Chef Peter Pepper race the maze to collect patties, cheese, lettuce and buns. As he crosses each ingredient, it falls onto a platter waiting below. Complete four burgers and you will feast on even more challenging mazes, build more burgers and score the biggest Burgertime score ever!

Destroy the pursuing Mr. Hot Dog, Mr. Egg and Mr. Pickle for bonus points! Hints: 1) Lure them onto burger parts right before they drop. 2) Smash the pursuers underneath a burger part.

Pepper! The Secret Ingredient

You can temporarily stun Mr. Hot Dog, Mr. Egg and Mr. Pickle by shaking pepper their way. Hint: Pepper supply is limited and should be used sparingly! Replenish your limited pepper power by snacking on ice cream, french fries and cups of tea as they're served.

Cabinet Specs.
Upright: Cocktail:
70" Height   29" Height
26½" Width   32" Width
34" Depth   22" Depth   ©1982 Bally-Midway Mfg. Co.

Bally
MIDWAY MFG. CO.
10601 W. Belmont Avenue
Franklin Park, Illinois 60131
Telephone (312) 451-9200

SHAFFER DISTRIBUTING COMPANY
1100 West Third Ave.
Columbus, OH 43212
(614) 224-6800

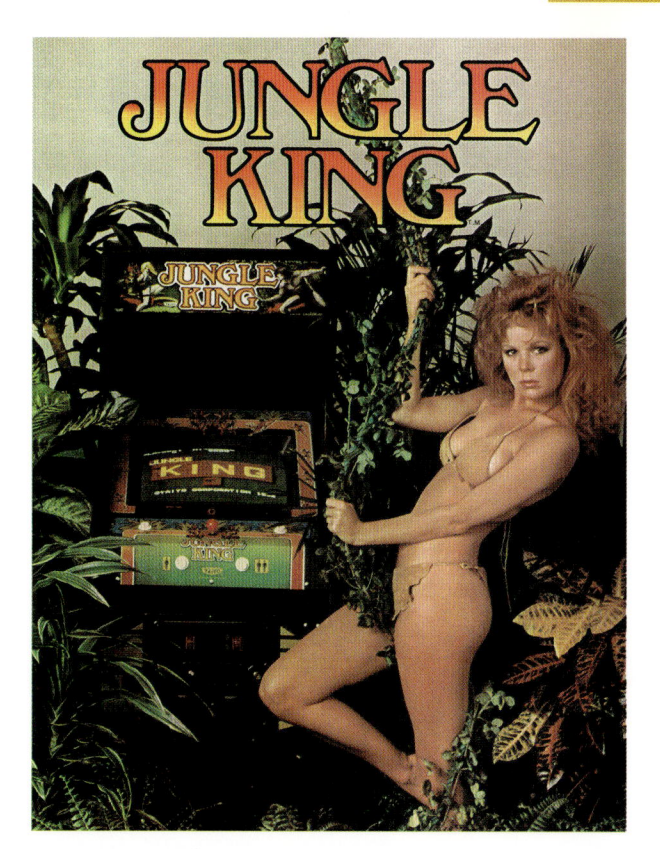

PRINTED IN U.S.A.

Taito's JUNGLE KING (also released as JUNGLE HUNT) looked like it came right out of a Tarzan movie. Swing through the forest on the vines and avoid the wild animals. Game shown in this period ad is $250-$300.

145

Taito's PIRATE PETE (1982) was similar to JUNGLE KING, except that PIRATE PETE was set on a pirate ship. $200-$250.

Gottlieb's REACTOR (1982) was set inside a radioactive reactor core and had a catchy background tune that often had players humming along. $250-$350.

Released in 1982, Universal's MR. DO was the first in a series of MR. DO games including MR. DO'S WILD RIDE and DO RUN RUN. Because the game was sold primarily as a conversion kit rather than a dedicated game, you'll find MR. DO in a variety of cabinet styles. $250-$300.

Battle the large one-eyed LAZARIAN in this 1982 Midway video game. $150-$250.

Lots of digging going on in 1982. Along with Atari's DIG DUG and Centuri's THE PIT, Midway's ROBBY ROTO let you dig underground tunnels while avoiding the bad guys (in this case, the Wicked Troll, the Evil Voltar, the Sinister Spider, and Jawbones). $200-$250.

Midway's BLUE PRINT (1982) was perfectly suited for architects! Follow the blueprints and build the house before the evil Ollie Ogre captures Daisy Damsel. $200-$250.

Explore the pyramids of ancient Egypt in Stern's TUTANKHAM (1982). $200-$300.

147

Centuri's TIME PILOT (1982) was set in five different time periods with the action going back to 1910 ("The Age of the Biplane") and into the "future" of 2001 ("The Age of the UFO"). $250-$350.

Originally titled KICK, Midway's 1982 KICKMAN featured a smiling clown on a unicycle trying to catch balloons on the top of his pointed hat. There was even a cameo appearance by Pac Man! $250-$350.

148

Part 4
THE EXPERIMENTAL YEARS
1983-1985

Video games had come a long way from PONG in the last decade. There was no doubt that games like CENTIPEDE and MS. PAC MAN helped capture female players, while BIRDIE KING and TEMPEST appealed to older players. But the core group of players was still teenage boys – and they were starting to tire of the same old outer space shoot-'em-up video games.

Many of the "new" video games elicited a "been there, done that" reaction from players. The concept of flying through space and firing at enemy ships while dodging their attacks had worn thin. There was a feeling that video game development had gone as far as it could go, that there were no frontiers left to explore.

Even worse, home video game systems like Atari's 2600 (introduced in the early 1980s) were starting to draw players out of the arcades and into their homes. Virtually every popular arcade video game had been released for the home units by the end of 1982, and even though many of these home games didn't play quite as smoothly as their coin-op counterparts, arcade video game manufacturers knew that something had to be done to reclaim the players that had been lost.

Video manufacturers took a cue from the pinball industry, which had been licensing popular themes for years. One of the first licensed video games was Midway's 1983 JOURNEY, which featured the internationally known rock band. You guided each of the five band members one by one through a different game screen, avoiding the screaming fans until all five reached the stage safely. JOURNEY also featured digitized photographic images of the performers incorporated into the game play.

Movies and TV shows provided a source of inspiration to video game manufacturers, as Gottlieb produced KRULL, based on the film of the same name. The company had created a KRULL pinball machine which reached the prototype stage, but the pinball concept was scrapped after Gottlieb built only nine of these games. Eager to recoup some of its investment in securing the license, Gottlieb released the KRULL video game which reused some of the same artwork and sound that had been created for the pinball.

Of course, it was only a matter of time before a video game appeared based on the *Star Trek* TV series, and the game arrived with lots of fanfare in the summer of 1983. Sega launched a massive promotional campaign for the STAR TREK video game with tournaments held in arcades

Midway's MAPPY (1983) had an attention-getting header on top of the cabinet. You're Mappy, the police mouse, who has to stop the tricky cats from stealing all of the valuables inside a home. $200-$300.

across the country complete with promotional T-shirts, coffee mugs, and other prizes. STAR TREK didn't do quite as well as expected in arcades, and Sega soon released the game as a conversion kit a few months after the machine had been unveiled.

On the other hand, Atari's STAR WARS video game was a huge success. With a steering unit that resembled the control panel of a tie fighter and music taken from the *Star Wars* soundtrack, STAR WARS was an instant hit and is still phenomenally popular among video game collectors today.

In the early summer of 1983, Cinematronics unveiled a new kind of video game, one which didn't have dots or lines on the screen. In fact, playing this game was almost like becoming part of a cartoon, because DRAGON'S LAIR featured high-quality laser disc animation. It looked like DRAGON'S LAIR would provide the video game industry with the boost that it so badly needed.

DRAGON'S LAIR was created by Don Bluth, a former Disney animator who had opened his own studio in the early '80s. Bluth sold the idea for DRAGON'S LAIR to Starcom, which in turn licensed the game to Cinematronics. Besides the dazzling graphics, DRAGON'S LAIR offered something else players had never seen before – a storyline. You would guide Dirk the Daring, a medieval knight, through the dark, winding corridors of a stone castle, heading for the final confrontation with the dragon inside. It took a lot of time – and a lot of quarters – to make it all the way through to the end of the plot.

DRAGON'S LAIR was an instant hit, and Cinematronics couldn't keep up with the demand for the game; in fact, the game was in production for over nine months, until early 1984. DRAGON'S LAIR came from the factory set at 50 cents per play and couldn't be adjusted to a quarter per game without a special modification kit. This was no accident on the part of Cinematronics; because DRAGON'S LAIR carried a higher price tag than other video games on the market, Cinematronics wanted to make sure that operators could quickly recoup their investment in the machine.

By the end of the summer, nearly every video game company had its own laser disc video game in production. These included ASTRON BELT and NFL FOOTBALL (Bally Midway), STAR RIDER (Williams), FIREFOX (Atari), CLIFFHANGER (Stern), LASER GRAND PRIX, (Taito), COBRA COMMAND and BEGA'S BATTLE (Data East), M.A.C.H. 3 and US VS. THEM (Gottlieb/Mylstar), BADLANDS (Centuri), and more. New companies like RDI and Funai sprang up, offering laser disc video games like THAYER'S QUEST and INTERSTELLAR, respectively.

While some of these laser disc video games featured high-quality animation similar to that of DRAGON'S LAIR, other games used actual video footage which was integrated with conventional video game technology. The most popular game of this type was Mylstar's M.A.C.H. 3, which put you in the cockpit of a fighter jet during a bombing mission.

Despite their success, laser disc video games were plagued with two inherent problems. First, the game play followed a storyline from beginning to end; once you reached the end of the game (which was the end of the disc), the game was over. Unlike conventional video games, laser games couldn't become progressively more challenging the longer you played.

The second problem was technological. Most laser disc games used a disc player manufactured by Pioneer. Although the player was state of the art at the time, it simply couldn't hold up to the constant use (and sometimes abuse) it was subjected to. Many of these laser disc games were operating in arcades and other locations that were open more than twelve hours a day, and these players would frequently overheat.

Midway introduced yet another Pac Man-themed game in 1983: PROFESSOR PAC MAN. Unlike all of the other Pac Man video games, PROFESSOR PAC MAN didn't have a yellow mouth traveling through a maze gobbling dots; instead, PROFESSOR PAC MAN was a quiz game in which the Pac character appeared wearing a mortarboard and holding a pointer, providing clues to the visual puzzles which appeared on the screen. Without question, this was the least successful PAC MAN-themed video game.

Midway's DISCS OF TRON, also released in 1983, fared much better. After the success of the TRON video game, DISCS OF TRON offered an entirely new game with graphics again taken from the Disney film. DISCS OF TRON was sold in a standard upright cabinet, but it was the first – and only – video game offered in what was called an environmental cabinet, arguably the most elaborate video game cabinet design ever created. This huge cabinet was more than five feet from front to back and weighed over 700 pounds. According to the sales brochure, "Exceptional sound acoustics, lighting and special effects in an enclosed environment enhance the game's challenges."

Atari's TX-1 driving game also weighed in at 650 pounds, and featured three screens which provided a panoramic view of the road during the game. Few collectors own TX-1 today; because of the game's size and factory cost (nearly three times as much as most upright video games), Atari made only a limited production run of this machine.

Nintendo's PUNCH OUT had two monitors mounted vertically in the cabinet. The lower screen showed the game action, while the upper monitor showed you the score and other game status information.

Williams unveiled its Duramold cabinet in 1983. Looking like a large black tube, this molded plastic cabinet was more durable than traditional wooden cabinets. Williams sold only two video games (BLASTER and BUBBLES) in Duramold cabinets, although some collectors have retrofitted other Williams games into Duramold cabinets.

Here's your chance to toss pies, bananas, and other fruit at the white-smocked chefs. Atari's 1983 FOOD FIGHT had an instant replay feature which would replay a sharp maneuver made by the player immediately after the close call. Game shown in this period ad is $300-$400.

CRYSTAL CASTLES (1983) was a 3-D maze game; the object was to move your figure over all the paths in the maze and gather up all the crystals to move on to the next level. $300-$400.

Nintendo's VS system, introduced in 1984, quite literally offered a new perspective on game play. Each VS game had two monitors, allowing each player to see the game action from his or her own perspective. For example, in VS TENNIS, when you hit the ball toward your opponent, you would see the ball moving away from you, while at the same time, your opponent would see the action from the other side of the court with the ball coming toward him.

By the time Cinematronics released SPACE ACE in January of 1984, the short-lived laser disc video game fad had ended, at least for the rest of the decade. SPACE ACE never came close to achieving the popularity of DRAGON'S LAIR. Probably the most ambitious laser disc video game was ATOMIC CASTLE, designed by Laser Disc Computer Systems of Cambridge, Massachusetts. ATOMIC CASTLE resembled a Hollywood production, with costumed actors and elaborate special effects. Stern Electronics bought the rights to market the game, but Stern went out of business in the fall of 1984 after building only two ATOMIC CASTLE prototypes. The following month, Game Plan acquired the rights to sell ATOMIC CASTLE as a conversion kit for existing laser disc video games, but Game Plan met the same fate as Stern, as the company closed its doors early in 1985 before the ATOMIC CASTLE kit could be marketed.

If you're a fan of the rock group Journey, then you'll love this 1983 Midway video game which featured five distinct game challenges as you tried to get all the members of the group past the audience and onto the stage. $500-$750.

Yet another high-profile video game manufacturer also called it quits in 1984. Mylstar Electronics, formerly D. Gottlieb and Co., went out of business in the late summer shortly after introducing its THREE STOOGES video game. Even the success of Q*BERT and M.A.C.H. 3 wasn't enough to keep this company open as the video game market was declining.

But in the midst of the downsizing in the video game industry, PONG inventor Nolan Bushnell took the bold step of opening a new company in the fall of 1984. Bushnell's Sente offered a line of economically priced video game kits, along with a new hardware system designed specifically for Sente games. SNAKE PIT, Sente's first offering, received a warm reception from video game operators partly on the basis of Bushnell's reputation in the industry. By the end of the year, Bally purchased the company from Bushnell, renaming it Bally Sente and using the slogan, "The All American Video Game Company." Sente invested a substantial amount of money to secure the rights to create licensed games like NAME THAT TUNE (based on the TV game show) and TRIVIAL PURSUIT (based on the popular board game), but the company's most successful video game was MINI GOLF, a video simulation of a miniature golf course. Less than two years later, however, after producing nearly two dozen different games, Bally shut down Sente following the limited production of MOONQUAKE, Bally Sente's final game.

By the mid 1980s, home video systems and a lack of new original game ideas spelled the end of what many collectors now call the golden age of video games. In the last decade, the first generation of video game players (some of whom had cut their teeth on games like PONG) had grown up and moved on to other interests, leaving a new generation of players to decide with their quarters the future of video games.

Midway's JOURNEY screen shot. Notice the digitized photos of the band members' faces.

SEGA/GREMLIN

Founded as separate companies on opposite sides of the world, Sega and Gremlin's paths became intertwined in the late 1970s. Tokyo-based Sega Enterprises was founded in 1952 as a game operator called Service Games by American businessman Martin Bromely. The company began manufacturing and exporting selected arcade games to the United States; its PERISCOPE game of 1966 was a big hit both in the U.S. and throughout the world – at seven feet tall and nearly nine feet deep, it couldn't be overlooked! Sega merged with Rosen Enterprises, Inc. in 1965, and by the mid 1960s, the company had produced several other moderately successful arcade games, including GRAND NATIONAL and COWBOY. The company also produced a line of pinball machines distributed primarily in Japan.

At about the same time, businessman Frank Fogleman founded Gremlin Industries in San Diego, California. Within a year, Gremlin had entered the fledgling video game industry, and became the leading manufacturer of wall games.

By the mid '70s, both Sega and Gremlin were producing video games. Sega had opened a manufacturing facility in Redondo Beach, California, where it was producing games like SECRET BASE, ROAD RACE, and THE FONZ, based on the popular character from TV's *Happy Days* sitcom. Gremlin had entered the video game market in 1976, and one of the firm's most successful video games (BLOCKADE) was even licensed to a Japanese firm.

On September 29, 1978, Gremlin became part of Sega through an exchange of stock between the two companies. For the next two years, all of the video games released by the now-combined company carried both firm's names, first as Gremlin/Sega, and then as Sega/Gremlin. The Gremlin name was phased out by 1981, and Sega introduced a string of video game blockbusters including CARNIVAL, TURBO, FROGGER, ZAXXON, and PENGO. In 1969, Sega had been purchased by Gulf & Western, an international conglomerate which also owned Paramount Pictures, which is how Sega acquired the rights to produce video games such as STAR TREK and MICHAEL JACKSON'S MOONWALKER, which were licensed from Paramount. Sega also owned the "Time Out" arcade chain in the United States. The company is still producing arcade video games today.

Check out the tilted cabinet on Midway's WACKO (1983). Even the control panel was slanted, which was disconcerting to some players. $150-$250.

Does the green Martian in the flying saucer look familiar? It's the same character who made his first appearance in WACKO. Midway's KOZMIK KROOZ'R was designed as a sort of sequel to WACKO, but neither game generated much interest from players. $200-$250.

Players looking for an original game theme found it in BUBBLES, a 1983 game from Williams. Clean up the kitchen sink while avoiding the razor blades and other items floating around. Players didn't care for the cockroaches which crawled out of the drain from time to time, though. $300-$400 (upright); $400-$500 (cocktail).

Centuri's AZTARAC appears on some video game collectors' lists of top ten games. Instead of a flat sheet of plastic over the monitor, you view the action on AZTARAC through a large convex bubble. $800-$1,000.

MAD PLANETS (1983) – another outer space shoot-'em-up, this one from Mylstar. $250-$300.

155

Produced in 1983, Sega's STAR TREK used a color X-Y vector monitor. The game had great *Star Trek* graphics on the header and cabinet, but the game play itself was rather generic. $500-$600.

STAR TREK was produced in a cockpit cabinet; it was also sold as a conversion kit for X-Y vector games produced by Sega and Atari so you might see the game in a wide variety of cabinet styles. $600-$750 (cockpit cabinet); $400-$600 (conversion games).

Atari introduced XEVIOUS, an aerial bombing game, in 1982. $150-$250.

XEVIOUS screen shot.

156

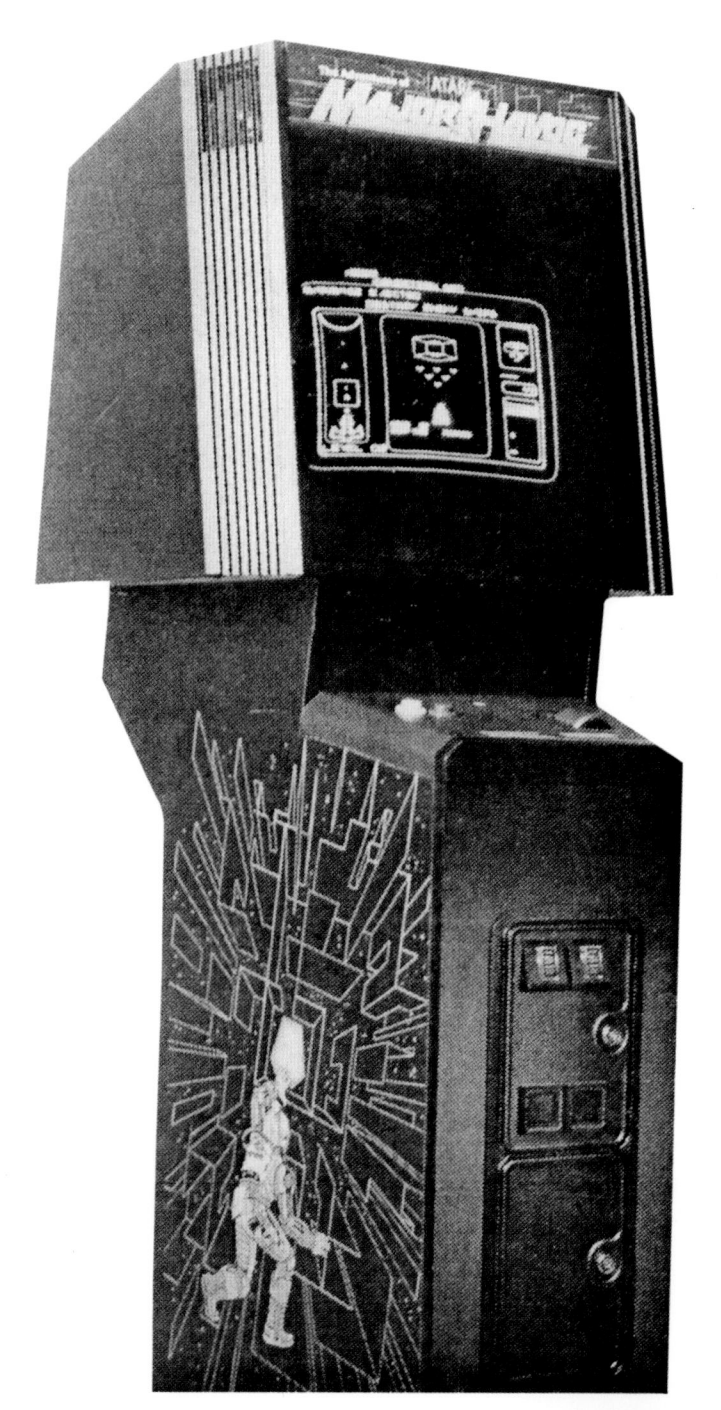

Nintendo's DONKEY KONG JUNIOR (1983) never quite captured the magic – or the players – of the original DONKEY KONG. $150-$250.

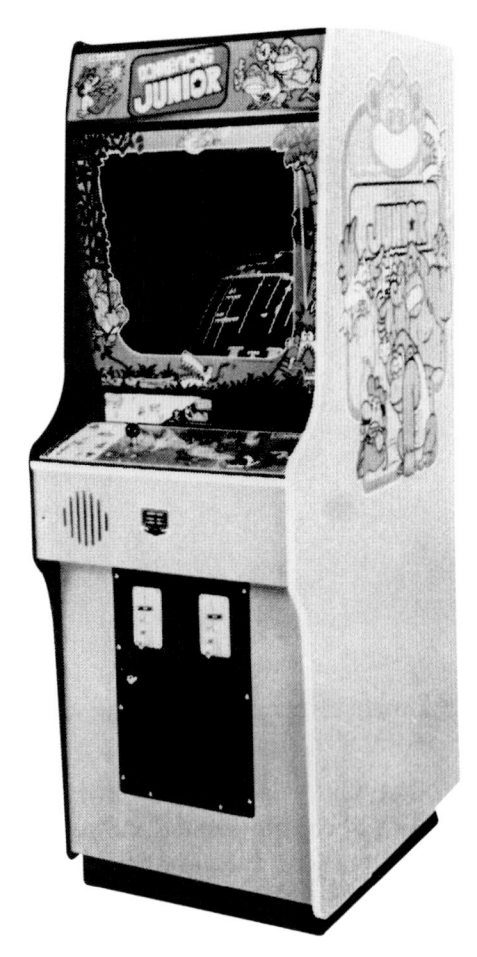

One of the most sought-after games among collectors is Atari's 1983 MAJOR HAVOC in the original dedicated cabinet shown here. When the initial response to the game was poor, Atari decided to sell MAJOR HAVOC in kit form and dismantled many of the games that were already built and ready to ship so that the circuit boards could be repackaged as conversion kits. Only a few dedicated MAJOR HAVOC machines were sold. $1,000-$1,500.

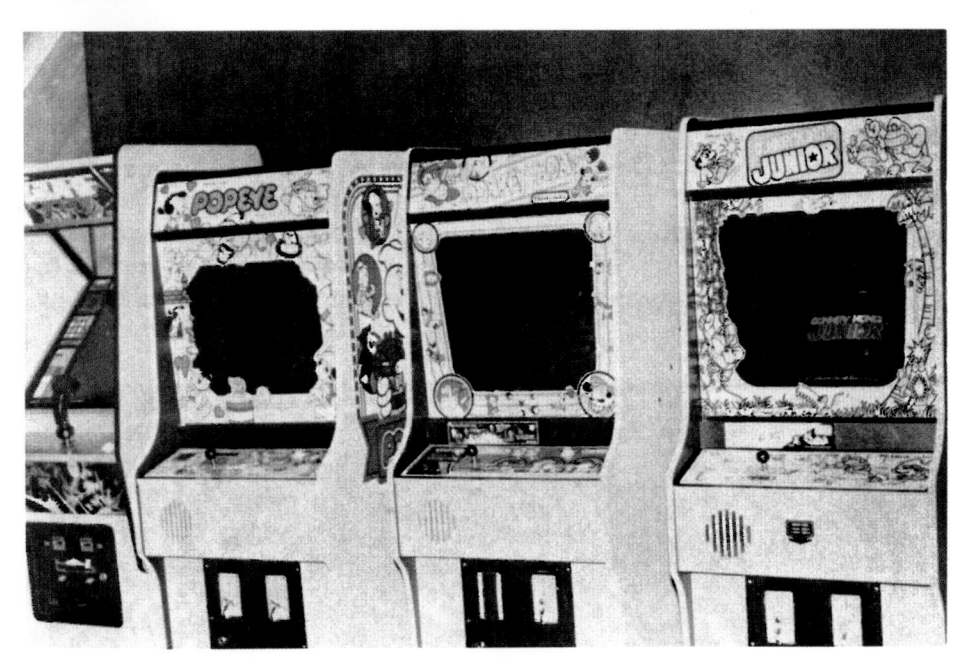

Nintendo used the same design on its video game cabinets for several years. Here's a 1983 arcade lineup of Nintendo games including POPEYE, DONKEY KONG, and DONKEY KONG JUNIOR.

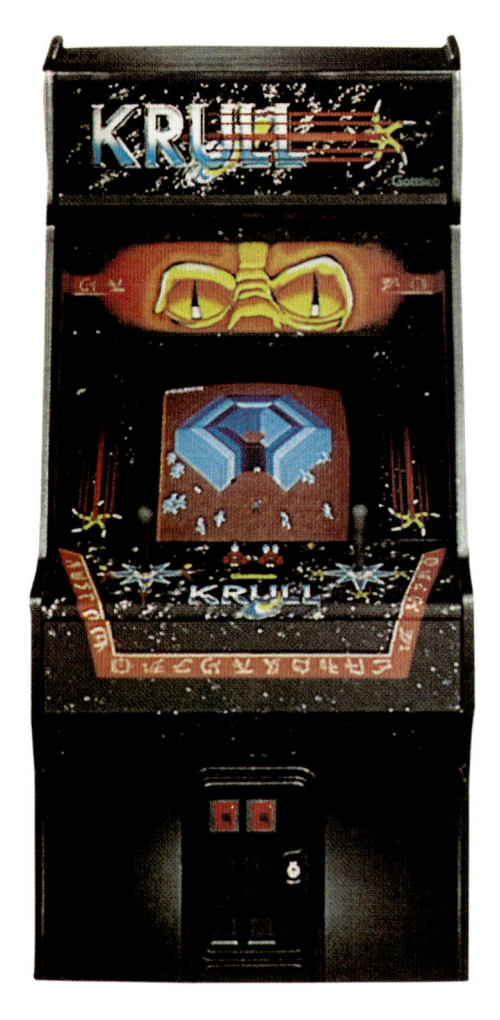

Gottlieb's KRULL (1983) was based on the film of the same name. The movie was released by Columbia Pictures, which owned Gottlieb at the time, and the game featured music from the soundtrack. $250-$350.

KRULL screen shots.

From the broad jump to the pole vault, you could participate in an Olympic decathlon on Centuri's TRACK & FIELD (1983). Some of the events required you to press the control buttons rapidly, and many of these machines couldn't stand up to the constant pounding they received. $200-$350.

Atari's STAR WARS was an instant hit with players when it was released in 1983, and it's still sought after by collectors today. The game featured music from the film's soundtrack, and was released in both the upright cabinet pictured here and a cockpit cabinet (pictured in Chapter 8). $600-$900.

Stern's GREAT GUNS (1983) was the first arcade gun game in years to use replica rifles. The game was designed by Joe Joos, a former Stern pinball designer who had been transferred to the company's video division when Stern shut down its pinball production in 1982. $250-$350.

Taito's LASER GRAND PRIX (1983) was Taito's only laser disc video game, but the machine sold poorly and is difficult to find today. $400-$500.

159

DRAGON'S LAIR screen shot.

Introduced in 1983, Cinematronics' DRAGON'S LAIR was the first laser disc video game. Created by former Disney animator Don Bluth, DRAGON'S LAIR featured movie-quality animation. Game shown in this period ad is $750-$1,200.

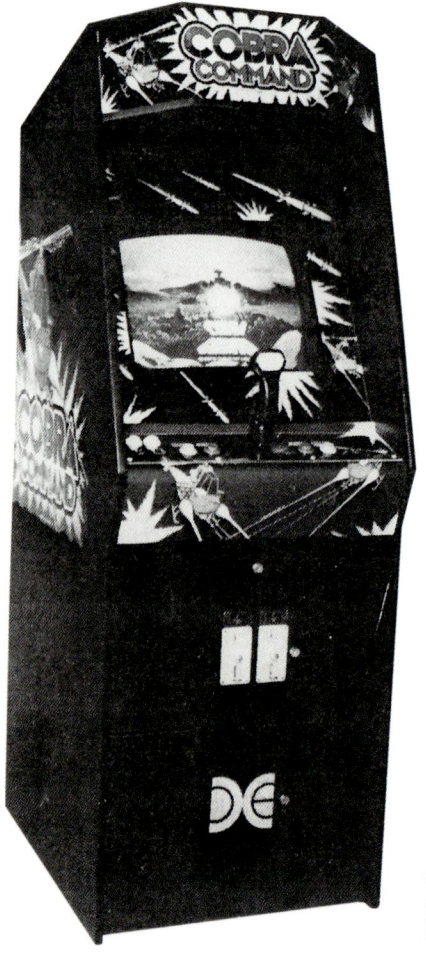

THE LASER'S EDGE

*DIAGNOSTICS
The Starcom system contains a complete diagnostic package which is enabled by an internal switch. This self-testing feature checks these aspects of your machine:

*General Malfunctions: Any malfunctioning in the machine is located and indicated to you by a written message on the screen.

*ROM and RAM: If your ROM or RAM are faulty, the screen produces a written message indicating which part or parts are malfunctioning.

*Sound: The diagnostic package allows you to hear the sound chip to insure that it is working.

*Keyboard Input: The Starcom keyboard, including the coin switch, is completely testable.

*LASER DISC: The Laser Disc is read and tested to make sure it is in perfect working order.

*CONVERTIBILITY
*The Starcom unit will come with convertible packages, making it substantially less expensive to install a completely new game in your arcade. Therefore, you can build up a library of game packages to be used on your original units.

*DIMENSIONS
Upright: Boxed:
72" height 77" height
25" width   27½" width
30" depth   33" depth
330 lb. weight

STARCOM
Distributed By:

starcom

*Manufactured and marketed by
Cinematronics Inc. El Cajon, CA. (619) 562-7000.

COBRA COMMAND (1983) was a laser disc video game produced by Data East which put you at the controls of a helicopter on a military rescue mission. $500-$600.

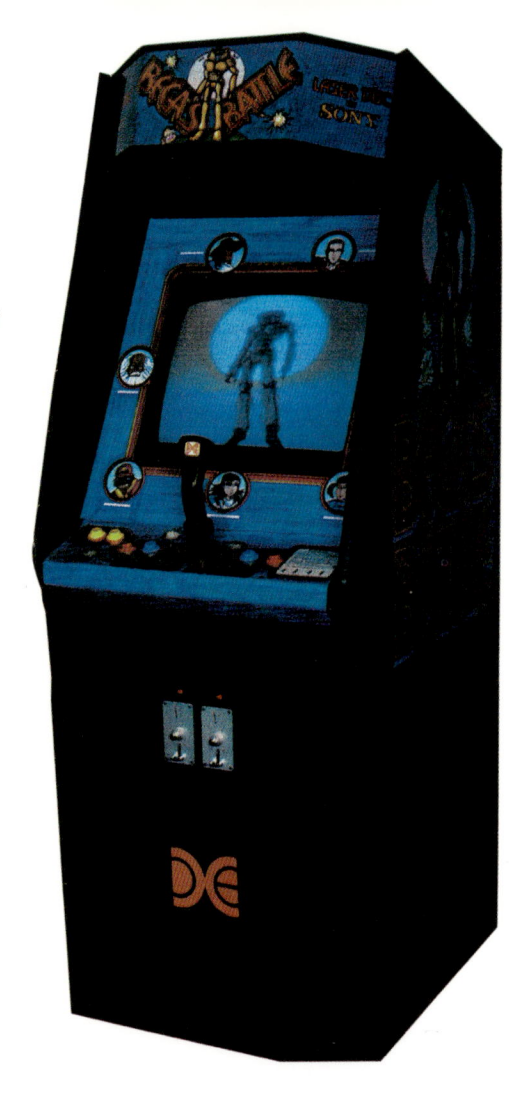

Produced in 1983, Data East's BEGA'S BATTLE laser disc video game used a Sony disc player to avoid some of the problems caused by the first generation of laser disc players, which often overheated after continued use. $500-$600.

CLIFF HANGER was produced by Stern in 1983. This laser disc game traced the adventures of Cliff, the hero who faced one peril after another in his attempt to rescue his girlfriend from the clutches of the evil Count Dreyco. $1,000-$1,500.

ASTRON BELT was a laser disc video game designed by Sega in late 1982 but released by Bally Midway in the United States in 1983. The combination of laser-quality graphics combined with traditional video images can be seen in this screen shot from ASTRON BELT. $500-$600.

NFL FOOTBALL screen shot showing traditional video image.

NFL FOOTBALL screen shot showing laser disc image.

Two players could play Bally Midway's 1983 NFL FOOTBALL laser disc video game simultaneously. All of the game play was shown with traditional video game images, while laser disc footage was shown between plays. NFL FOOTBALL was the first game which came from the factory with a bill acceptor that could take $5 bills along with $1 bills. $500-$600.

162

Funai unveiled INTERSTELLAR, its first game, in 1983. This laser disc game suffered from poor distribution and the company closed up the following year after producing three more ill-fated laser disc games: INTERSTELLAR II, ESH'S TYRANNY, and ZANGUS. $1,500-$2,000.

STAR RIDER was the only laser disc video game ever produced by Williams. The motorcycle seat tilted from side to side, adding to the illusion of riding on this 1983 game. Game shown in this period ad is $750-$1,000.

Mylstar's M.A.C.H. 3 laser disc video game (1983) was offered in both a cockpit cabinet (shown here) and an upright model. $600-$750.

163

Atari's FIREFOX laser disc video used film footage and sound clips from the film *Firefox* starring Clint Eastwood. When the game was unveiled in Atari's booth at the 1983 national coin-op games trade show, Atari's technicians couldn't keep the game running for more than a few minutes at a time and showgoers lost confidence in the game. $1,000-$1,200.

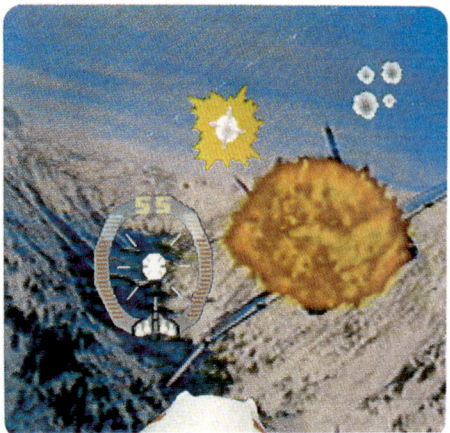

FIREFOX screen shots.

164

Nintendo's MARIO BROTHERS brought back the Mario character which had been introduced in the firm's DONKEY KONG video game. And this time, Mario's brother Luigi was around, too. This 1983 game came in a wide cabinet so two players could stand comfortably side by side. $150-$200.

Released in 1983, Mylstar's US VS. THEM laser disc game was offered as both a dedicated game in an upright cabinet and as a conversion kit designed to convert both upright and cockpit M.A.C.H. 3 laser disc games. $500-$600.

MARIO BROTHERS screen shot. The little pests coming out of the pipes are called sidewinders and shellcreepers.

165

Bally Midway's PROFESSOR PAC MAN (1983) was a disaster for operators. Because of its small production run, this game is quite difficult to find today and is in high demand among PAC MAN fans. $1,000-$1,200.

Introduced in 1983, Taito's ELEVATOR ACTION was available as both a dedicated game and a conversion kit. Most of the action in this spy-themed game takes place in an elevator shaft! $150-$200.

Zeke the Zookeeper must rescue Zelda, who's being held hostage by a renegade monkey, in Taito's ZOOKEEPER (1983). ZOOKEEPER was one of the only video games produced in the 1980s that could award players a free game for a high score. $125-$175.

DISCS OF TRON was the second and final Midway video game based on Disney's *Tron* movie, and was also the only video game produced in an environmental stand-up cabinet. When the game didn't sell very well, Midway chopped up the unused cabinets and reused the wood paneling in the assembly of other video game cabinets – it's not unusual to find other Midway video games from the mid 1980s with DISCS OF TRON artwork on the bottom of the game cabinet or the inside of the back door. $700-$1,000.

DISCS OF TRON screen shot.

Taito's 1983 video driving game was CHANGE LANES. $125-$200.

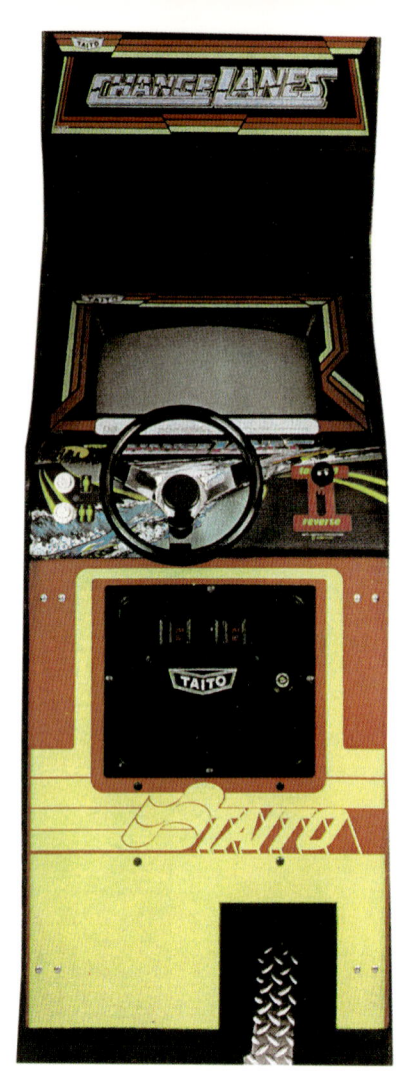

It's an old-fashioned wild west shootout with Taito's TIN STAR (1983). $100-$150.

Atari's TX-1 was a monster of a game that used three separate video screens to give you a panoramic view of the roadway. Try to fit this 1983 game through a doorway! $500-$600.

Williams' BLASTER (1983) was available in both a cockpit and an upright cabinet; the game was also sold as a conversion kit. BLASTER was designed with a 49-way joystick and stereo sound. $250-$400.

BLASTER was also sold in this black fiberglass Duramold cabinet. Because of the shape of the cabinet, the control panel and header had to be specially designed for a Duramold game. Williams' BUBBLES was also sold in a Duramold cabinet, although the production runs for both BLASTER and BUBBLES in this cabinet were very limited. $800-$1,200 (BLASTER Duramold); $750-$1,000 (BUBBLES Duramold).

Exidy's FAX trivia game was intended for adult players who weren't interested in the outer space shoot-'em-ups that were so common in arcades in 1983. $100-$150.

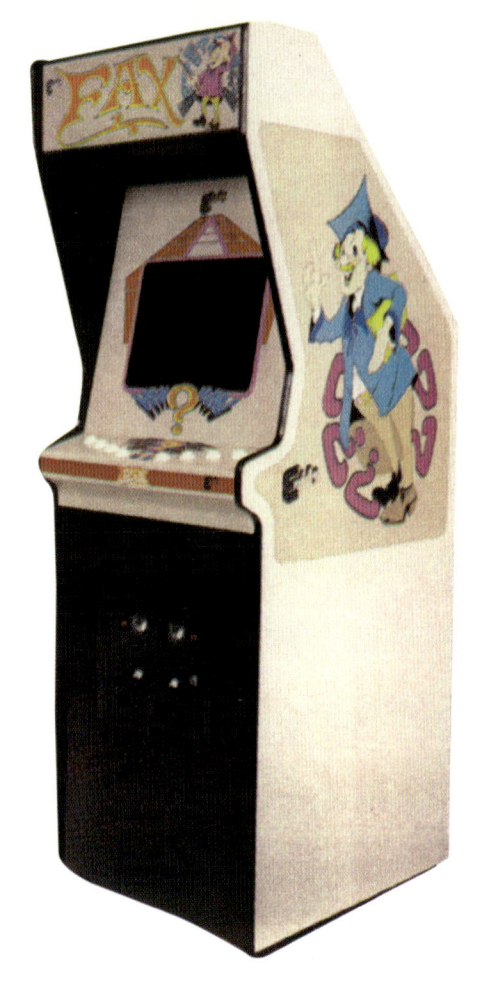

Instead of a rifle, you shot a bow in Exidy's 1983 CROSSBOW. At the start of each game, you selected which forest path you chose to follow, with each of the paths offering different challenges. CROSSBOW was the first of several convertible gun games produced by Exidy. $350-$450.

FAX was also sold in a sophisticated "Elegante" cabinet designed for upscale locations. $100-$150.

170

Video driving games are always dependable (if not hot) earners. MOTORACE U.S.A. (1983) was a standard driving game with a motorcycle theme. $250-$350.

With Stern's 1983 MAZER BLAZER you fired a metal gun inside the cabinet at an array of alien monsters including The Tongue, The Eyeball, and Jaws. $250-$400.

MOTORACE U.S.A. screen shot.

171

No, it's not a video game – it's just a pinball machine disguised as a video game to try to attract video game players to the silver ball. Williams built 78 VARKON pinball machines in cabinets left over at the end of the MOTORACE U.S.A. production run. Only a few VARKON machines are known to exist today. $1,500-$2,000.

Atari's ARABIAN (1983) was set in the magical world of flying carpets and magic lamps. You must complete each of the four "pages" (missions) to make it to the end of the story and rescue the princess. $150-$200.

ARABIAN screen shot.

Nintendo's VS. TENNIS had two screens positioned side by side for two-player action; each player would see the game from his own perspective. VS. TENNIS could also be played by one player against the game. The cocktail table version of this 1983 game is pictured in Chapter 8. $250-$400.

Nintendo's PUNCH OUT (1983) had two screens; the lower screen showed the game action while the upper screen showed the game status. Knock out opponents like Glass Joe and Bald Bull to become the heavyweight champ. $200-$300.

Go on safari in Sega's CONGO BONGO (1983). $125-$200.

173

Bally Midway's SPY HUNTER (1983) was more than a driving game; it was also a shooting game, because you fired an arsenal of weapons at the escaping crooks as you sped down the road. $250-$350.

The second video game in Atari's *Star Wars* series was RETURN OF THE JEDI. The game had everything that a *Star Wars* fan could want: Scout Walkers, Ewoks, the Millennium Falcon, and, of course, Chewbacca, Lando Calrissian, Princess Leia, and Hans Solo. This 1984 game is still sought after by both *Star Wars* enthusiasts and video game collectors. $800-$1,200.

Bally Midway's SPY HUNTER was also sold in a cockpit format. $500-$650.

174

One of the last X-Y vector games, Sega's ZEKTOR (1984) was offered as part of the company's Convert-A-Game series. $250-$350.

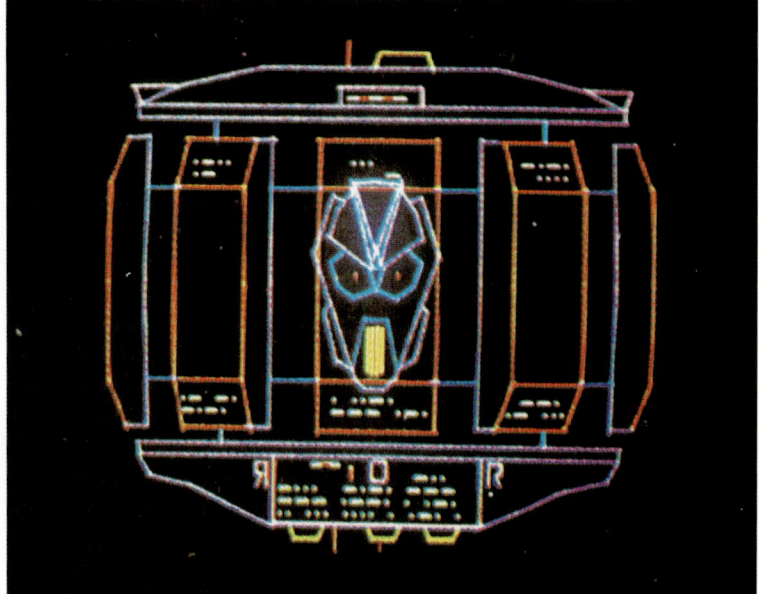

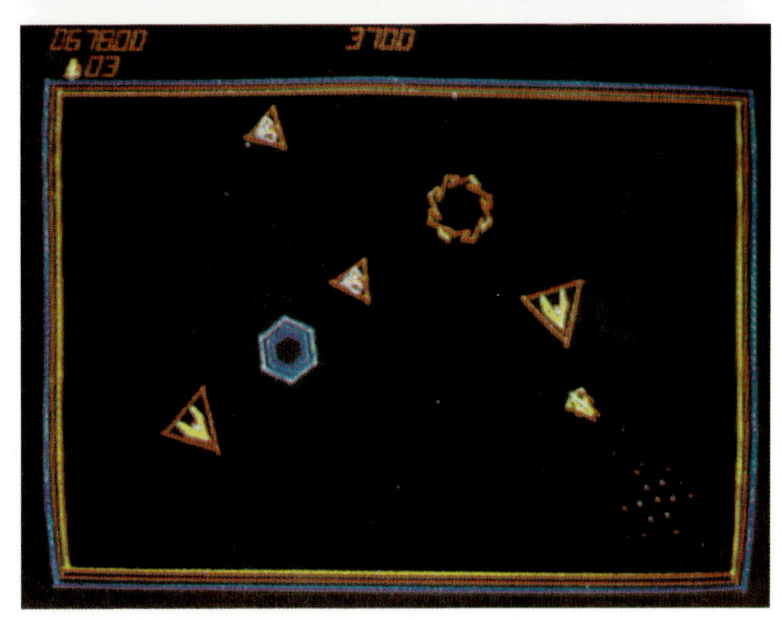

ZEKTOR screen shots.

175

SPACE ACE (1984) was Cinematronics' follow-up to DRAGON'S LAIR. Like DRAGON'S LAIR, SPACE ACE was a laser disc video game with animation created by Don Bluth (as shown in this screen shot), although SPACE ACE was an outer space adventure set on a remote planet. $750-$1,200.

Midway's third (and final) laser disc video game was GALAXY RANGER (1984), an outer space shoot-'em-up game. $500-$600.

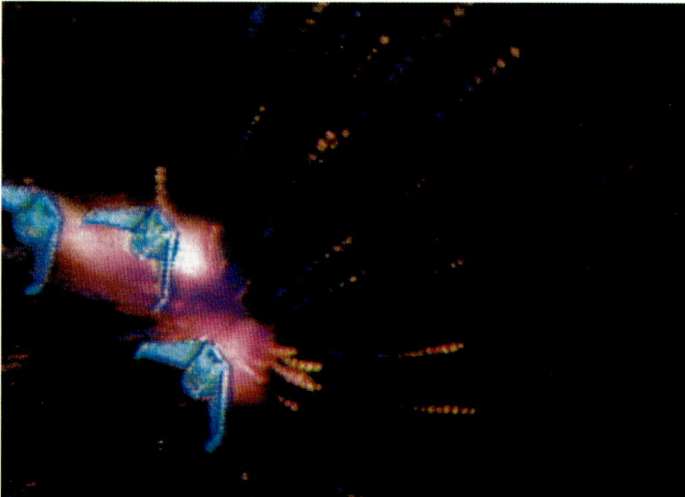

GALAXY RANGER screen shots.

176

THAYER'S QUEST (1984) was the only video game produced by RDI. Players used a computer keyboard to control the action on this laser disc video game, probably the most sophisticated player control panel ever found on any arcade game. $800-$1,000.

Unlike Bally's NFL FOOTBALL laser disc game which showed footage of professional football players, Stern's GOAL TO GOAL laser disc game (1984) contained live-action scenes of amateur football players practicing on a high school field with cars driving by in the background. Production of GOAL TO GO was very limited. $600-$700.

Stern had planned to offer SUPER BAGMAN (1984) as both a dedicated game and a conversion kit, but the company closed before the game went into production. SUPER BAGMAN was a sequel to the company's BAGMAN video game, and offered the same colorful comic-strip graphics as its predecessor. $250-$350.

SUPER DON QUIX-OTE (1984) was the first of two laser disc video games produced by Universal of Tokyo, Japan. Notice the unique cabinet design – the entire front of the cabinet swung open to make it easy to access the components inside. Game shown in this period ad is $600-$800.

Stern previewed ATOMIC CASTLE in the fall of 1984 at the national coin-op games trade show. Before the game went into production, however, Stern went out of business and Game Plan acquired the rights to market ATOMIC CASTLE as a conversion kit. Game advertised in this period ad is $3,000-$4,000.

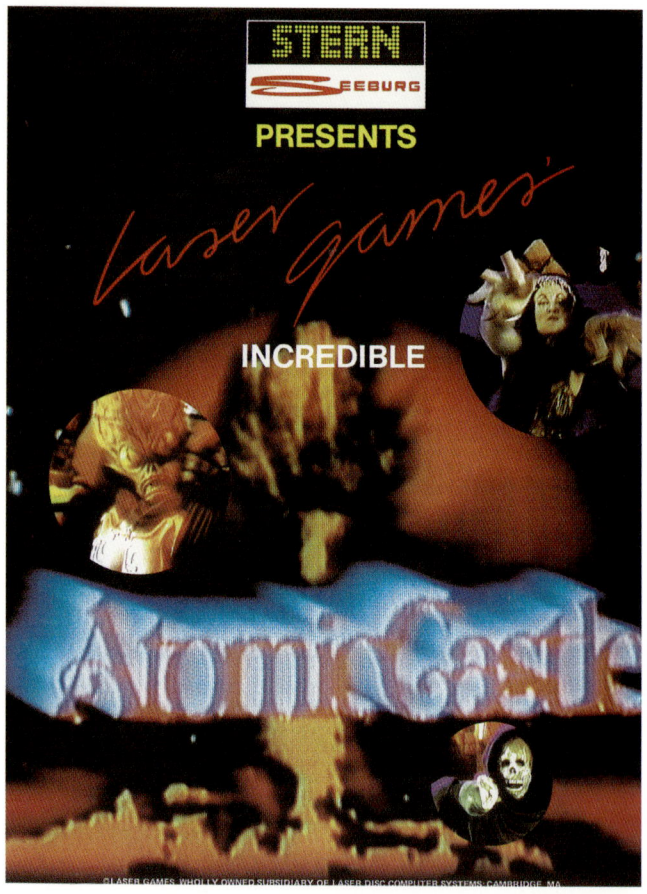

Mylstar's THREE STOOGES (1984) let you select whether you wanted to be Larry, Curly, or Moe as you made your way from room to room to rescue the girl held captive by the mad scientist. You could throw pies and slap your enemies to momentarily stun them during the game! Limited production makes this video game difficult to find today. $750-$1,200

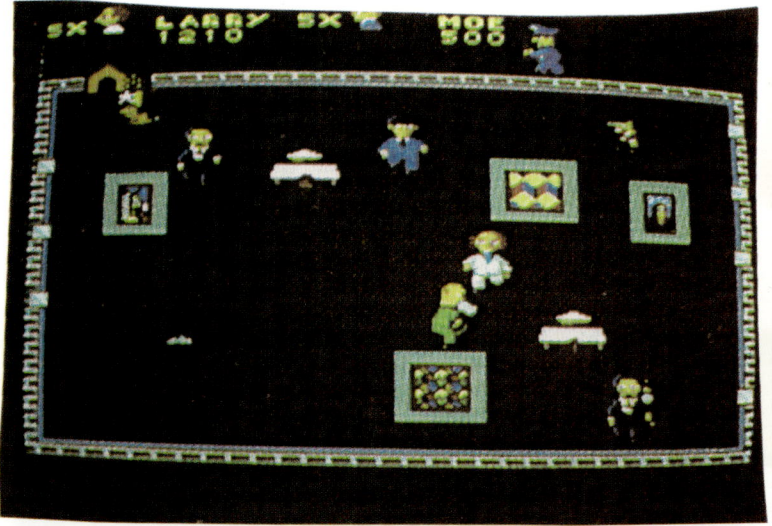

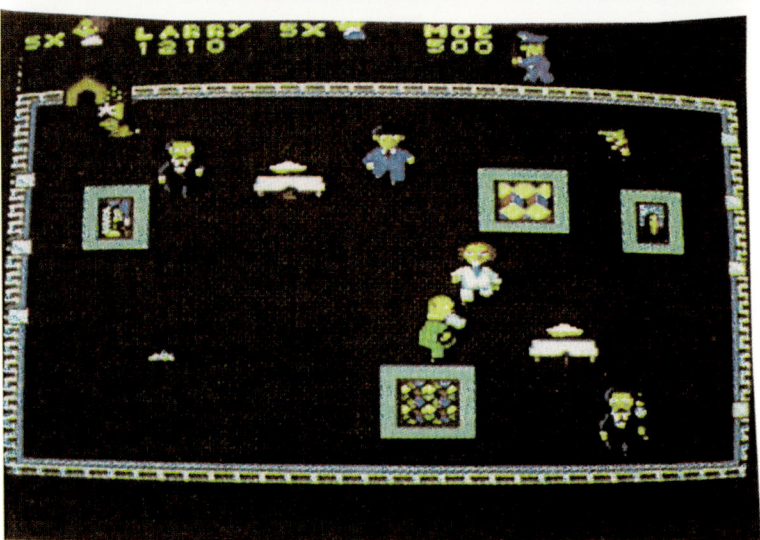

THREE STOOGES screen shots.

Exidy's CHEYENNE (1984) offered seven different screens of western action, including a graveyard, a mineshaft, and a ghost town. Help good guy Buster Badshot hunt down the gold hidden throughout the old west as you face a pitchfork-throwing undertaker, vampire bats, flaming arrows, skeletal birds, and more. $350-$450.

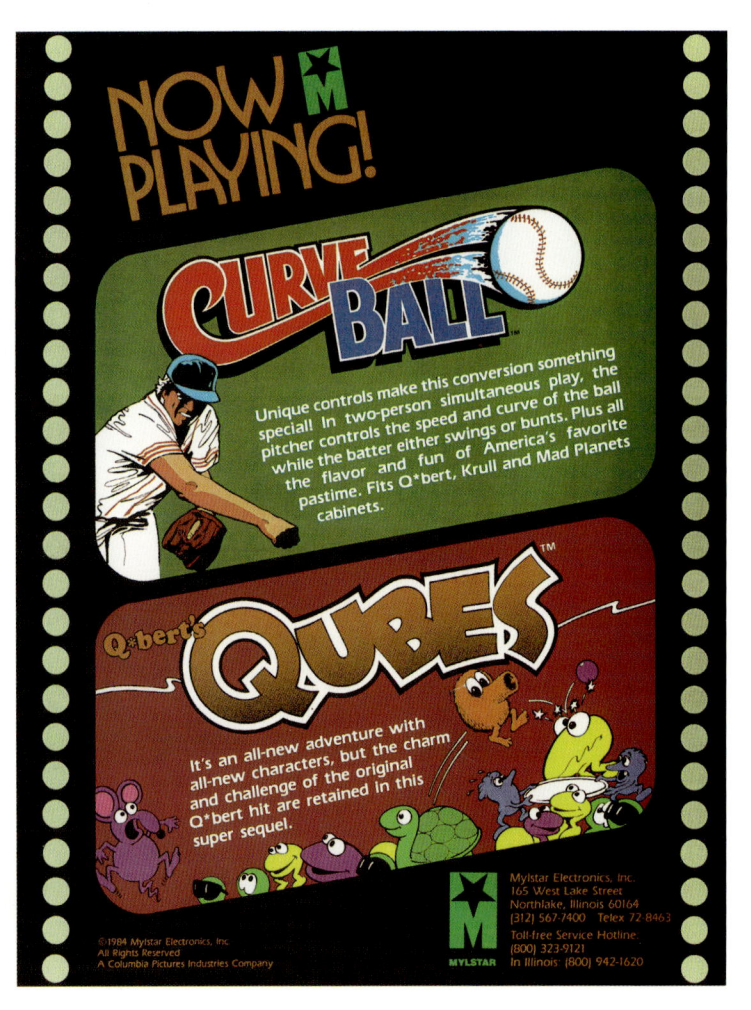

Join the magical race through a forest with a variety of gnomes, elves, wizards, and other mythical creatures. Williams MYSTIC MARATHON (1984) was sold only as a kit which could convert older Williams' video games. A few of these kits were installed into some of the empty video game cabinets which Williams had in inventory at the time the kits were being assembled, so a few "dedicated" MYSTIC MARATHON games left the Williams plant in a variety of cabinet designs. $300-$400.

Trade ad for CURVE BALL and Q*BERT'S QUBES (1984), two games which Mylstar offered as conversion kits shortly before the firm closed its doors. Q*BERT'S QUBES featured the same orange guy with the snout from the original Q*BERT video games, although the sequel had little else going for it. Games advertised in this period ad are $200-$250 (CURVE BALL); $400-$500 (Q*BERT'S QUBES).

180

Outwit the evil eye and jump past him when he's not looking in Atari's 1984 I, ROBOT. Lots of enemies to face including killer birds, giant beach balls, pyramid mines, and buzz saws. Atari heavily promoted this game with I, ROBOT wall posters and T-shirts. Approximately 700 of these machines were built. $800-$1,200.

HYPERSPORTS (1984) was the sequel to TRACK & FIELD. Produced by Centuri in 1984, HYPERSPORTS never had the player attraction of TRACK & FIELD, however. $150-$250.

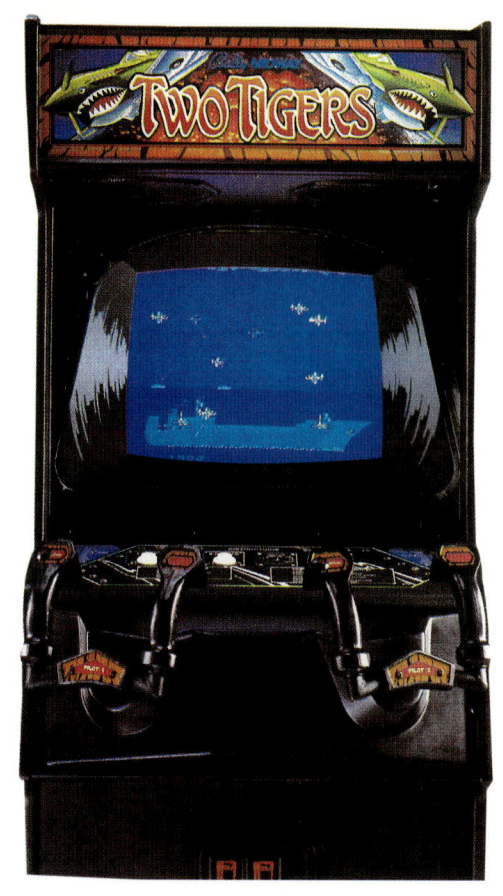

Two players could team up to fight off the enemy squadrons in Midway's TWO TIGERS (1984). This World War II aerial combat game put you in the cockpit of a small but heavily armed fighter plane. $200-$300.

Instead of athletic events, you guided a clown through a series of circus stunts in Centuri's CIRCUS CHARLIE (1984). The six stunts included the fire rings, tight rope, ball walk, horseback riding, trampoline, and the flying trapeze. The game was designed by Konami of Japan and licensed to Centuri. $150-$200.

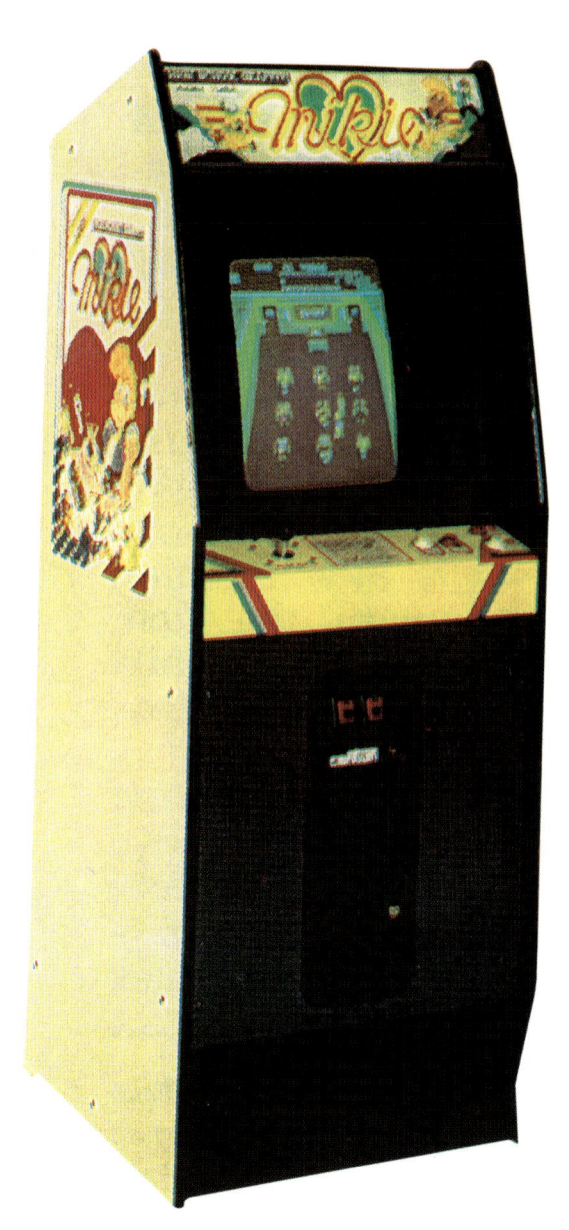

MIKIE (1985) was the last game produced by Centuri. The game had been licensed from Konami of Japan, and after Centuri's demise, Konami began selling its video games directly to distributors in the United States rather than licensing the games to U.S. manufacturers. $300-$300.

Catch the eggs as they're laid and fall down the barnyard chutes! Two players could play cooperatively or as opponents – or one person could play alone. CHICKEN SHIFT (1984) was one of the first games produced by Nolan Bushnell's newly established Sente and was sold as part of the firm's S.A.C. conversion system. Game advertised in this period ad is $300-$400.

MARBLE MADNESS screen shot. The timer at the top center of the screen let you know how many seconds you had to guide your marble through the challenge.

Use the trackball to guide the rolling marbles through obstacles, along narrow walls, and past dangerous enemies. MARBLE MADNESS was introduced by Atari in the fall of 1984. The game had an incredible musical soundtrack and high-resolution graphics. $500-$700.

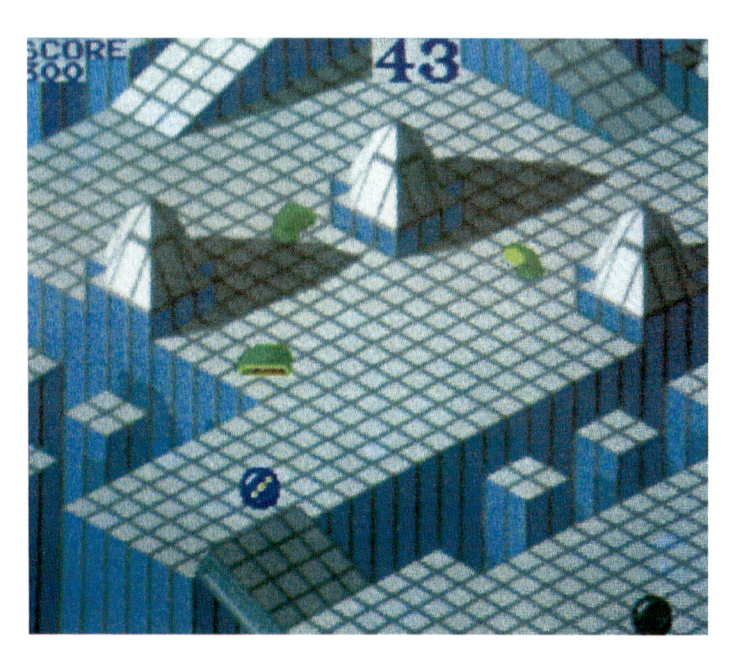

MARBLE MADNESS screen shot.

183

ROOT BEER TAPPER screen shot. You moved your soda fountain attendant up and down the screen to catch the empty root beer mugs which the thirsty customers slid along the bar. Don't let the mugs fall off the edge of the bar, though!

Bally Midway's ROOT BEER TAPPER (1984) was the family oriented arcade version of TAPPER, pictured in Chapter 8. An original game concept, clever music, and color graphics make this one of the most collectible video games of the mid 1980s. $400-$600.

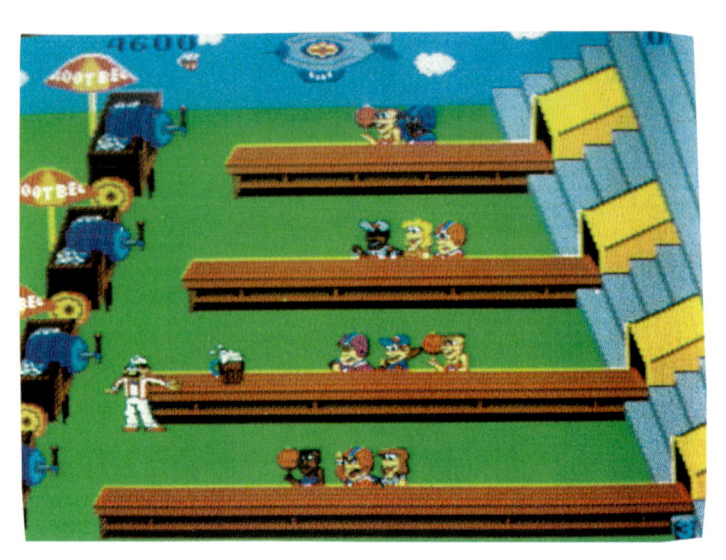

ROOT BEER TAPPER screen shot. Catch the empty root beer mugs before they slide off the bar – and don't let the customers reach the root beer barrel on the right wall.

184

Data East's GRAPLOP (1984) was a low-production conversion game which is seldom found today. $250-$350.

TAPPER screen shot. Notice the Budweiser logo, which has replaced the root beer logo seen in the previous photograph in this scene from TAPPER, designed for bars and taverns.

TAPPER screen shot showing the Budweiser logo again prominently featured in the game.

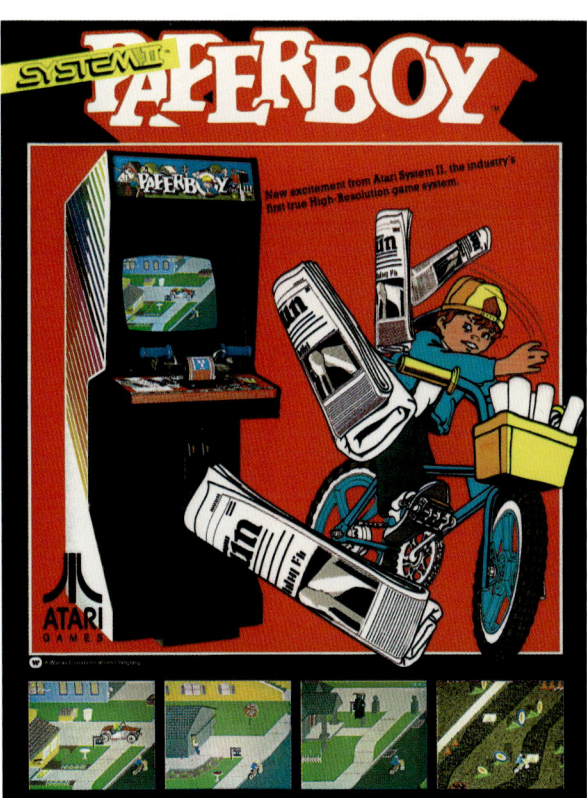

If you've ever had your paper carrier throw your newspaper into the bushes, then you'll appreciate PAPERBOY. This 1984 Atari game put you behind the handlebars of a teenager as he rides up and down neighborhood streets on his morning route. You had to hit the control button at just the right time to toss the newspaper close to your customers' homes. $300-$500.

185

It was up to you to foil the robbers in Bally Midway's 1984 BANK PANIC. Shoot at the outlaws, but be careful not to hit the innocent citizens being held hostage. $200-$250.

Hit the turkeys and watch the feathers fly! Williams' TURKEY SHOOT (1984) was not your typical gun game. Set in February of 1989 after the turkeys of the world had organized themselves into violent gangs, this game had you shoot at Pilot Turkeys, Boss Turkeys, Cyborg Turkeys, and Thug Turkeys. And when you hit the turkeys, a fan inside the cabinet would blow real feathers in front of the screen! $400-$500.

Bally Midway licensed UP 'N DOWN, a cute driving game, from Sega for U.S. production. Your drove your ATV along the narrow roads, gathering up all the flags along the way. There were lots of forks in the road, so you had to choose your path carefully to collect the flags as quickly as possible before your time ran out. $200-$250.

UP 'N DOWN screen shot.

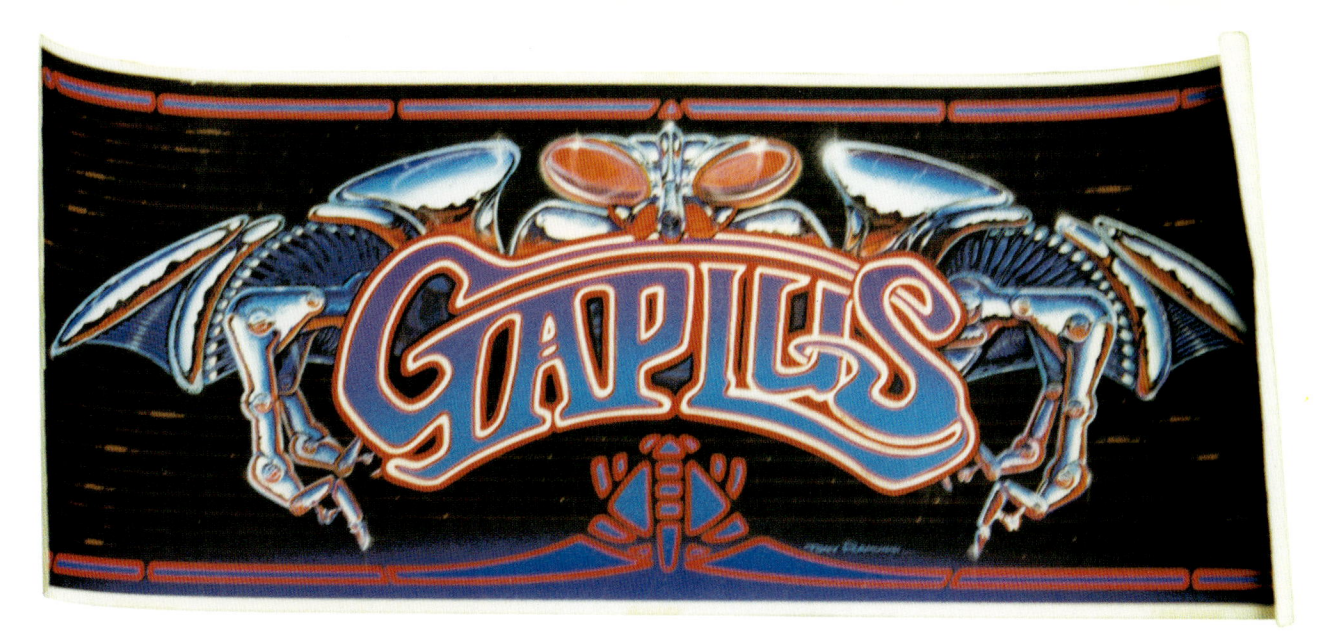

Original hand-drawn artwork for the GAPLUS header. Notice that the Bally Midway logo has not yet been added to the top left corner of the header (it can be seen in the next photo). Original game artwork such as this is usually created as an oil on canvas painting, although it is sometimes created on posterboard, depending on the artist's preference. $2,500-$3,500.

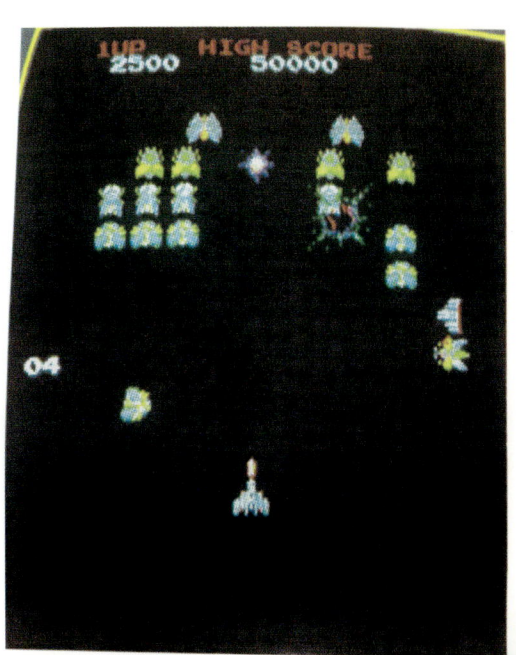

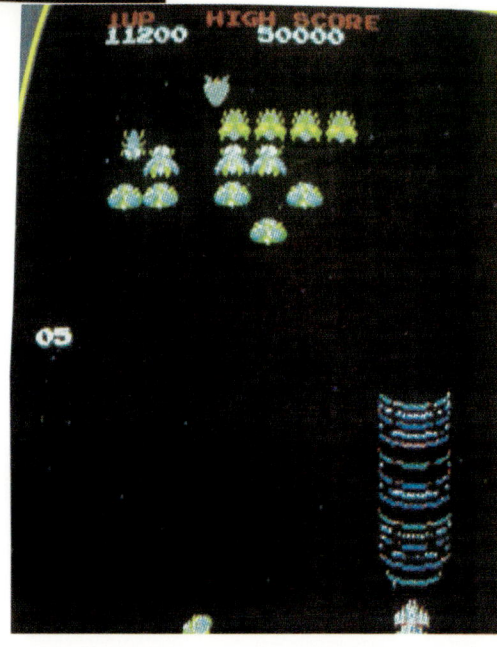

GAPLUS/GALAGA 3 screen shots.

Bally Midway's GAPLUS (1984) was designed as a sequel to GALAGA. You could move your fighter ship anywhere around the lower half of the screen (not just from side to side), so enemy ships could now get underneath you and attack you from behind. Midway released GAPLUS as a conversion kit under the name GALAGA 3 a few months later. $350-$500.

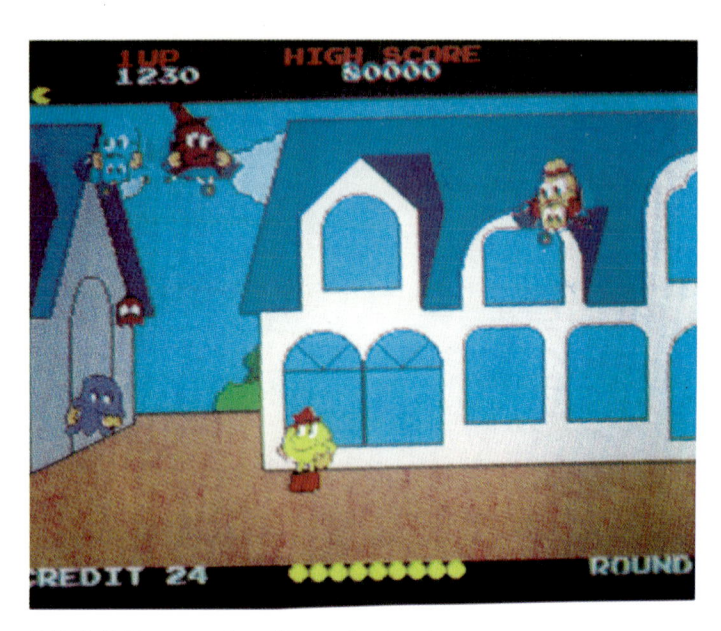

PAC LAND screen shot. Notice the detailing in the characters – Pac Man finally has eyes, along with arms and legs.

PAC LAND screen shot. Guide Pac Man through the forest to Fairyland.

No dots for Pac Man to munch on here. Guide Pac Man to Fairyland by having him run through the woods and hopping over the objects in his way. When he arrives in Fairyland, he'll receive a pair of magic boots which will make his return trip easier. PAC LAND (1984) was the last Bally Midway game featuring the Pac Man character. $300-$400.

188

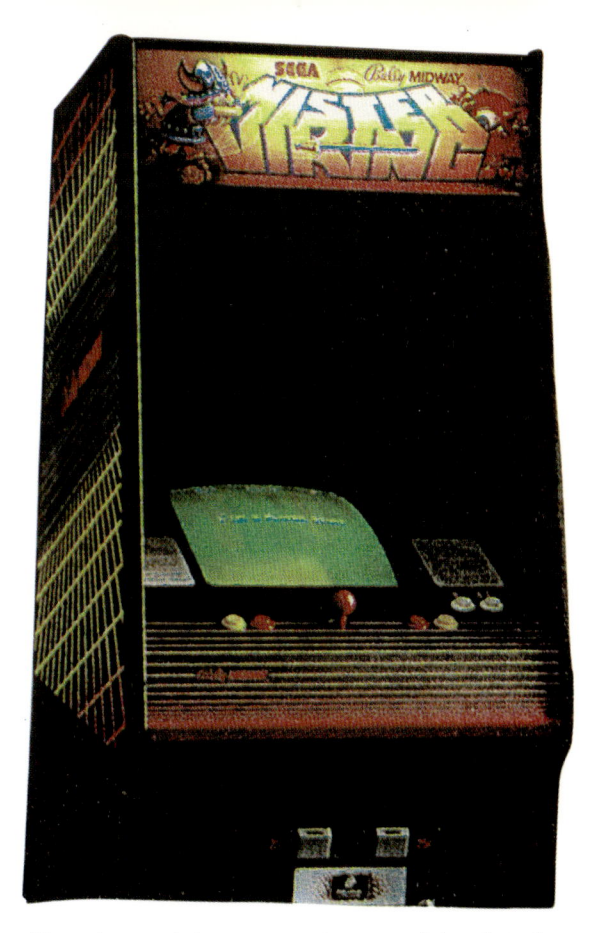

Tornadoes and dinosaurs are just two of the obstacles you'll have to overcome as you search for the hidden treasure on Bally Midway's MISTER VIKING (1984). $175-$250.

Peter Pack Rat goes from the junkyard to the sewer in search of treasure, always trying to stay one step ahead of the nefarious Riff Rat and the other villains. Atari released PETER PACK RAT in 1985. $300-$400.

New opponents didn't add up to new excitement for players on Nintendo's SUPER PUNCH OUT (1985), which was sold as a conversion kit to update the original PUNCH OUT game. SUPER PUNCH OUT was also available as a new dedicated game. $150-$250.

TIMBER screen shot.

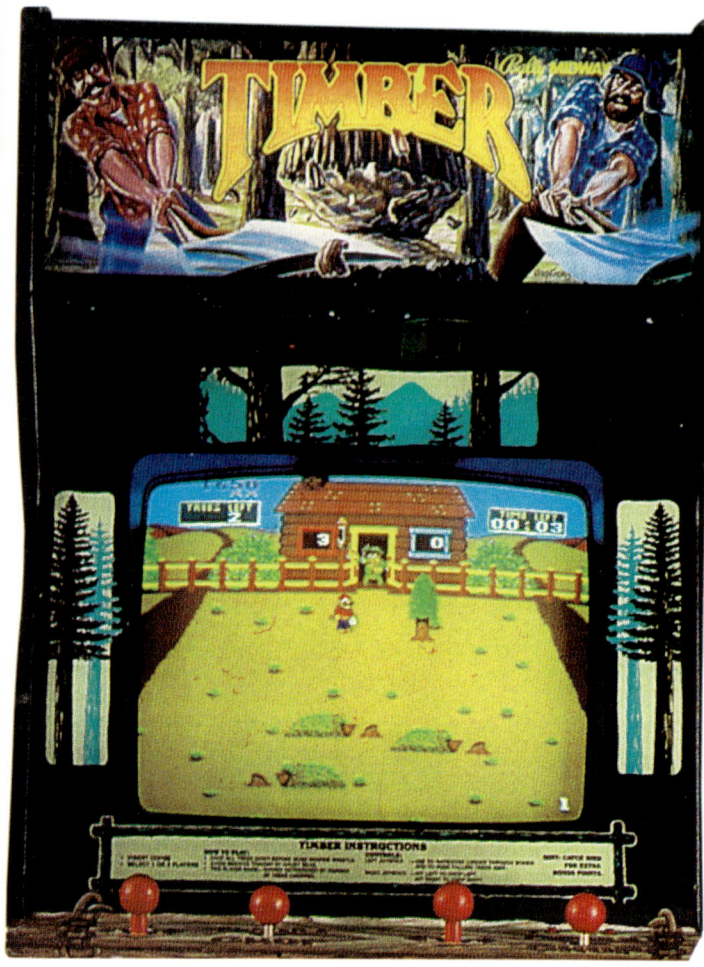

Bally's Midway's 1985 TIMBER game featured the same mustached character who appeared as the bartender in TAPPER and ROOT BEER TAPPER. You earned points by chopping down trees and balancing atop rolling logs. $400-$600.

TIMBER screen shot.

190

INDIANA JONES AND THE TEMPLE OF DOOM screen shot.

For fans of the movie, Atari's INDIANA JONES AND THE TEMPLE OF DOOM was the perfect adventure. Featuring music taken from the film's soundtrack along with speech, the game recreated several scenes from the popular movie with scenes set in a mine, on a rope bridge, and in the Temple of Doom. $400-$500.

INDIANA JONES AND THE TEMPLE OF DOOM screen shot – the mine shaft.

191

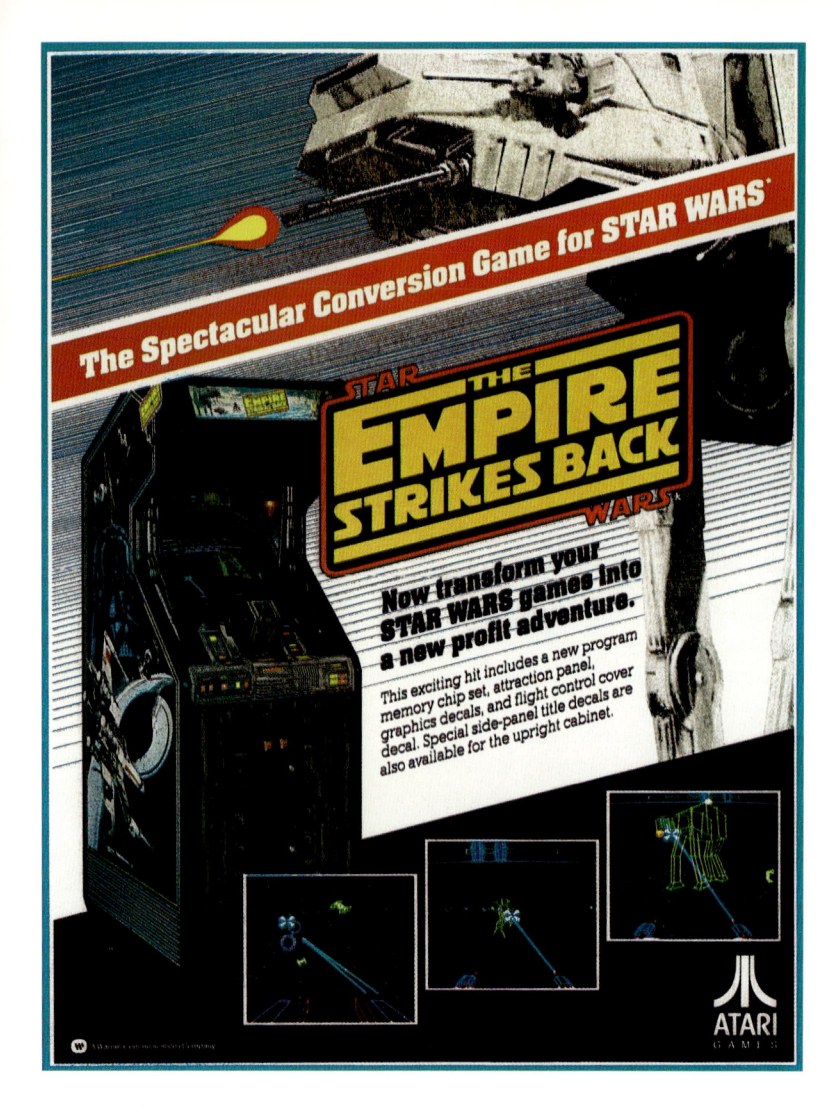

Atari's THE EMPIRE STRIKES BACK (1985) was sold only as a conversion kit for STAR WARS; it was never available as a complete game from Atari. Many video game collectors and *Star Wars* enthusiasts regard the original STAR WARS video game as superior to THE EMPIRE STRIKES BACK, and some of these collectors have converted THE EMPIRE STRIKES BACK back into STAR WARS. Game shown in this period ad is $500-$750.

Nintendo's ARM WRESTLING (1985) used the same dual-monitor cabinet as PUNCH OUT and SUPER PUNCH OUT. $150-$200.

Up to four people could play Atari's 1985 GAUNTLET simultaneously, with each person selecting a different character who possessed different magical powers. GAUNTLET was the first video game with an exposed monitor that wasn't recessed inside the cabinet. $250-$350.

An attractive video model wished you good luck at the beginning of your game on Bally Midway's DEMOLITION DERBY. One or two people could play the upright version of this 1985 game, and the company also produced the machine in a four-player "island" cabinet design. $150-$200 (upright); $250-$400 (island cabinet).

Bally Midway's SARGE (1985) had a "Join the Action" feature which let players start a game anytime, even joining a game that was already in progress. SARGE was a tank combat game set in World War II. $200-$250.

Sente's NAME THAT TUNE (1985) was based on the popular TV game show. The clever graphics included a video hand playing a piano keyboard as each note was sounded. Game shown in this period ad is $250-$350.

193

Released in 1984, MINI GOLF was Sente's most popular video game. $300-$400.

STREET FOOTBALL, released in 1984, was not a big seller for Sente. $250-$350.

Sente's SPIKER (1984) was based on the game of volleyball, and was the first volleyball-themed video game since Atari's REBOUND a decade earlier. $250-$350.

An extra pair of hands would be useful when playing Sente's NIGHT STOCKER (1984). You had to steer your car with your left hand while firing the gun with your right! $300-$400.

By 1986, Sente's game lineup included some hits like MINI GOLF and TRIVIAL PURSUIT, the latter based on the board game. This trade brochure pictures all of the games which Sente had produced by 1986, a little over a year after the company's inception.

Sente's TRIVIAL PURSUIT (1984) is rarely found in the cocktail table cabinet pictured here; most TRIVIAL PURSUIT games were installed into upright video game cabinets. $300-$500.

Part 5
THE MODERN ERA
1986-PRESENT

It's impossible to say with certainty what led to the decline in the popularity of video games starting in the mid 1980s. Some said it was the introduction of the home computer and economically priced home video games that rivaled those available in the arcades. Others said it was a lack of fresh game ideas. And still others said it was that the Generation X players who had been feeding quarters into the machines for the last decade had simply outgrown video games. The golden age of video games was over, but the video game industry still had some surprises up its sleeve for players.

Cinematronics released its WORLD SERIES: THE SEASON in both upright and bartop configurations. While countertop games had been around for several years, WORLD SERIES was one of the few top-earning video games released in this format since HEAD ON was sold by Gremlin nearly a decade earlier. By the early 1990s, countertop games like Merit's MEGATOUCH were found in virtually every tavern and are still popular with players today.

Sente's STOMPIN' was the first foot-controlled video game. Using nine pressure-sensitive footpads, you hopped around on the Floorplay controller to squash a variety of bugs and rodents as they appeared on the screen in front of you. The concept was revived in 2000 with DANCE DANCE REVOLUTION, which featured an elaborate musical score.

While STOMPIN' was an innovative game (maybe even ahead of its time, considering the success of DANCE DANCE REVOLUTION), it wasn't enough to keep Bally Sente afloat. The firm introduced its final video game – MOONQUAKE – later in 1986 before fading into oblivion.

Exidy, which had faced criticism in the mid 1970s for its DEATH RACE video game, was prepared to deal with the outcry that erupted with the release of CHILLER in 1987. Set in a chamber of horrors, CHILLER was a rifle game which let you shoot at ghouls and monsters. Nothing new here – except that CHILLER was designed with lots of blood and gore in every scene. To silence critics who were sure to claim that the game was too violent, Exidy designed the game with an operator setting which could turn the blood from red to green for a less gory effect.

Williams' 1986 INFERNO was an outer space shoot-'em-up game with an unusual twist. As many as four people could play simultaneously, each on his own machine! Up to four INFERNO cabinets could be linked together with external cables, and each player would view the action from his own perspective. Players could either work together to defeat the aliens or battle the enemies individually. Williams promoted the linked-play feature of INFERNO in its marketing, and although the game earned reasonably well, most operators didn't want to invest in what amounted to four video games that could be operated in only a few locations because of the space required.

Sega's GALAXY FORCE was also designed for arcades which had plenty of space. Released in 1988, GALAXY FORCE was part video game and part amusement park ride. You were rocked from side to side along with

Whether you chose the character patterned after King Kong, Godzilla, or the Wolfman, you could keep dropping in quarters to extend the game in Bally Midway's 1986 RAMPAGE so you could complete all 768 screens and reach the end of the game. One, two, or three people could play simultaneously. $250-$350.

Midway's 1991 REVOLUTION X featured the rock group Aerosmith in a video gun game that played several of the Grammy award winning band's hits. And Sega's MICHAEL JACKSON'S MOONWALKER featured the King of Pop dancing along to his songs. Scenes from Jackson's *Moonwalker* video were digitized and played during the game.

Midway introduced one of the biggest hits of the decade in the early 1990s – MORTAL KOMBAT. Several sequels were produced for this martial arts video game. Capcom's STREET FIGHTER video game series was also popular among players.

American Laser Games introduced a new generation of players to laser disc video games with its CRIME PATROL games. The games featured movie-quality footage of drug busts, strip bars, and car chases – far more dramatic and intense than the laser disc games of a decade earlier, most of which had featured aerial combat scenes.

Sega's HOUSE OF THE DEAD was a modern-day gun game. Set in a deserted building where the dead have come back to life, you had to shoot the attacking zombies while being careful not to hit the living who were wandering throughout the building. Atari's AREA 51 was another gun game, and was based on the secret government installation of the same name. AREA 51 gave you a choice of adventures at the start of the game, which each adventure offering different challenges and requiring different skills.

Starting in the early 1990s, video games began carrying ratings for violence, much like TV shows and CDs, because games like HOUSE OF THE DEAD contained many gruesome scenes and a great deal of blood. Not surprisingly, these games were particularly popular with teens.

Anyone who enjoys skateboarding will instantly recognize the name 720, which refers to a 720 degree maneuver, one of the most difficult skateboarding stunts to perfect. Atari's 720 (1986) let you perform tricky maneuvers while avoiding hazards including BMX bikers, Frisbee throwers, street traffic, and skater gangs. $300-$400.

the action which was taking place on the screen, making GALAXY FORCE a full sensory experience. The game even came with a safety chain around the base to keep spectators from getting too close to the machine during play.

Although Midway had secured the rights to GALAXIAN, GALAGA, and GAPLUS (also released as GALAGA 3) from Namco of Japan, Midway's contract with Namco expired in the mid 1980s. Atari's GALAGA 88 received only a lukewarm response from players and was the final entry in the series.

Superheroes hit the arcades with Taito's SUPERMAN and Atari's BATMAN video games, released in 1989 and 1990, respectively. Neither the Man of Steel nor the Caped Crusader fared too well, however. Even Sega's SPIDERMAN video game failed to lure players into its web.

Atari's three-player SUPER SPRINT (1986) was the final entry in the firm's popular SPRINT series, and the first SPRINT game produced in nearly a decade. $250-$350.

A number of video games were produced strictly for older players. One of the most successful of these was BIG BUCK HUNTER, a gun game designed for taverns rather than arcades. Several other adult-oriented gun games have also proven popular in bars.

In fact, by the late 1990s, more and more video games were being designed for adult players rather than teens, as arcades closed across the country. And many of the arcades that remained open were phasing out video games and replacing them with redemption machines that dispensed tickets which could be redeemed for prizes.

Sadly, the coin-op video game industry is now only a shadow of what it was in the glory days of the early 1980s. In 1988, Williams Electronics purchased Bally Midway, and a couple of years later, Williams acquired Atari as well. By the end of the decade, though, Williams pulled the plug on its amusement game division to concentrate its efforts in the area of coin-operated gambling equipment. Nintendo had left the coin-op game industry several years earlier to concentrate on producing home video game systems, and firms like Konami, Centuri, Data East, Cinematronics, Taito, Exidy, and others simply closed their doors when the video boom went bust.

The only major manufacturer from the 1980s still producing video games is Sega, which owns a chain of arcades across the country. Namco, which had licensed games like PAC MAN and GALAGA to Midway and other U.S. manufacturers in the 1970s and '80s is now producing and selling games directly in the U.S. market. In fact, Namco has even reissued several classic arcade video games in recent years, including GALAGA/MS. PAC MAN 20th ANNIVERSARY REUNION and CENTIPEDE/MILLIPEDE/MISSILE COMMAND. These reissue games re-

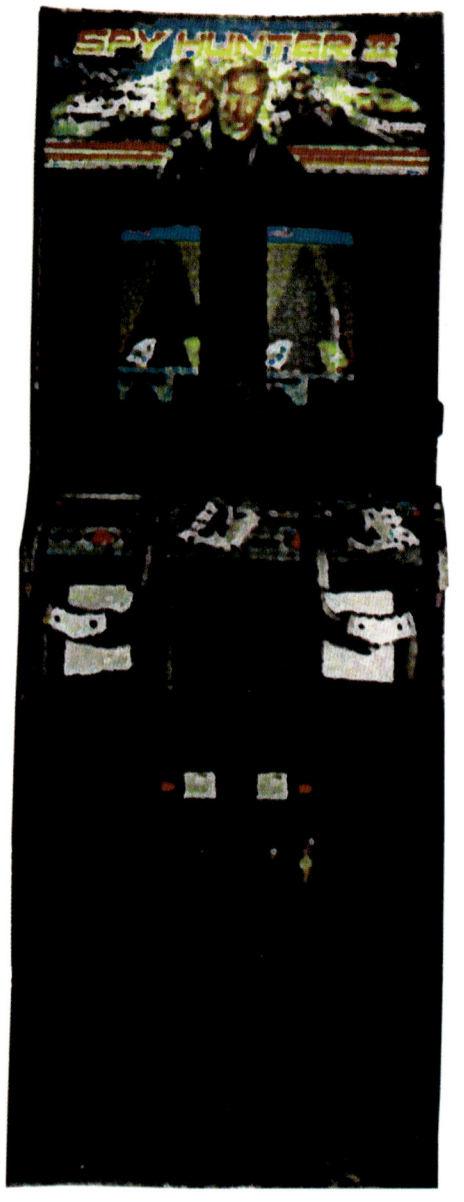

Bally Midway's SPY HUNTER II was produced in 1986 and featured a 25" split screen monitor so each player could independently follow the action on this dual-player game. $200-$250.

Original hand-painted header artwork for Bally Midway's SPY HUNTER II, drawn by Bally Midway artist Tony Ramunni. $2,500-$3,500.

main true to the original video games, with the graphics, sound, and game play reproduced exactly.

Without a doubt, the most popular video game in recent years has been GOLDEN TEE, manufactured by Incredible Technologies. If a tavern has only video game, chances are good that it's GOLDEN TEE. While this machine offers challenging game play and great graphics, it's the linked competition that has hooked players across the United States. When you play GOLDEN TEE, you're not playing against the machine – you're competing with players from across the country. Tournaments offering high-ticket prizes have kept players coming back to this machine, often feeding $20 bills into the game to hone their skills. Some players have even spent upwards of $4,000 to purchase their own GOLDEN TEE machine so they can spend hours practicing to enter the national tournaments. Update kits are offered annually to keep the game play challenging, as GOLDEN TEE 2002 games around the country were transformed into GOLDEN TEE 2003 machines.

It's too soon to tell if the video games produced in the 1990s will become classics. One thing is certain, however: Video games will continue to evolve, and will continue to offer thrills and excitement to new generations of players.

Trade brochure for Sente's STOMPIN' (1986). The idea was to step on the proper square of the footpad at the same time and place as the rodents appeared on the corresponding square on the screen. STOMPIN' was sold as a kit (including the footpad) for Sente's conversion system. Game shown in this period ad is $400-$500.

MORE THAN JUST VIDEO GAMES

Most video game manufacturers have produced other coin-op arcade machines along with video games. Here are some of the more notable arcade games produced by these manufacturers after the introduction of video games in 1972.

Atari produced a novelty game called TOUCH ME in 1974 and a coin-op photo booth in 1975. The firm unveiled the first widebody pinball machine, THE ATARIANS, in 1976 and built several more pinball games before pulling out of the pinball market following the success of the company's SUPERMAN pinball machine in 1980. Atari built several redemption games in the 1990s including POT SHOT.

Allied Leisure had a long history of building pinball and arcade machines before the company's first video game, PADDLE BATTLE, was introduced in 1973. Allied continued to produce pinball machines until 1980 when the firm was purchased by Centuri.

Like Allied Leisure, Chicago Coin had been in the arcade game business for many years before the video game era. After building only a handful of video games, Chicago Coin continued to manufacture pinball machines, gun games, and bowling machines until the firm was purchased by Sam Stern in 1976 and renamed Stern Electronics.

Exidy was best known for its video games, but one of the first items produced by the company shortly after it was founded in 1975 was a coin-operated player piano! Exidy also built an old-style electromechanical arcade basketball game called ALL-AMERICAN BASKETBALL. In the 1990s, the firm began producing redemption games.

Game Plan started out in the pinball business in 1978, and introduced its first video game, TORA TORA, in 1980. The company built slot machines and pinball games until it closed in 1985.

Gottlieb was the oldest pinball manufacturer, founded in 1927 by David Gottlieb. The company's first product was a countertop grip tester, although the company quickly jumped into the pinball market in 1931 and began producing video games in 1980. The company's name was changed to Mylstar in the early 1980s, although the video games still carried the well-known Gottlieb name. In 1985, the company's name was changed yet again to Premier Technology. Premier built only one video game, EXTERMINATOR, and concentrated most of its efforts on pinball production. Premier went out of business in 1996.

Midway was a diverse company which was purchased by Bally in 1976. Although the firm produced primarily video games after 1973, it did market one pinball machine called ROTATION VIII in 1978. In the 1990s, after Bally Midway was purchased by Williams Electronics, a number of redemption games were produced under the Bally Midway name.

Mirco produced several video games in the mid 1970s, including CHALLENGE, SLAM, and PT-109. The company also produced one pinball machine (SPIRIT OF 76, the first solid-state pin) but was best known for its line of table soccer (foosball) tables.

Stern Electronics introduced its first video game, ASTRO INVADER, in 1980, after the company had already established itself as a leading pinball manufacturer. The company continued building pinball machines as well as Seeburg jukeboxes until 1982, before closing its doors in the fall of 1984.

Taito's ICE COLD BEER was an electromechanical novelty game designed for bars and taverns and was introduced in 1983. The company also produced other novelty arcade games in the late 1980s and early '90s.

Williams was the most diverse arcade game manufacturer, producing top earning video games and pinball machines in the early 1980s. In 1988, Williams bought Bally Midway and later acquired Atari as well. The company withdrew from the amusement game field in 1999.

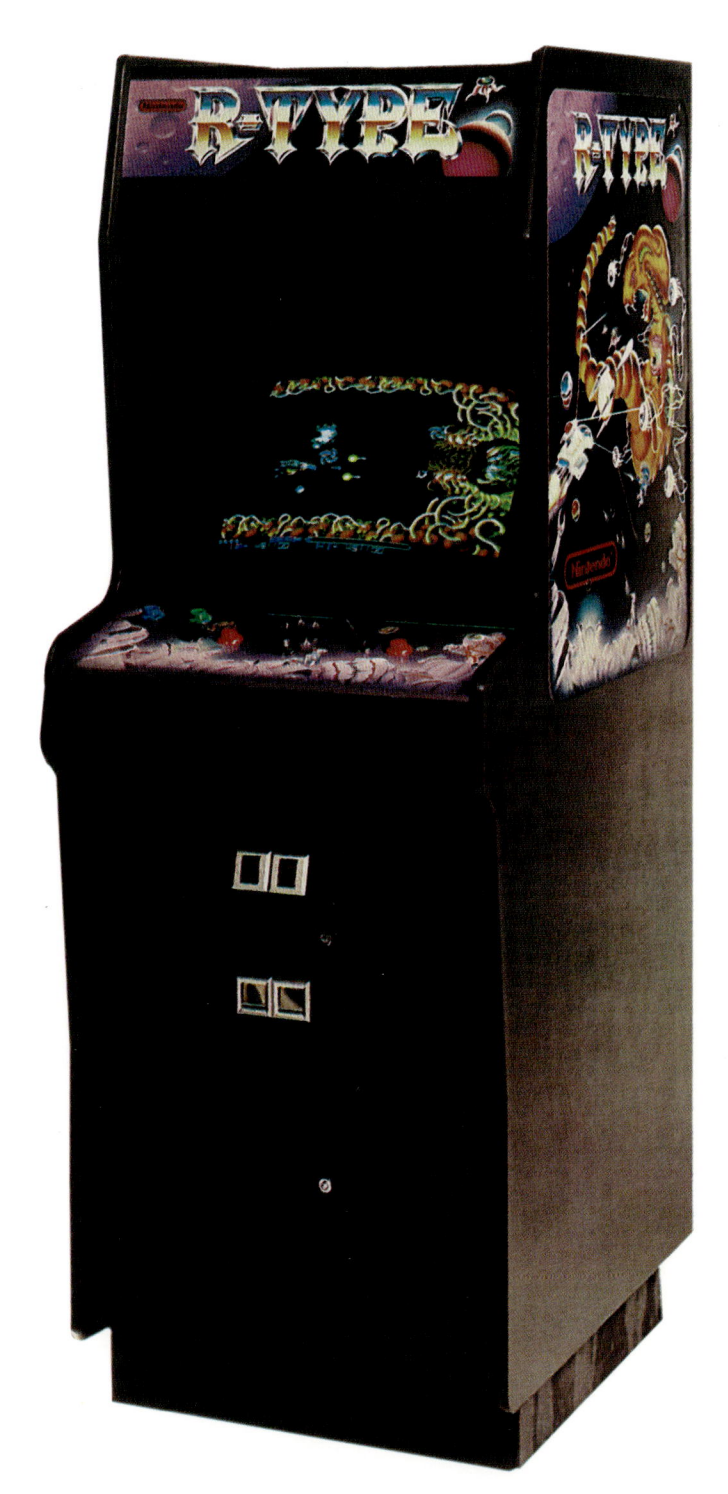

Cinematronics' WORLD SERIES: THE SEASON (1986) was offered in this countertop model, as well as in a standard upright cabinet. $150-$200 (countertop or upright).

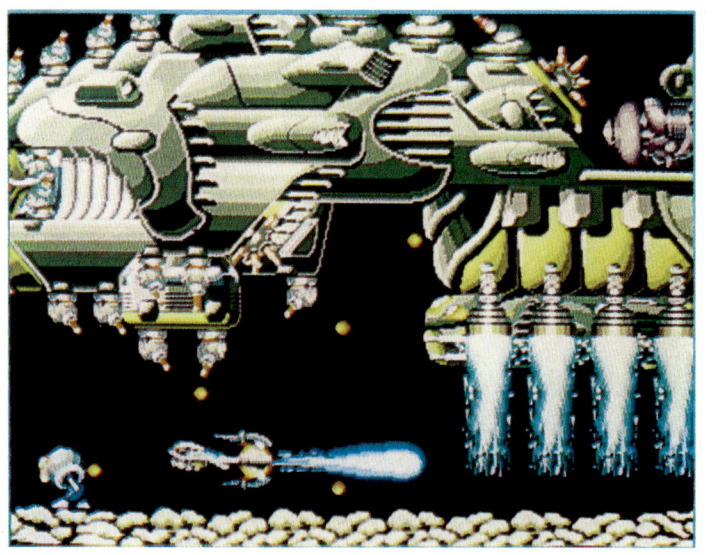

Nintendo's R-TYPE (1987) was the dedicated version of the company's GRADIUS, which had been released a few months earlier as a conversion game for Nintendo's VS system. $350-$450.

R-TYPE screen shot. The game featured elaborate, detailed graphics.

201

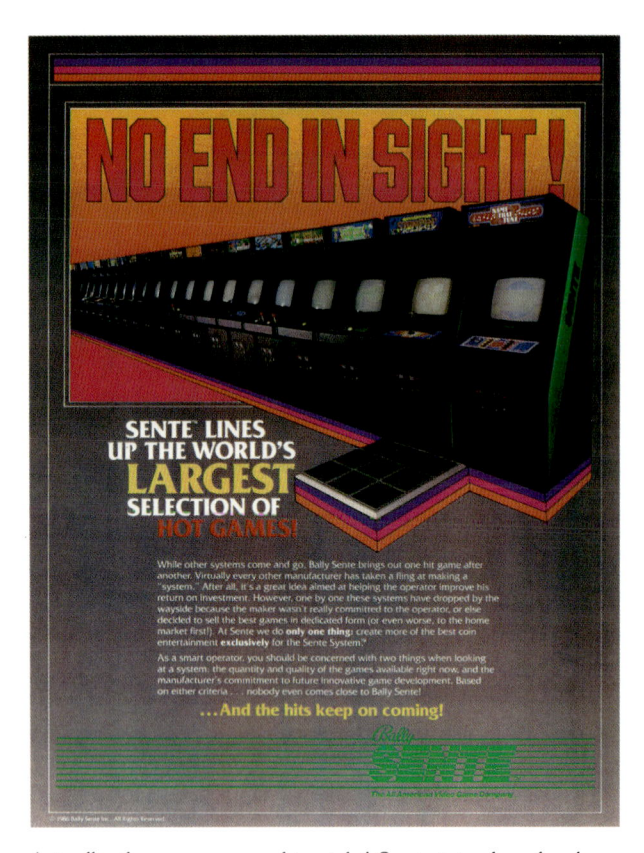

Actually, there was an end in sight! Sente introduced only one more game after STOMPIN' – MOONQUAKE – in 1986 before the firm closed its doors.

Williams' 1986 AEROBOTO was another outer space shoot-'em-up game; because of its low production, it's rarely seen today. $300-$500.

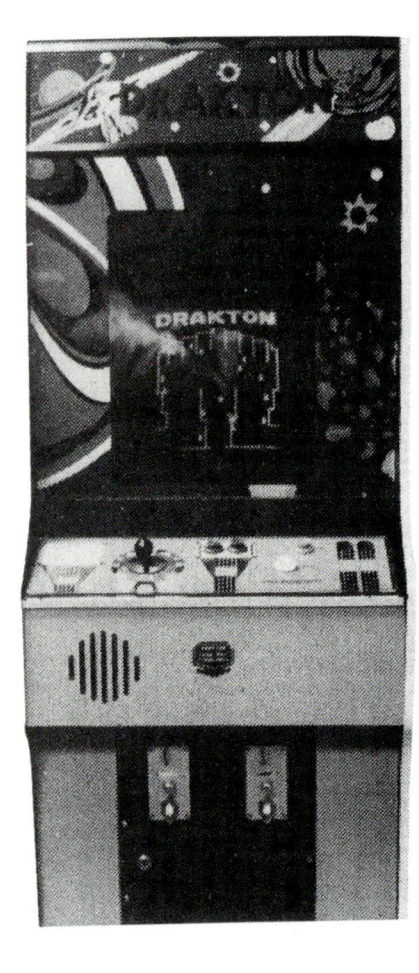

If the cabinet on Cardinal's DRAKTON (1986) looks like the same cabinet used on Nintendo's DONKEY KONG, you're right. Cardinal released DRAKTON as a conversion kit specifically designed to convert DONKEY KONG games. $150-$200.

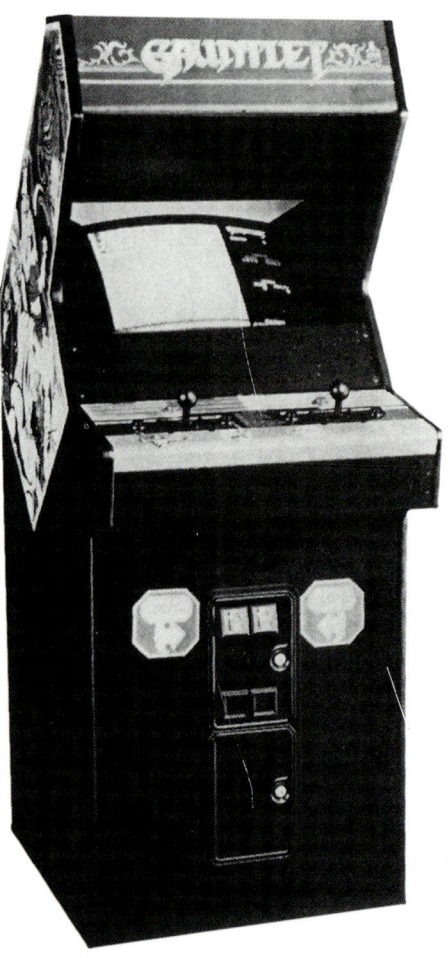

Atari released a two-player version of its popular GAUNTLET video game in 1986. $200-$350.

202

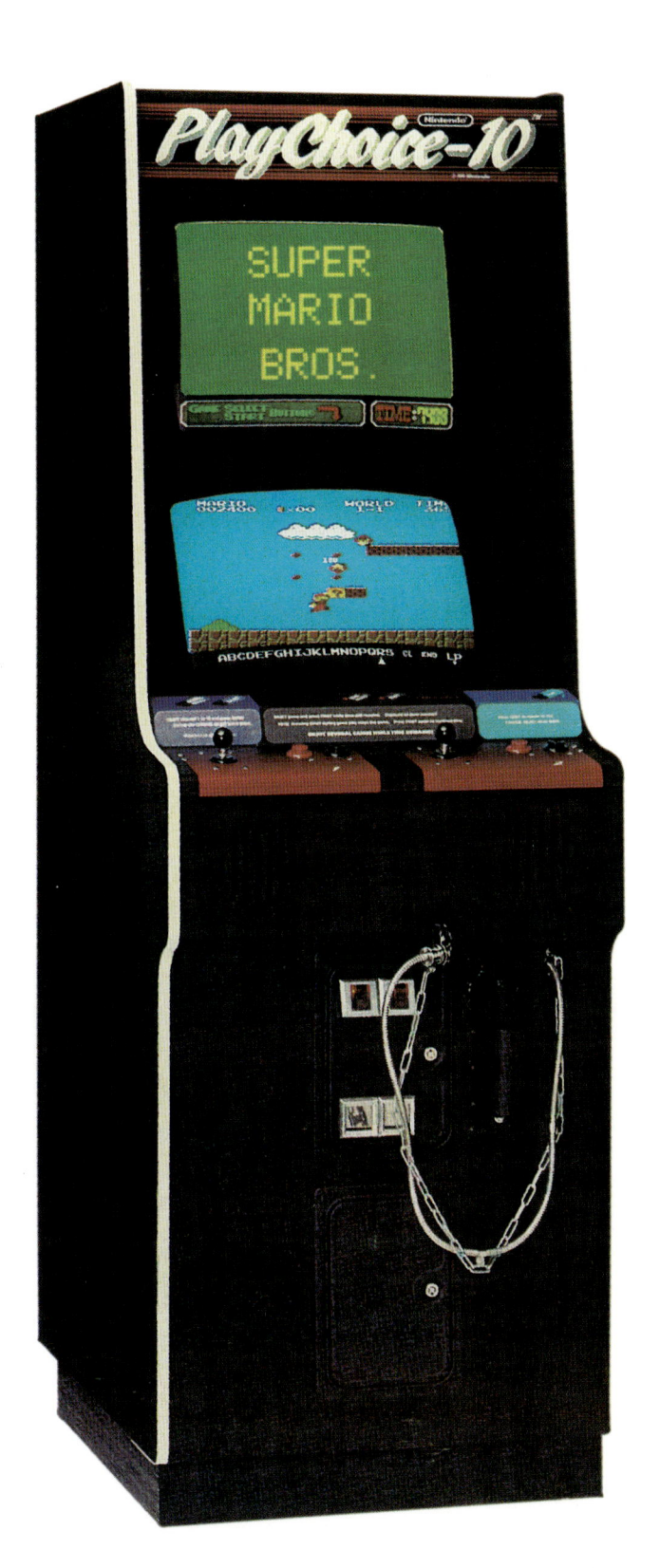

Atari released ROLLING THUNDER, a futuristic shoot-'em-up, in 1987. $200-$300.

Nintendo's PLAY CHOICE 10 video game system (1987) offered ten different video games in one cabinet; the control panel had joysticks, buttons, and even a handgun to accommodate all of the game choices. Nintendo offered new games periodically for several years. $300-$400.

Atari's DRAGON SPIRIT (1987) had a futuristic sword and sorcery theme. Game shown in this period ad is $200-$300.

203

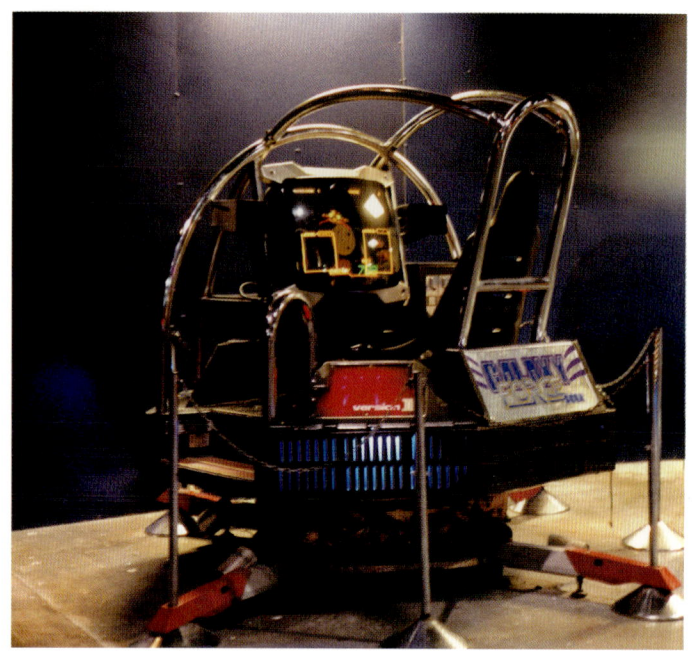

Sega introduced GALAXY FORCE in 1988. You moved from side to side in this video game, which in some ways resembled an amusement park ride. $800-$1,000.

With its unique cabinet, it was hard to miss Atari's 1988 XYBOTS in any arcade. $250-$350.

GALAGA '88 was produced by Atari rather than Bally Midway, which had produced GALAGA, GAPLUS, and GALAGA 3. GALAGA '88 was licensed from Namco, which had also created and licensed the earlier games in the series. $350-$450.

Released in 1988, Taito's SUPERMAN had the Man of Steel battling the Emperor Zaas. Two people could play SUPERMAN cooperatively to defeat Zaas' henchmen more quickly. Notice in this screen shot that one of the Superman characters is wearing a red outfit with a blue cape rather than the traditional blue outfit with the red cape; that's to distinguish one player's Superman character from the other. $350-$450.

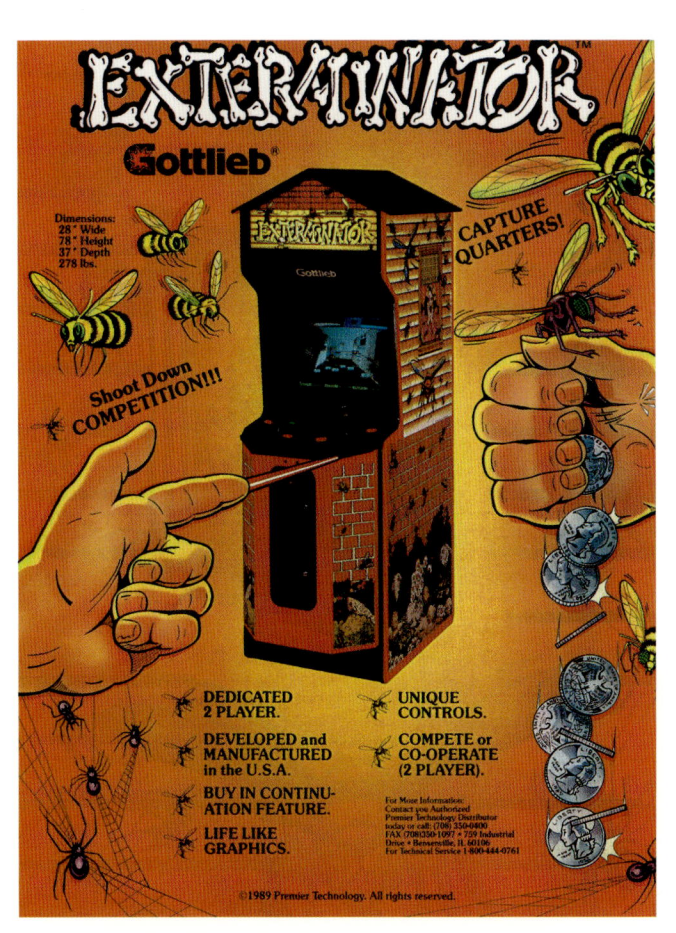

After the 1984 closing of Mylstar, Premier Technology purchased the assets of the company, along with the Gottlieb name, from Columbia Pictures. Although Premier focused its efforts primarily on pinball machines, the company did build one video game – EXTERMINATOR (1988), which has the Gottlieb name above the screen. Game shown in this period ad is $250-$350.

SUPERMAN screen shot. Mount Rushmore is in the background.

205

Atari's BATMAN arrived in arcades in 1990, shortly after the first *Batman* movie was released, and included music and sound from the film. BATMAN had everything you would expect in a video game – the Batrope, Batarangs, the Batmobile, and the Batwing plane. And the Joker, too! Game advertised in this period ad is $300-$400.

Produced by Betson in 1990, MAD DOG MCCREE was a laser disc shooting game which challenged you to outdraw the wild west desperados.

206

TIME TRAVELER featured holographic footage of actors in scenes set in both the past and the future. The holographic images were projected onto a small screen in the center of the cabinet.

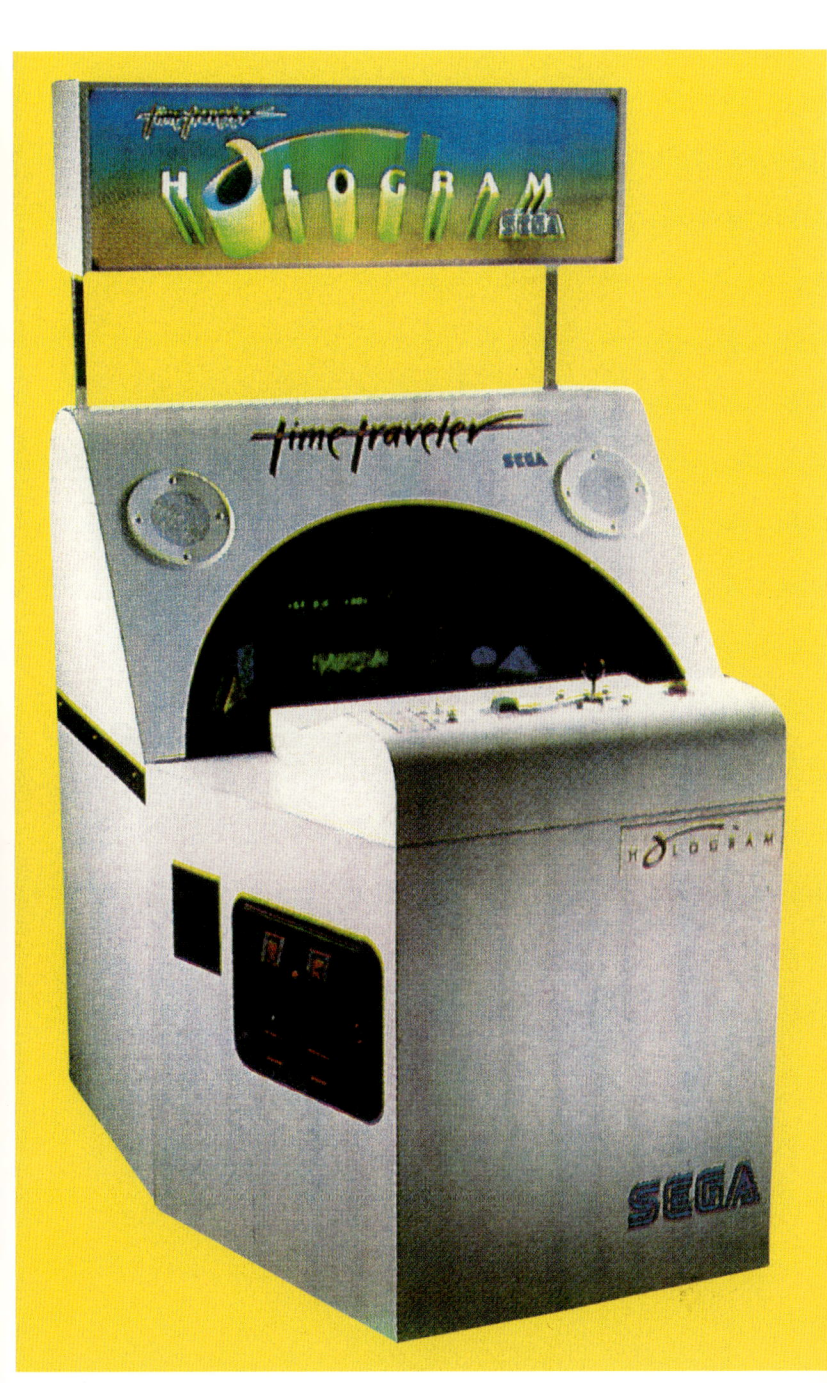

This 1991 Sega video game cabinet design moved you forward and backward along with the action on the screen. Spectators could watch the video game being played on the small screen attached to the cashbox, visible on the left side of the photo. $800-$1,200.

Sega's TIME TRAVELER (1991) was the first holographic video game. Because of the high retail price on this 1990 video game, most TIME TRAVELER machines were set on either 75 cents or one dollar per play to help operators recoup their investment. $800-$1,200.

207

The rock group Aerosmith was featured in this three-player gun game produced by Bally Midway in 1994. Game shown in this period ad is $500-$750.

208

The King of Pop started showing up in arcades in 1991 with the release of Sega's MICHAEL JACKSON'S MOONWALKER. The game featured sounds and images taken from Jackson's *Moonwalker* video, including some of his most famous dance moves. $450-$550.

MICHAEL JACKSON'S MOONWALKER screen shot.

MICHAEL JACKSON'S MOONWALKER screen shot.

209

Midway's TROG (1991) featured the cartoon adventures of a one-eyed caveman. Because the images in the game strongly resembled the animation style called Claymation, the company advertised TROG as being in Playmation. $300-$400.

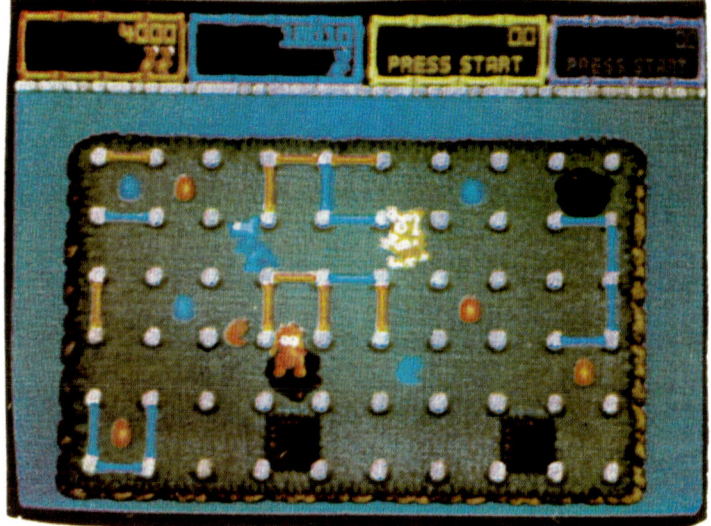

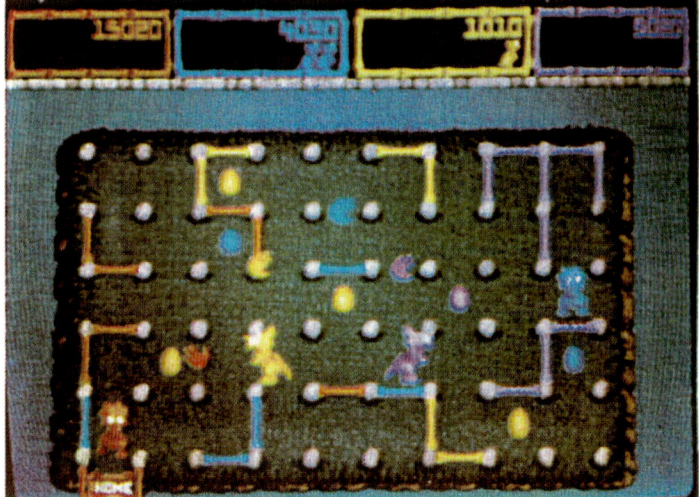

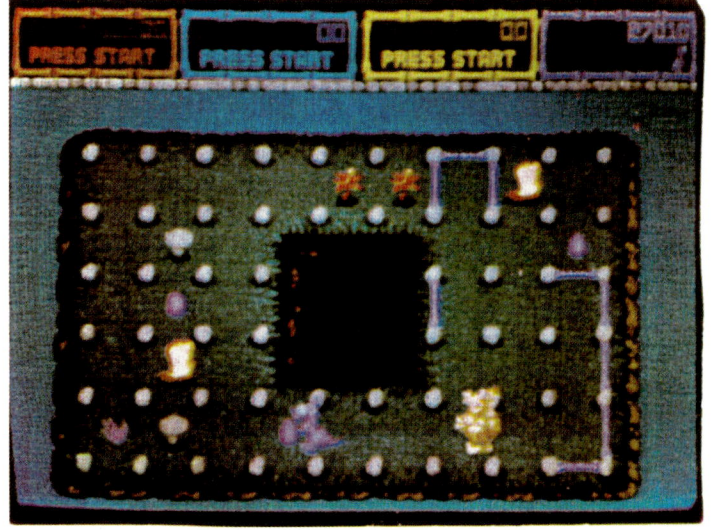

TROG screen shots.

Trade brochure for LEE TREVINO'S FIGHTING GOLF, produced by SNK in 1990. SNK produced only conversion kits, rather than dedicated games. Game advertised in this period brochure is $200-$300.

Released in 1991, Leland's DRAGON'S LAIR II never attained the following of the original DRAGON'S LAIR laser disc game. Many operators decided not to purchase the machine because they remembered the service problems caused by malfunctioning laser disc players on the original game eight years earlier. $1,000-$1,200.

Up to three players could compete in medieval battle on Atari's RAMPART (1991). $200-$300.

211

This game was designed to take a beating! Throw punches at your opponent by pushing the handgrip controls. Sega released TITLE FIGHT in 1992. $300-$400.

Midway's TERMINATOR II gun game featured digitized images and music from the popular *Terminator* movies. And it was impossible to miss the lifesize photo of Arnold on the side of the cabinet. Game shown in this period ad is $500-$650.

TERMINATOR II screen shot.

TERMINATOR II screen shot.

TERMINATOR II screen shot. Notice the digitized image of one of the film's characters in the left foreground.

213

You could play pool, miniature golf, or bowling on Midway's TRI-SPORTS, released in 1990. $200-$350.

Midway's MORTAL KOMBAT (1992), was the most popular of the martial arts genre of video games that dominated the arcade scene in the 1990s. You could select from one of seven different fighters – one of them a woman – at the beginning of the game, with each fighter specializing in a different martial arts technique. $300-$400.

Walk through any arcade near the end of 1991 and you could hear Bart Simpson's voice coming from Konami's THE SIMPSONS. Nothing spectacular about the game play, but the name alone has made this game a favorite among both video game collectors and fans of *The Simpsons*. Game shown in this period ad is $300-$500.

Laser disc video games made something of a comeback in the early 1990s with games like CRIME PATROL by American Laser Games (1992). These games featured more dramatic footage and were far more interactive than the laser games introduced a decade earlier. $750-$1,000.

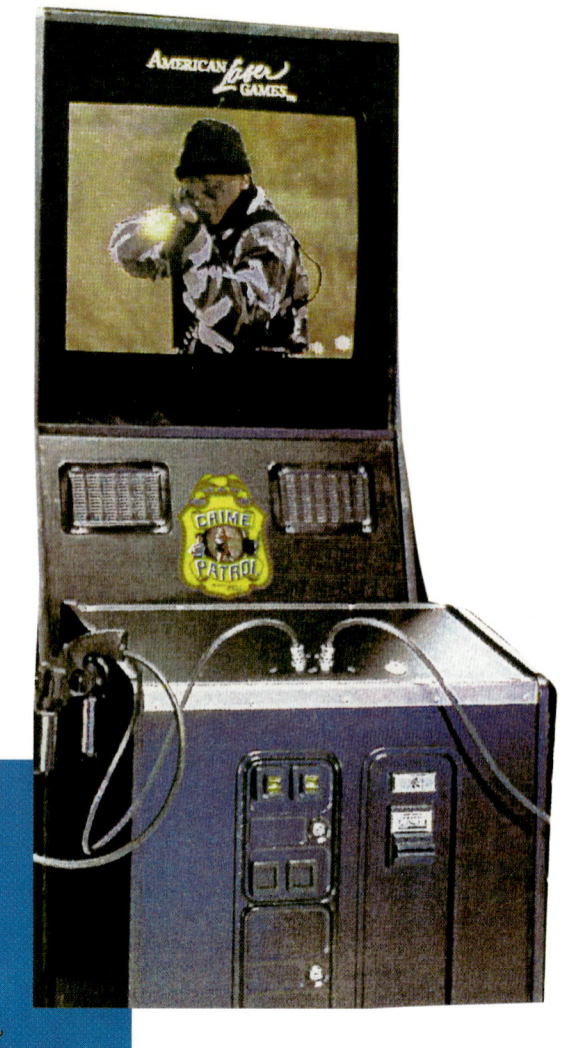

Hi-tech virtual reality arrived in arcades in April of 1993 when VR8 Inc. introduced VIRTUAL COMBAT, the first virtual reality coin-op game. Despite the dazzling graphics, the game play failed to draw players and both the company and the concept faded quickly. $2,000-$2,500.

Konami's ALIENS (1991) was based on the popular series of *Alien* movies starring Sigourney Weaver. Game advertised in this period ad is $300-$400.

Today's arcades feature large video games with linked play.

HOUSE OF THE DEAD screen shot.

HOUSE OF THE DEAD screen shot.

Sega promised operators "disgustingly large collections" on the brochure for HOUSE OF THE DEAD, a gun game released in the late 1990s. The game is still a top earner in most arcades. Operators could change the blood from red to green for a less gruesome game. Video games had certainly changed in the two decades since Exidy's DEATH RACE stirred up controversy for its violent theme. $7,500-$9,000

Part 6
VIDEO GAMES OF THE WORLD

It's often been said that video games were invented in the United States and perfected in Japan, and there's a lot of truth to that statement. Although Nolan Bushnell was responsible for creating both COMPUTER SPACE and PONG, it was Japanese companies like Taito and Namco whose games led to the video boom of the late 1970s and early '80s.

Only a few weeks after the release of PONG, Bushnell licensed the concept to Sega of Tokyo, which started building PONG-TRON in Japan under license from Atari. Dozens of Japanese companies began building PONG-style video games, but the technology advanced more rapidly in Japan than in the U.S. Less than three years later, Midway licensed the game GUNFIGHT from Taito, the first time that a U.S. manufacturer licensed a video game from abroad. Many of the most popular games from the golden age of video games were created in Japan, including SPACE INVADERS, GALAXIAN, GALAGA, PAC MAN, and MS. PAC MAN.

But Japan wasn't the only country to produce arcade video games. Several pinball and arcade game manufacturers were based in Italy and Spain, but these companies were rooted in electromechanical technology. It took a few years for these companies to enter the video game field, but by the mid 1970s, a number of European manufacturers were producing video games.

Several of these companies entered the field by licensing games from Taito, Namco, and other manufacturers. Most manufacturers sold video games only in their home country, which left the production and distribution rights for many games throughout the rest of the world up for grabs. The situation can get very confusing; for example, Sonic (of Barcelona) licensed the rights to Atari's POLE POSITION for manufacture and distribution in Spain, while Atari (rather than Cinematronics) had the license to sell DRAGON'S LAIR in the United Kingdom.

One of the few European companies to successfully design and market video games was Zaccaria. Based in Bologna, Italy, Zaccaria began producing pinball machines in 1975, and by the mid '80s, entered the video game field with MONEY MONEY. The company's most popular game was JACKRABBIT, a cute game (strongly resembling Mylstar's Q*BERT) which featured a smiling rabbit hopping around a field looking for carrots.

Inder (of Madrid) began building pinball machines for the Spanish market in the mid 1970s before adding video games to its product line near the end of the decade. And Model Racing, based in Italy, originally manufactured slot cars but entered the coin-op game market in the mid '70s with DYNAMITE JOE, a projection gun game, before producing more traditional video games a few years later.

There are no European companies developing video games today; the few remaining video game manufacturers are based in the United States and Japan. But there certainly won't be a shortage of video games in Europe, because U.S. and Japanese firms continue to license popular games for production and distribution in Europe.

HILL CLIMB (1976) was produced and sold in Italy by an unidentified Italian video game manufacturer. The game was a copy of Atari's STUNT CYCLE. $100-$150.

It looks like Midway's SPACE INVADERS – and it is SPACE INVADERS, just under a different name. Taito sold SPACE INVADERS in Spain under the name SPACE KING II. $350-$450.

This bootleg SPACE INVADERS clone was sold only in Europe. It's no wonder that the manufacturer of SPACE DRAGON preferred to remain anonymous. $100-$200.

Made in England, BATTLE ATLANTIS was produced by Game World and had a World War II naval combat theme. It was sold only in the United Kingdom. $150-$200.

Zaccaria, a game manufacturer headquartered in Bologna, Italy, introduced JACKRABBIT in 1984. The game featured a rabbit hopping around a field looking for carrots, similar to Mylstar's popular Q*BERT video game. Unlike most games produced in Europe, JACKRABBIT was sold in the United States. $200-$250.

JACKRABBIT screen shot.

221

EUROPA was produced by a small Japanese manufacturer in the 1990s. $100-$150.

Look at the unusual cabinet on Taito's GRAND CHAMPION, licensed to Electron Games for distribution in Germany. $200-$300.

Europa Coin of Kent, England, introduced SUPER PINBALL '91 in 1991. Europa Coin had announced plans to introduce update kits with new pinball designs periodically, but these conversion kits were never produced. $250-$350.

SUPER SHOT was one of the few video games produced by Model Racing of Italy, a company which was known for producing coin-operated slot car games. $150-$200.

222

Inder's FLIP-VI (1995) combined a full-sized pinball playfield with a sophisticated video game. Notice that the game has two joysticks and two sets of control buttons just below the playfield so two players could compete on the video game simultaneously. $500-$600.

Use your machine gun to battle the 1920s gangsters when you play GANG HUNTER, a game produced in the mid 1990s by an unknown Italian manufacturer. $150-$250.

Franco Cinea of Coal, Italy, produced MEGA SHOW, a giant, four-player video unit, which was designed to work with any standard video game. Notice the numbering on the back of the chairs, which determines where each player must be seated. Produced in the early 1990s, these units were seldom found outside of Italy. $3,000-$4,000.

223

Part 7
VIDEO GAME COLLECTIBLES

If you're like many video game enthusiasts, your collection goes beyond simply owning several machines. You might have the original sales flyers that were distributed to the trade to promote your games, or some of the promotional items that were created to catch your eye. You may even own a few of the toys and novelties that were sold commercially to cash in on the popularity of some games. Some dealers even specialize in these items, which can often be more difficult to locate than the games themselves.

Very few promotional items were produced to advertise video games prior to the late 1970s. Game manufacturers relied on sales brochures (also called flyers) to sell the machines, and original brochures can sometimes be difficult to find today, especially for popular games. As each new machine was introduced, video game distributors received a supply of flyers from the manufacturer which described the game's features and usually had a color photograph of the machine. Nearly every distributor had a table or a rack in the showroom where customers could pick up these brochures, but because they were given away for free, distributors figured that they had no value and most distributors disposed of their leftover brochures every few weeks. It wasn't until the early 1980s that a handful of collectors recognized the nostalgic and historic value of these flyers, but by then, many collectible brochures had already been lost.

Some collectors use flyers to help in game restoration, while others frame the brochures and display them near the machine. Prices can vary widely on original video game flyers; an original color PONG flyer can sell for over $200, while the black and white PONG flyer will go for more than $125. Another high-priced flyer would be the brochure produced to advertise COMPUTER SPACE; this flyer usually sells for about $100. The prices of most video game flyers, however, are usually a reflection of the popularity of the machine. Even though there are only a few original flyers still around for Williams' 1973 PADDLE BALL, the company's first video game, you can pick up one of these for about $15, while more recent flyers for games like Atari's TEMPEST and MAJOR HAVOC can easily sell for more than $35.

Some flyers were produced for distribution only at the national coin-op games trade shows and were never circulated to video game distributors. Atari's BLACK WIDOW flyer, for example, was available only from Atari's

Cute packaging made this Pac Man candy by Fleer a big seller back in 1981 but most people tore open the card and ate the candy, so this item is difficult to find today. $5-$10.

booth at the 1983 trade show; expect to pay at least $200 for this flyer if you're lucky enough to find it.

Even harder to find than sales brochures are the large promotional posters which were issued starting in the late 1970s. These posters were often distributed at the national trade shows where attendees had to carry them around the exhibit hall; because they're so large and often difficult to handle, many posters never left the trade show floor, while others were folded or damaged. Most often, these posters pictured the cartoon graphics which appeared on the sides of the cabinet.

Most video games came shipped from the factory with an instruction manual inside, but the manual often became separated from the machine as routine maintenance and service was performed over the years. The manual is a valuable tool, because it contains information about parts, troubleshooting, scoring, and other important items. You'll also find information in the manual about changing the settings on your machine to adjust the length of the game, sound, and other options. And most manuals come with a schematic (or wiring diagram) which tells you how the circuitry is connected inside your game; it can sometimes mean the difference between having a working or a non-working machine. Without a schematic, it can be difficult – or even impossible – to track down problems, so even if you can't read a schematic yourself, you should have it available in case an experienced mechanic works on your game. For some collectors, a photocopy or a manual downloaded from the Internet will work just fine, but for others, only an original will do.

As video games started growing in popularity in the late '70s, manufacturers were willing to spend more money on promotional items which were distributed to game operators and arcade owners. T-shirts, hats, key rings, and coffee mugs with game artwork and logos were frequently given away at trade shows, although some manufacturers were more creative in their promo items. Centuri created a set of sweatbands to promote TRACK AND FIELD (1983),

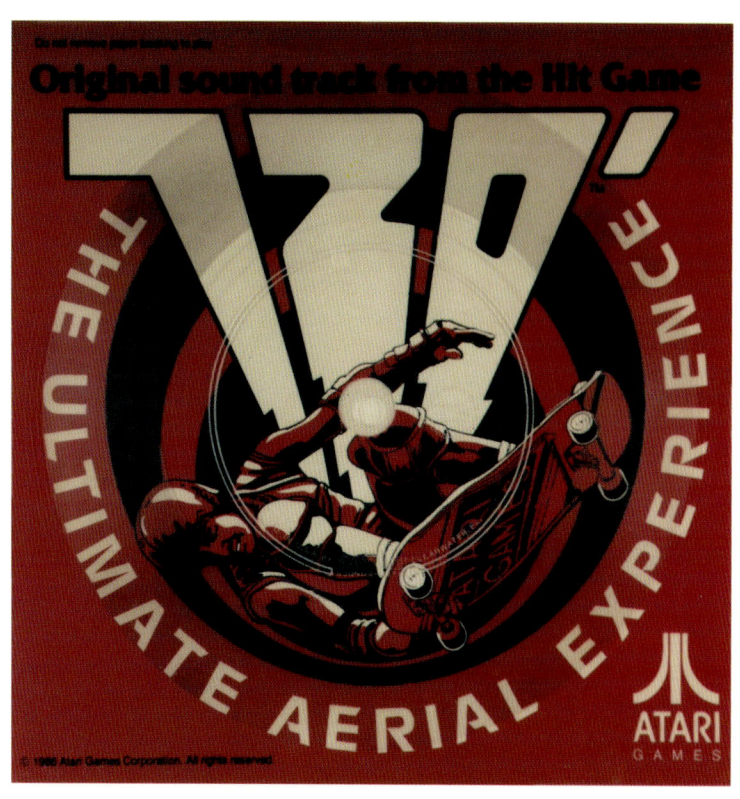

It never made the Billboard Top 100, but Atari released a record with some of original music used in the company's 720 video game. Few people ever heard this record, though, because it was available only to video game operators and distributors, not the general public. $15-$25.

which featured a series of athletic events. Midway distributed a set of paper coasters to promote its bar-themed TAPPER video game in 1984. Exidy distributed straw cowboy hats with the CHEYENNE logo to promote its 1984 video game. And Stern gave out plastic shopping bags to draw attention to its BAGMAN video game in 1983.

Some video game collectibles were sold commercially. You could find PAC MAN drinking glasses, Q*BERT banks, a CENTIPEDE board game, DONKEY KONG bubble gum cards, and many more items. Most of these items were mass produced in such vast quantities that they have little value today.

If you're looking for any video game collectibles, the Internet auction site eBay is the place to start. You'll find hundreds of flyers, manuals, and all sorts of promotional items listed every day, with most of these selling for $10 or less. As more and more collectors learn about the variety of promotional items that have been produced for video games, you can expect their value to increase. If you don't have the space or the money for a large collection of arcade video games, then you might want to consider adding some promotional items to your collection.

Many collectors like to have the original manuals to go along with their machines, while others are satisfied with a photocopy or even a computer download. Expect to pay anywhere from $5 to $30 for an original manual, depending on the popularity of the game and whether or not schematics are included in the manual.

Williams' PRO-HOCKEY

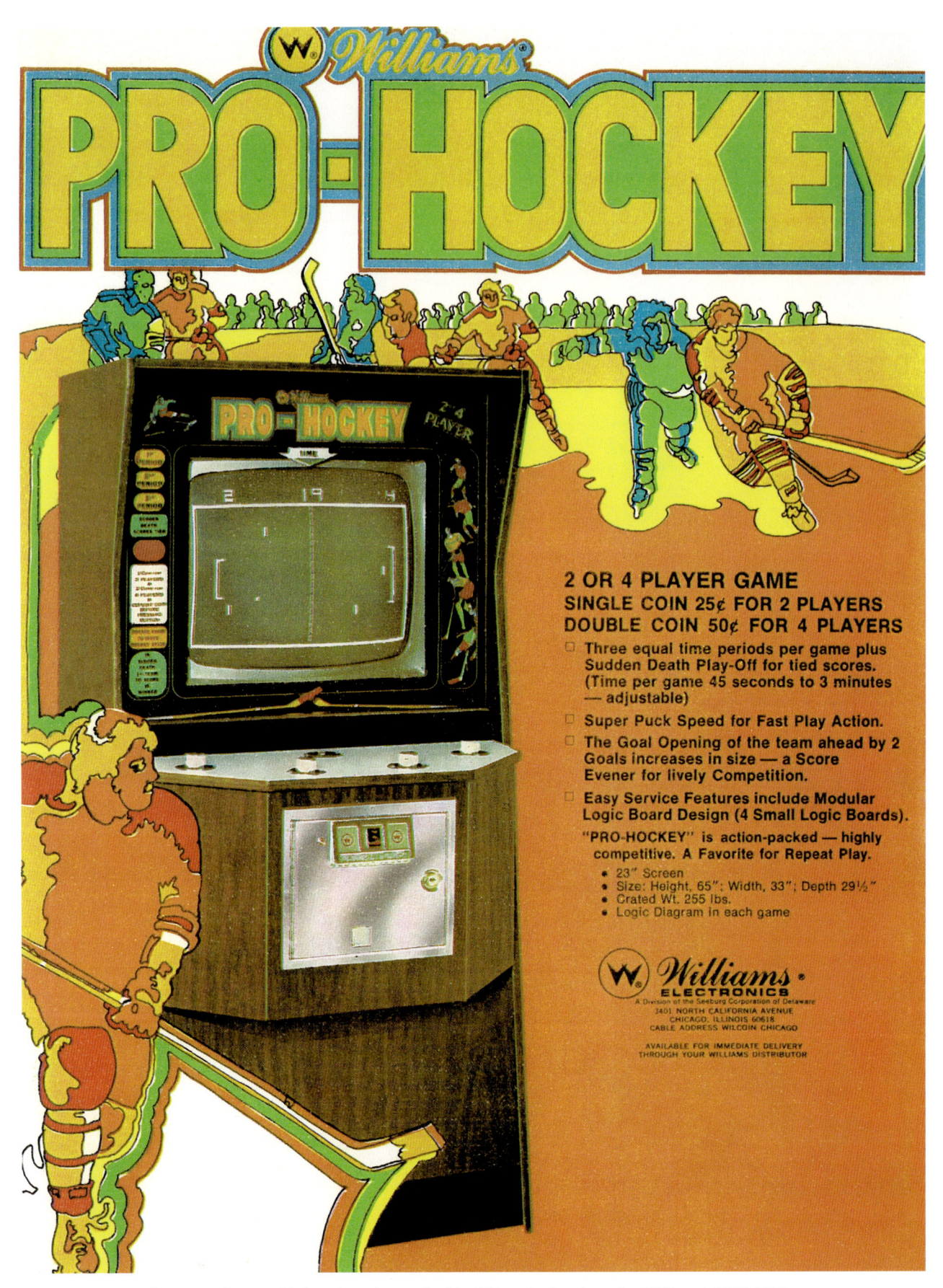

2 OR 4 PLAYER GAME
SINGLE COIN 25¢ FOR 2 PLAYERS
DOUBLE COIN 50¢ FOR 4 PLAYERS

- Three equal time periods per game plus Sudden Death Play-Off for tied scores. (Time per game 45 seconds to 3 minutes — adjustable)
- Super Puck Speed for Fast Play Action.
- The Goal Opening of the team ahead by 2 Goals increases in size — a Score Evener for lively Competition.
- Easy Service Features include Modular Logic Board Design (4 Small Logic Boards).

"PRO-HOCKEY" is action-packed — highly competitive. A Favorite for Repeat Play.

- 23" Screen
- Size: Height, 65"; Width, 33"; Depth 29½"
- Crated Wt. 255 lbs.
- Logic Diagram in each game

Williams ELECTRONICS
A Division of the Seeburg Corporation of Delaware
3401 NORTH CALIFORNIA AVENUE
CHICAGO, ILLINOIS 60618
CABLE ADDRESS WILCOIN CHICAGO

AVAILABLE FOR IMMEDIATE DELIVERY
THROUGH YOUR WILLIAMS DISTRIBUTOR

Just because a video game flyer is old doesn't make it valuable. This sales brochure for Williams' 1973 PRO HOCKEY, one of the company's first video games, usually sells for between $15 and $20, while flyers for many of the PONG-style paddle games from companies like Amutronics can be found for only a dollar or two.

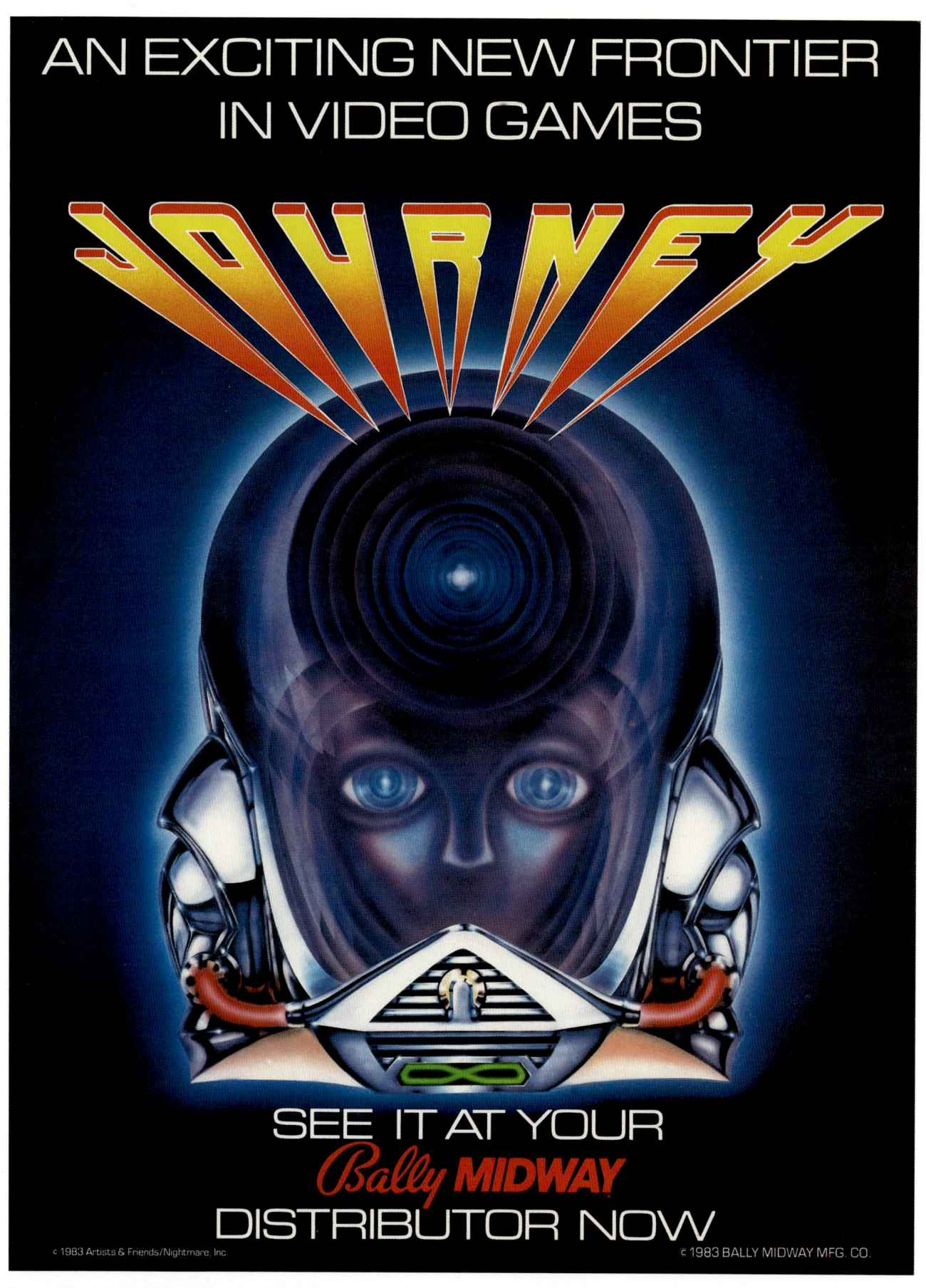

Posters like this for Bally Midway's JOURNEY were available only to arcade owners and video game operators, not to players or collectors. $25-$35.

Bally Midway created a neat paper chef's hat to promote the company's 1983 BURGERTIME video game. $15-$20.

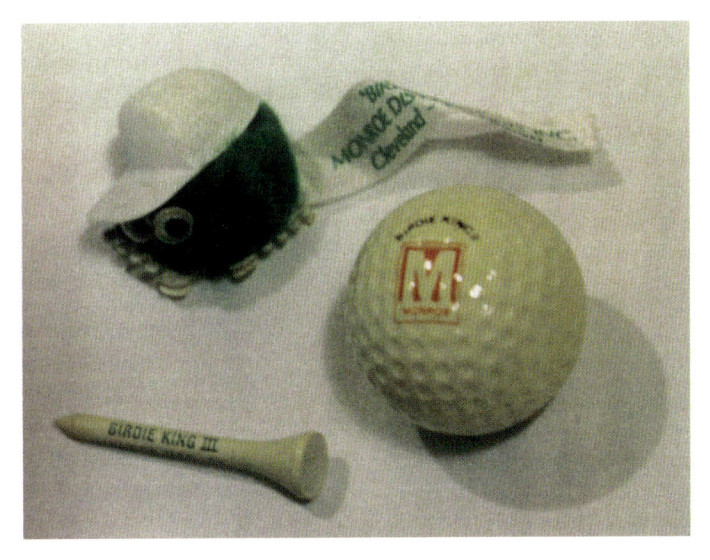

Here's an assortment of promotional items from Monroe Manufacturing for the company's BIRDIE KING II and BIRDIE KING III video games. $5-$10 each item.

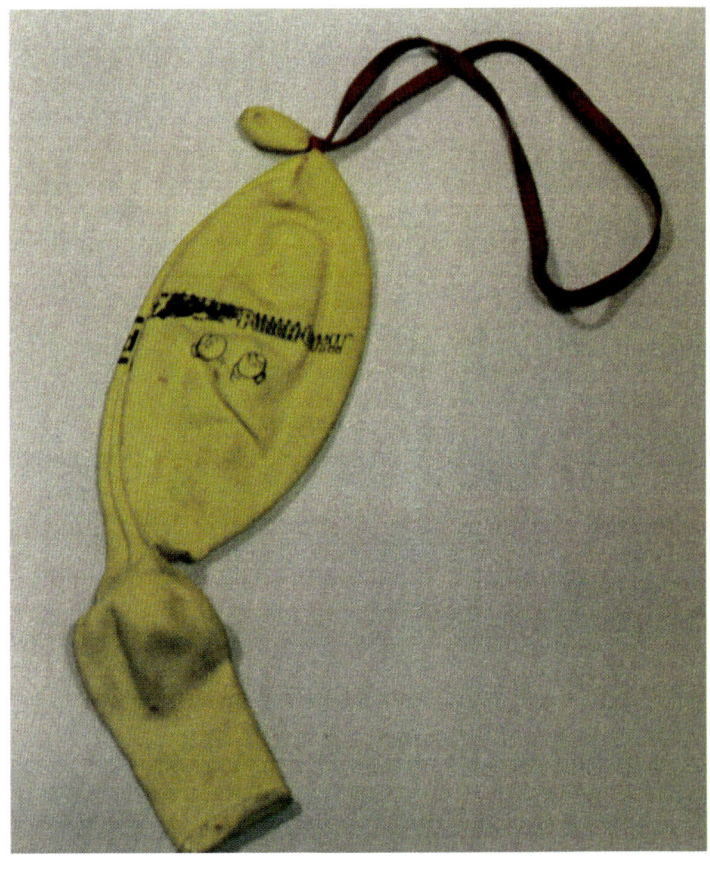

Nintendo used giant inflatable punchballs to promote SUPER PUNCH OUT. $5-$10.

Cinematronics created flip books and pinback buttons to promote its laser disc games in the mid 1980s. The flip books usually sell for between $25 and $50, while the pinback button is generally priced between $10 and $20.

T-shirts like these were available to video game operators and arcade owners at the national coin-op games trade shows; they were never sold commercially. $25-$35 (FOOD FIGHT); $20-$30 (MILLIPEDE).

Nichibutsu distributed these fuzzies with sticky feet to promote its MAG MAX and ROLLER JAMMER video games. These creatures resemble owls because Nichibutsu used an owl in the company logo. $3-$5 each.

Williams produced several different pinback buttons to promote its 1984 TURKEY SHOOT video game, including this button which reads: "Make Your Day . . . Shoot Turkeys." $15-$20.

Centuri passed out heart-shaped stickers to game operators to promote the firm's MIKIE video game. $3-$5.

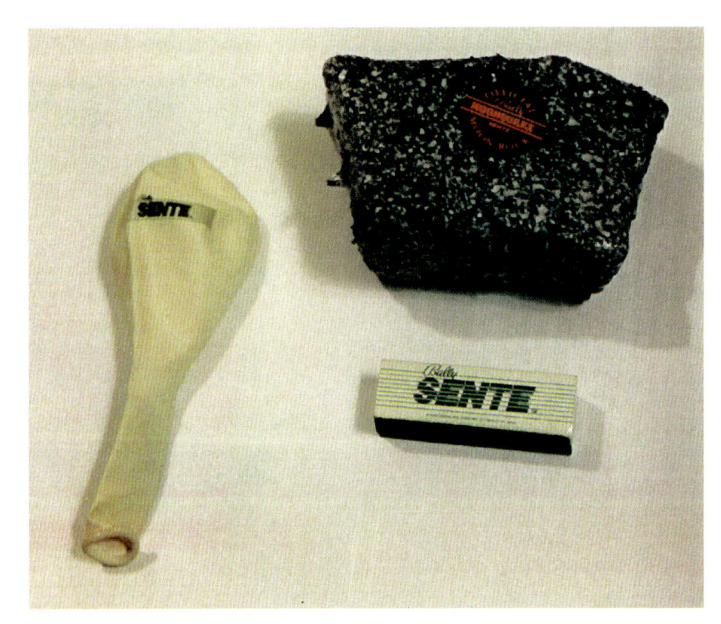

An assortment of promotional items for Sente video games: a balloon, a matchbox, and a foam "rock" advertising the company's MOONQUAKE video game. $2-$3 each (balloon and matchbox); $15-$20 (foam rock).

DONKEY KONG, PAC MAN, and MS. PAC MAN were just three of the video games for which trading cards were produced. Each wrapper originally came packaged with a stick of bubble gum. $5-$8 (unopened wrappers); $3-$5 (empty wrappers).

230

The Q*BERT Eraser-Mate pen was sold commercially; the fuzzy with the sticky feet was a handout at the Gottlieb/Mylstar booth at the 1982 coin-op games trade show. $15-$20 (pen); $5-$8 (fuzzy).

This tabletop toy version of Midway's GALAXIAN was sold in retail stores in the late '80s. It was licensed from Midway, and featured the same graphics as the arcade game. $35-$50 (without box); $60-$75 (with box).

If you couldn't get enough PAC MAN in the arcade and wanted to buy your own PAC MAN machine back in 1980, you might have to settle for this tabletop version produced by Coleco. $50-$75 (without box); $75-$100 (with box).

Part 8
OWNING YOUR OWN MACHINE

Collecting arcade video games is a fascinating and enjoyable hobby. Video games can offer you more adventures than you could hope to experience in a lifetime, and they're instant attention getters in any rec room. Best of all, your machine is always waiting for you – at the drop of a coin, you can suspend reality and enter a fantasy world where anything is possible.

Buying your first machine can be an overwhelming experience, though. Where do you begin? First, a couple of don'ts. Don't buy a video game as an investment. Very few games appreciate in value. Next, don't buy a machine simply for the artwork or the sounds – buy it because you enjoy playing the game. No matter how avid a fan of the rock group Journey you may be, if you buy a Midway JOURNEY video game simply because it features your favorite band, you'll ultimately be disappointed in the game.

Most people buy machines that they remember playing when they were younger. Did you drop hundreds of tokens into that FROGGER game at the arcade? Then FROGGER might be the game for you. Did you play PAC MAN until your elbow hurt? There's your game. Just be sure to play the machine again before you purchase it. No matter how much time you spent engrossed in games like TANK and BREAKOUT, you may find these games hopelessly dated when you play them again after twenty-five years.

You can probably find a video game to suit your taste no matter what your interests are. If you're an auto racing fan, then you might enjoy Atari's POLE POSITION or Sega's TURBO. Do you enjoy classic movies? Then Atari's INDIANA JONES AND THE TEMPLE OF DOOM or Midway's TERMINATOR 2 – or even Mylstar's THREE STOOGES – could be just what you're looking for. If you're a sports fan, you might want Midway's EXTRA BASES, Atari's BASKETBALL, or Centuri's TRACK & FIELD. From underwater games like Midway's SUBMARINE to aerial flying games like Sega's ZAXXON, you're sure to find something that appeals to you.

You might want to consider how the game's theme will fit into your rec room's décor. If you have a bar set up in your basement, then Midway's TAPPER would complement the surroundings. Western motif? Consider Atari's OUTLAW or Taito's WILD WESTERN. And if you do a lot of cooking, then Midway's BURGERTIME or Atari's FOOD FIGHT would be perfect.

So where do you begin to look for a game? There are lots of options available. Most large cities have one or two retail stores which sell reconditioned video games

Are you a football fan? Then Taito's 1984 TEN YARD FIGHT might be perfect for your rec room. $150-$200.

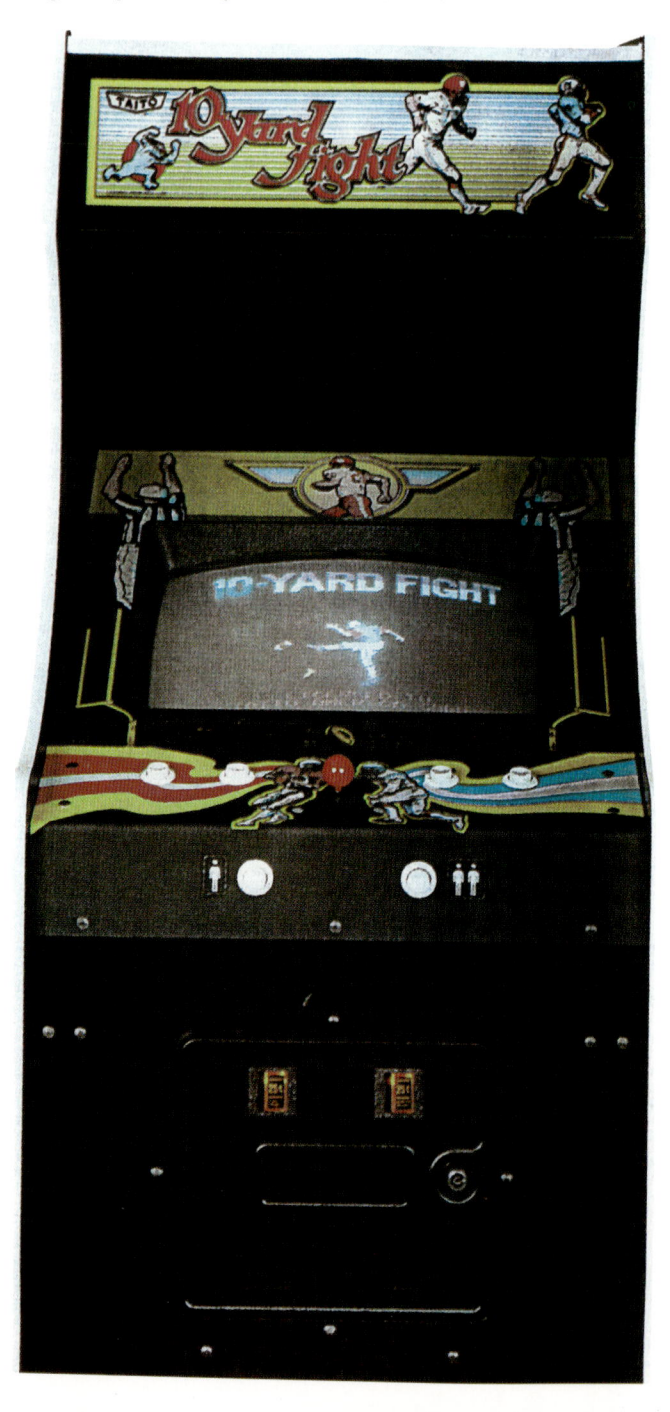

Sega's 1983 STAR TREK video game would make a perfect addition to any collection of *Star Trek* memorabilia. $400-$600.

along with pinball machines, pool tables, and slot machines. These stores usually offer professionally reconditioned games, usually at premium prices. Still, you'll have the assurance of knowing that you're buying an expertly restored game, and many of these shops include a 30-day warranty as part of the sale.

Arcade game auctions are another source for used machines. The games are sometimes reconditioned, although more often than not, they've just been removed from an operator's route and may need some service. At most auctions, you'll have a chance to play the machines before the bidding begins. Be sure that you're satisfied that the game is operating properly, though, because most auction machines are sold "as is." You can sometimes find video games in antique and liquidation auctions, but these machines often sell for high prices because you'll often find a number of bidders competing for only one or two machines at these events. You'll find more bargains at auctions that offer only coin-op games. Keep in mind that many of these auctions require minimum bids on some items or have a "buyer's premium" added to the hammer price.

You can also find video games in the classified ads of your local newspaper, where you may stumble across a game that's been sitting unused in someone's basement for years. Video games are usually listed in categories such as "Sale Miscellaneous," "Rec Room Furnishings," and even "Antiques." These machines will often need some minor repair work, so you may be able to negotiate a break on the selling price. If an advertisement catches your eye, it's usually best to call immediately because many coin-op game dealers scan the ads for machines they can resell at a profit. You may also want to check the yard and garage sale ads, as video games are often sold at these locations. And don't overlook second-hand thrift stores, which may contain a bargain.

One of the best sources for locating a specific video game is eBay. If you have your heart set on owning a specific machine, be sure to check out the listings frequently, at least to get an idea of how much others are paying for the same game. Remember that many eBay sellers are able to ship machines for an additional $100 to $200 or so, depending on where you are located. Of course, buying on eBay has the drawback of not being able to play the machine before you buy, so it's essential that your seller has established a good reputation through positive feedback.

And while you're on your computer, you might want to check out the video game newsgroups on the Internet: rec.games.video.arcade.collecting and rec.games.video.arcade.marketplace. There's lots of cross-posting between the two groups, but the collecting group focus primarily on service and technical tips while the marketplace group leans more heavily toward buying and selling games. There are lots of knowledgeable people who post on these newsgroups and are willing to answer your questions like "How can I fix the garbled sound on my CENTIPEDE?" or "Where I can I find parts or service for my DONKEY KONG?" Unfortunately, as with any Internet newsgroup, there are also many uninformed and misinformed people who frequent these newsgroups; lots of incorrect information is disseminated here, so be careful.

If you want to mingle and talk with other video game collectors in person, then the California Extreme show is for you. Held annually in California, this show features hundreds of classic and modern video games, all fully restored and playable, with most of them for sale. More information about the show can be found on the convention website (www.caextreme.org). Another national show is the Classic Gaming Expo, generally held in Las

Vegas every August. Several game designers attend the show regularly and often address the crowd at seminars. More information can be found at www.dragons-lair-project.com/community/cge/cge2003.asp.

If you're going to pick up your machine locally, remember that most upright video games weigh between 250 and 300 pounds, and can fit in a pickup truck, minivan, or SUV. Don't try to move your machine by yourself – two people can move a game much easier than one person alone.

Video games come in a variety of sizes and shapes. If an upright video game would look out of place in your rec room, then a cocktail table video game might be the answer. On the other hand, if space is not an issue in your rec room, then you might want to consider getting a cockpit-style video game. These cockpit games are large and bulky, though; most weigh over 500 pounds and may be too wide to fit through a doorway.

One of the most difficult video games to find is the cockpit version of Atari's STAR WARS (1983). These cockpit games may be too large to fit down your stairway, so be sure to measure your doorways and stairways before buying a video game, either an upright or a cockpit model. $1,500-$1,800.

Newer video games usually have fewer service problems than older games. Most game distributors and some operators have technicians that make home service calls, although these visits can be pricey, with most techs charging between $75 and $125 for the first hour. You might also be able to find some service assistance on one of the Internet newsgroups mentioned above.

Several dealers sell replacement parts for video games. For example, Marco Specialties in South Carolina has a large stock of parts in inventory for games going back more

Bally Midway's TAPPER (1984) has brass cup holders at each end of the control panel and a brass footrest at the bottom of the cabinet – perfect for anyone who has a bar in his rec room. $400-$600.

234

than twenty years. And Two-Bit Score offers not only parts but also service assistance. Many of these dealers have websites with computerized inventory lists, so you can pick up the parts you need without even picking up a phone.

Bringing home your first video game is an experience you'll always remember. And you'll find that it's addictive. After you begin your collection, you'll find that arcade games multiply very quickly. Start with one, and before long, you'll own several.

TUGBOAT was one of the games produced by Moppet Video. This easy-to-play game let children sound the horn anytime throughout the game simply by pressing the button on the control panel. $300-$400.

Moppet Video games were designed especially for children under ten. Not only were the cabinets child-sized, but the games themselves were created to appeal to children and were simpler to play than most arcade video games. If you have children in your home, a Moppet Video game might be just their speed.

Moppet Video's NOAH'S ARK screen shot. $300-$400.

235

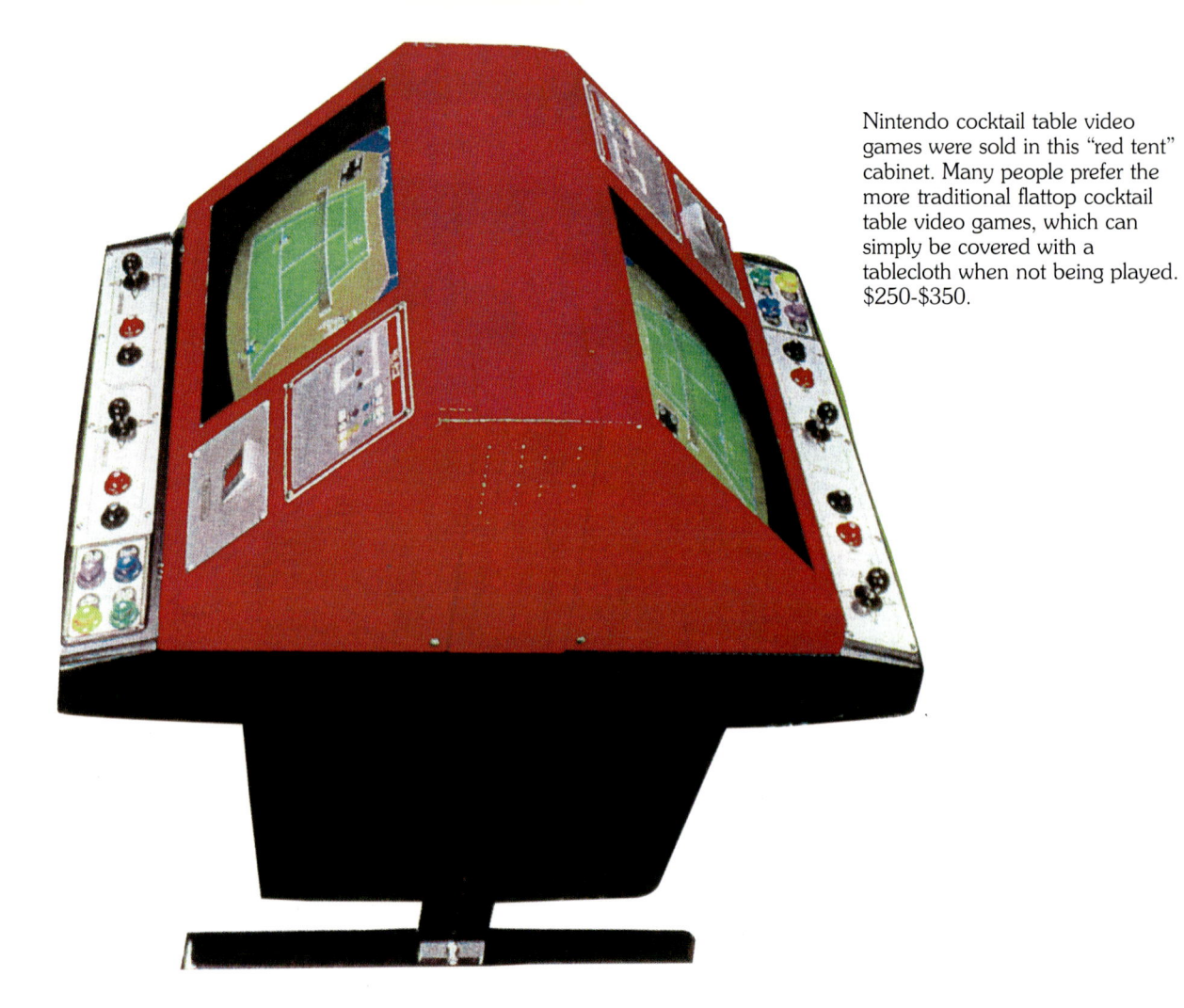

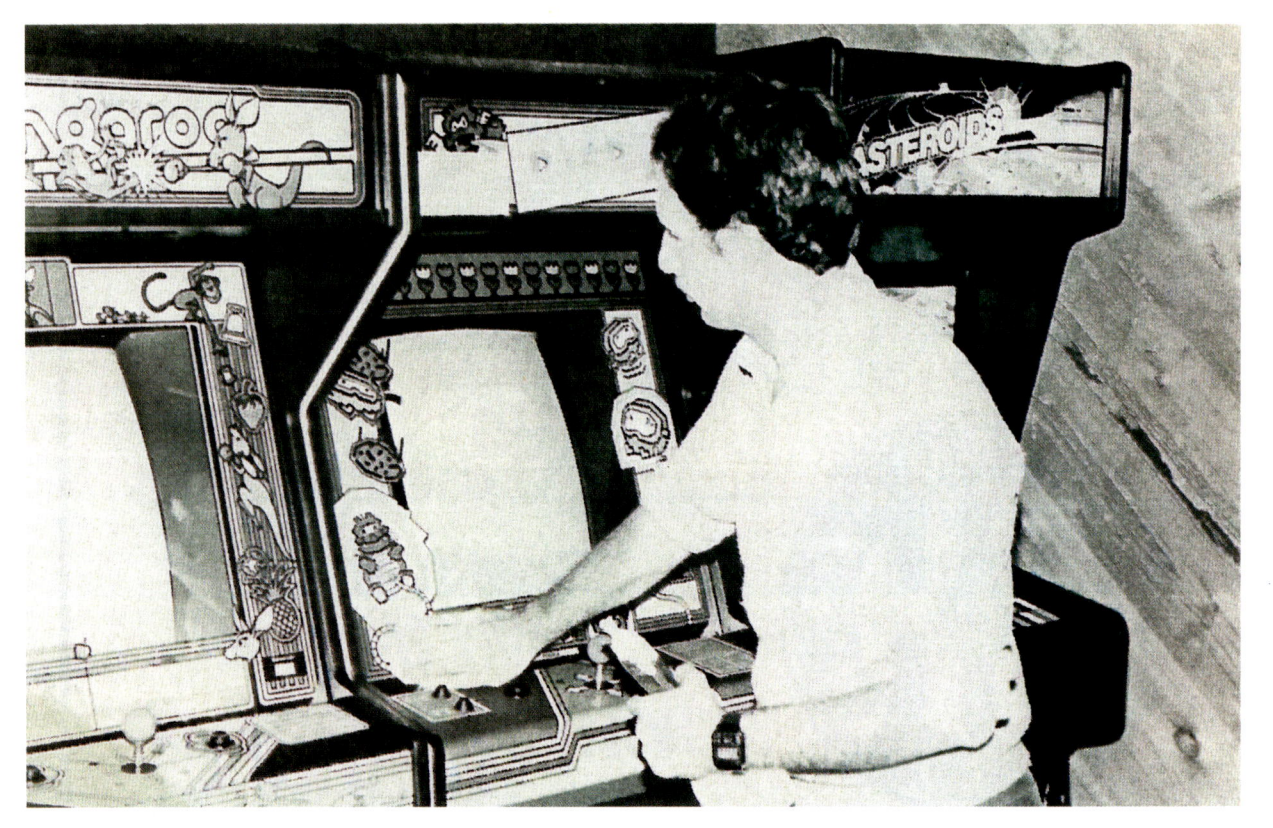

Nintendo cocktail table video games were sold in this "red tent" cabinet. Many people prefer the more traditional flattop cocktail table video games, which can simply be covered with a tablecloth when not being played. $250-$350.

Video game collector and expert player Jeff Siegel of Cincinnati always polishes the video games in his collection to keep them looking sharp. Most video games will require only an occasional cleaning to keep them looking and running fine.

Can't decide if you want a video game or a pinball machine for your collection? Why not get both? Bally Midway's 1984 GRANNY AND THE GATORS has both video and pinball games in the same machine. Other video/pinball combo games include Bally Midway's BABY PAC MAN and Gottlieb's CAVEMAN. $600-$1,000.

237

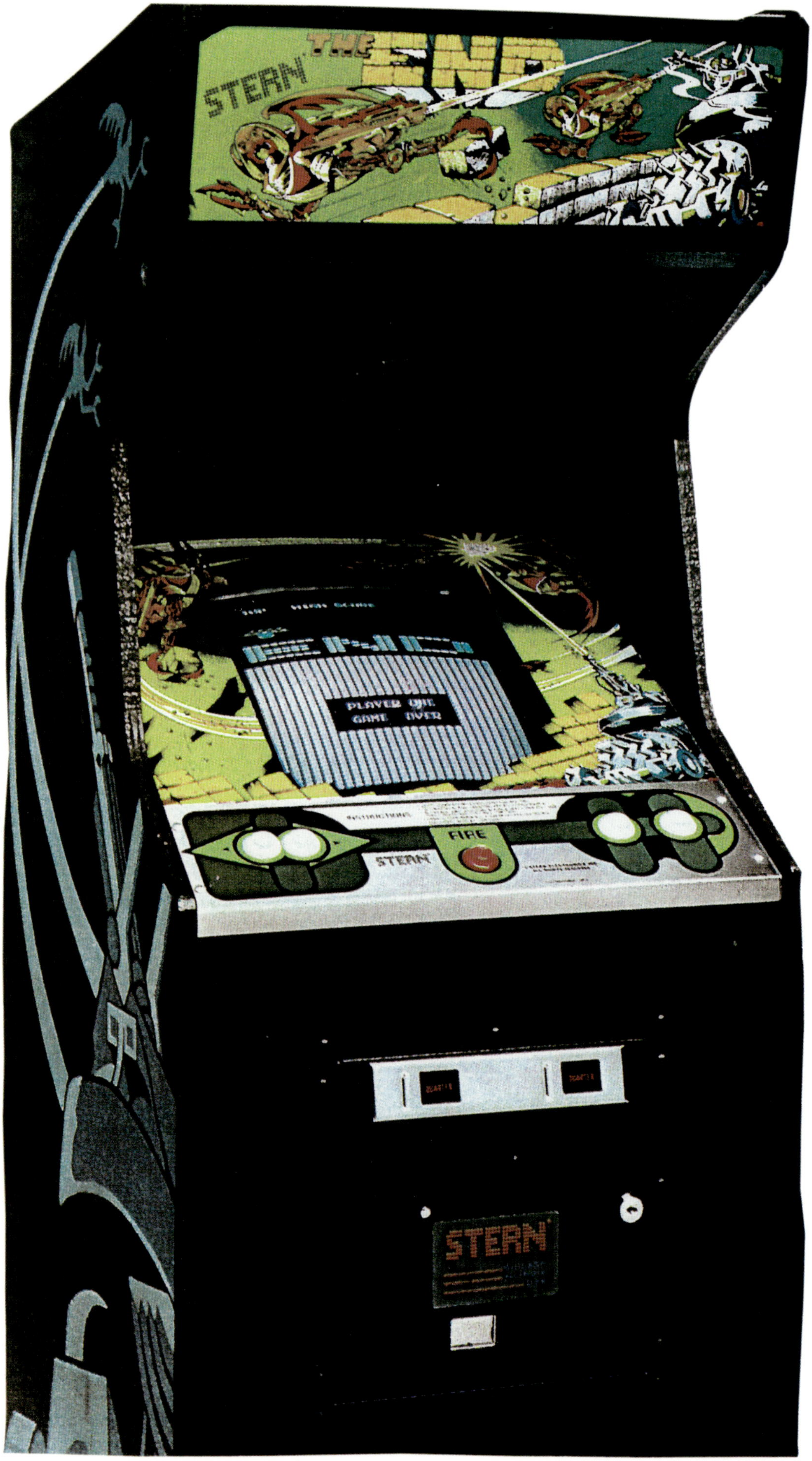
STERN
THE END
PLAYER ONE
GAME OVER
FIRE
STERN
STERN

NOTES

NOTES